Data Structures With Ada®

Data Structures With Ada®

MICHAEL B. FELDMAN

The George Washington University

RESTON PUBLISHING COMPANY, INC.
A PRENTICE-HALL COMPANY
RESTON, VIRGINIA

Library of Congress Cataloging in Publication Data

Feldman, Michael (Michael B.)
    Data structures with Ada.

    1. Ada ® (computer program language)
    2. Data structures (Computer science)   I. Title.
QA76.73.A35F45 1985   001.64′24   85-589
ISBN 0-8359-1220-5

© 1985 by Reston Publishing Company, Inc.
A Prentice-Hall Company
Reston, Virginia

1   3   5   7   9   10   8   6   4   2

Printed in the United States of America

Ada® is a registered trademark of the U.S. Government, Ada Joint Program Office

TO

My Father who, sadly, did not live to see it in print

and

My Mother, who, happily did.

Contents

Preface   xiii

1   Abstraction and Abstract Data Types   1
   1.1   GOAL STATEMENT   1
   1.2   ABSTRACTION VS. IMPLEMENTATION   1
   1.3   ABSTRACT DATA TYPES (ADTS)   4
   1.4   AN ABSTRACT DATA TYPE FOR FRACTIONS (OR RATIONALS)   7
   1.5   ADA AS A DESIGN LANGUAGE FOR ADTS   9
      The General Structure of an Ada Package   9
      Package Specifications and Package Bodies   10
      Private Types   12
      Using an Ada ADT Package   15
   1.6   DESIGN ONE: AN ABSTRACT DATA TYPE FOR SETS   16
   1.7   DESIGN TWO: AN ABSTRACT DATA TYPE FOR TEXT STRINGS   20
   1.8   STYLE GUIDE: AN ADT FOR COMPLEX NUMBERS IN STANDARD PASCAL   23
      Packages in Standard Pascal   24
      A Pascal Complex-number Package   25
      The Pointer in Pascal   26
      What Happens to the Allocated Memory?   29
      The Specification Part   29
   1.9   SUMMARY   29
   1.10 EXERCISES   31

2 **Algorithms, Recursion, and Performance Prediction 32**
2.1 GOAL STATEMENT 32
2.2 ALGORITHMS AND ALGORITHM DESIGN 33
2.3 RECURSIVE ALGORITHMS 34
Reversal of a String 35
Permutations of a Set 37
Recursive Binary Search 39
Recursive Merge Sort 42
2.4 PERFORMANCE PREDICTION AND THE "BIG O" NOTATION 43
Algorithm Growth Rates 44
Estimating the Growth Rate of an Algorithm 45
Some Examples of Performance Prediction 53
2.5 DESIGN: MAINTAINING A DYNAMIC TABLE AS AN ARRAY 54
Implementation One: Unordered Array 56
Implementation Two: Array Ordered by Key 58
2.6 SUMMARY 59
2.7 EXERCISES 60

3 **Arrays, Vectors, Matrices, and Lists 62**
3.1 GOAL STATEMENT 62
3.2 "CLASSICAL" REPRESENTATION OF VECTORS AND MATRICES 63
Vectors or One-Dimensional Arrays 63
Matrices and Two-Dimensional Arrays 66
Higher-Dimensional Structures 69
3.3 DENSELY-PACKED STRUCTURES WITH MANY "ZERO" ELEMENTS 71
Lower Triangular Matrices 71
Symmetric Matrices 73
"Band" Matrices 73
3.4 SPARSE VECTORS AND MATRICES 74
Sparse Vectors 75
Linking the Elements Together 79
3.5 DESIGN: VECTOR AND MATRIX OPERATIONS IN ADA 84
Vector Arithmetic and Ada Arrays 84
Matrix Arithmetic 89
3.6 STYLE GUIDE: WORKING IN LANGUAGE WITHOUT RECORD TYPES 93
3.7 SUMMARY 95
3.8 EXERCISES 96

4 **Linear Linked Lists, Pointers, and Cursors 98**
4.1 GOAL STATEMENT 98
4.2 LINKED STRUCTURES 99
4.3 POINTERS AND DYNAMIC MEMORY MANAGEMENT 99
4.4 USING DYNAMIC ALLOCATION FOR LINKED STRUCTURES 101
Creating a One-Way Linked List 103
An ADT For One-Way Linked Lists 105

One-Way Lists With Head and Tail Pointers   109
Building an Ordered List   112
Two-Way Linked Lists   116
4.5   DESIGN ONE: SPARSE VECTORS AND MATRICES REVISITED   116
Vector Arithmetic   117
Sparse Matrices   121
4.6   DESIGN TWO: TEXT HANDLING REVISITED   123
4.7   STYLE GUIDE ONE: SIMULATING DYNAMIC MEMORY MANAGEMENT   126
4.8   STYLE GUIDE TWO: ANOTHER VISIT TO PASCAL COMPLEX NUMBERS   131
4.9   SUMMARY   135
4.10 EXERCISES   136

5   **Queues and Stacks   138**
5.1   GOAL STATEMENT   138
5.2   QUEUES AND STACKS INTRODUCED   139
5.3   QUEUES   139
Array Implementation of Queues   140
Circular Array Implementation of Queues   143
Linked Implementation of Queues   143
5.4   STACKS   147
Array Implementation of Stacks   147
Linked Implementation of Stacks   148
5.5   STACKS, EXPRESSION EVALUATION AND POLISH NOTATION   149
Evaluating RPN Expressions   151
Converting Manually From Infix to RPN Form   153
5.6   DESIGN: AN INFIX-TO-RPN TRANSLATOR PROGRAM   156
5.7   SUMMARY   162
5.8   EXERCISES   162

6   **Directed Graphs   164**
6.1   GOAL STATEMENT   164
6.2   INTRODUCTION   165
6.3   PROPERTIES OF DIGRAPHS   166
6.4   IMPLEMENTATIONS FOR DIRECTED GRAPHS   170
Adjacency Matrix   171
Adjacency List   172
Weighted Adjacency Matrix   173
State Table   174
6.5   GRAPH TRAVERSALS   175
Depth-First Search   175
Breadth-First Search   176
6.6   DESIGN: A SIMPLE LEXICAL SCANNER   179
6.7   SUMMARY   182
6.8   EXERCISES   182

7 Tree Structures 184

7.1 GOAL STATEMENT 184

7.2 INTRODUCTION 185

7.3 BINARY TREES 189

Properties of Binary Trees 190

Implementing Binary Trees 193

Traversals of Binary Trees 194

7.4 EXPRESSION TREES 196

Constructing Expression Trees 198

Traversing Expression Trees 200

7.5 BINARY SEARCH TREES (BSTS) 202

The Report Operation: Traversing a BST 202

The Update Operation: Inserting a Record in a BST 205

The Search Operation: Finding a Record in a BST 207

The Delete Operation: Deleting a Record From a BST 208

7.6 GENERAL TREES 211

Digital Search Trees 212

B-Trees 215

7.7 DESIGN ONE: BUILDING AN EXPRESSION TREE 217

7.8 DESIGN TWO: A CROSS-REFERENCE GENERATOR 218

The Table Handler 220

The Scanner 224

7.9 STYLE GUIDE: THREADING TREES FOR EFFICIENCY 228

7.10 SUMMARY 236

7.11 EXERCISES 236

8 Hash Table Methods 238

8.1 GOAL STATEMENT 238

8.2 SEQUENTIAL AND BINARY SEARCH REVISITED 239

8.3 THE HASH TABLE 240

8.4 CHOOSING A HASH FUNCTION 242

Truncation 242

Division 243

Mid-Square 243

Folding or Partitioning 243

8.5 RESOLVING COLLISIONS IN HASH TABLES 244

Linear Probing 245

Non-Linear Probing 247

Bucket Hashing 248

Ordered Hashing 249

8.6 DESIGN: HYBRID SEARCH STRATEGIES 250

8.7 SUMMARY 250

8.8 EXERCISES 251

9   Internal Sorting Methods   253

   9.1 GOAL STATEMENT   253
   9.2 INTRODUCTION   254
   9.3 SORT ALGORITHMS WITH GROWTH RATE O (N^2)   254
      Simple Selection Sort   255
      Delayed Selection Sort   256
      Bubble Sort   257
      Linear Insertion Sort   259
      Binary Insertion Sort   262
   9.4 INTERNAL SORTS WITH GROWTH RATE O (N × LOG (N))   262
      Merge Sort   262
      Heap Sort   266
      Quicksort   277
   9.5 OTHER INTERNAL SORT ALGORITHMS   281
      Shell Sort   281
      Quadratic Selection Sort   283
      Radix Sort   284
   9.6 SUMMARY   287
   9.7 EXERCISES   288

10   Sorting External Files   290

   10.1 GOAL STATEMENT   290
   10.2 THE TWO-WAY MERGE   291
   10.3 THE K-WAY MERGE   291
   10.4 SIMPLE MERGE SORTING   219
   10.5 THE "NATURAL" DISTRIBUTION   294
   10.6 POLYPHASE SORTING   296
   10.7 FIBONACCI DISTRIBUTION FOR POLYPHASE MERGING   296
   10.8 SUMMARY   300
   10.9 EXERCISES   300

Bibliography   301

Index   305

Preface

The textbook literature in the area of what is generically called "data structures" falls generally into two categories: the theoretical and the practical. In the former category, the emphasis is on the axiomatic specification of data types; there tends to be heavy treatment of algorithm performance prediction ("big O" and the like); and the actual implementation of the structures is often presented in a pseudo-language not directly compilable on any computer.

Books in the latter category emphasize the programming side: there is relatively little mention of algorithm performance (and it is concentrated in the chapter on sorting); abstract data types are treated cursorily if at all; but there is helpful concentration on the implemention of data structures in a real-world programming language, Pascal in most recent cases.

This book attempts a compromise. Many students take only a single course in the data structures area; industry programmers often read only a single book. A blend of the theoretical and the applied is quite in order. The careful reader should come away from this book equipped to understand and design data structures and their implementations, with an emphasis on the information-hiding principle to encourage system decomposition and "hiding" implementation details.

Such abstraction is not always free of costs, however, and can seriously affect the growth rate or "big O" of an algorithm if not handled carefully. Therefore some attention is paid to performance prediction, at least to the degree that a reader will learn the earmarks of linear, quadratic, and logarithmic growth rates.

It is important to develop an understanding of the tradeoffs between space and time and between abstraction and program performance. Equally important is to learn that while micro-"efficiency" is less crucial than it was in the days of slow processors and limited, expensive memory, macro-"performance" needs to be considered right along with other factors in designing and implementing algorithms. Indeed, using an algorithm with a slow(er) growth rate often makes feasible the very solution of a problem.

Those who continue in the formal study of data structures and algorithms will certainly have ample opportunity to cover these performance issues more rigorously. Those who do not continue with more theoretical study need at least to experience some "consciousness-raising": sensitivity to the necessity to get an approximate idea of their programs' likely performance and to the fact that there is rarely a "free lunch." This will encourage a certain amount of "back-of-the-envelope" performance estimation, and may forestall grievous waste of machine resources and human time to correct errors in algorithm selection.

This book was developed to support a semester course at The George Washington University entitled "Programming and Data Structures." It is a second or third course in programming, populated by juniors, seniors, and some graduate students. Some institutions might offer it in the sophomore year. In such a course, this book can be used straight through from beginning to end. Our experience is that students and instructors alike are more comfortable with such a book than with one where chapters must be taken out of sequence or skipped altogether to fit a one-semester course.

"Structured programming" in the sense of block structuring, use of procedures and functions, and strictly-controlled use of the "goto" statement, is taught almost universally in entry-level programming courses, and is in ever-wider use in industry as well. We therefore feel safe in assuming that the reader already is comfortable with a modern language like Pascal, PL/1, Algol-W, C, or Fortran-77.

ADA AS A LANGUAGE FOR DATA STRUCTURES

We believe that the reader of a book in this field should be able to see algorithms presented in a real programming language, not as a "toy" synthesized for the purpose. In this book, we have chosen Ada as the language of our algorithms.

Ada is named for Ada Augusta, Countess of Lovelace, the daughter of the nineteenth-century English poet Lord Byron and the assistant to Charles Babbage, the computer pioneer. Ada, the person, is thought to have been the very first programmer. Ada, the language, was intended originally for the development of embedded computer systems for the U.S. Department of Defense. Many in the industry believe that Ada embodies enough of the state of the art in programming language design to be useful to a much more widespread constituency.

Ada's most significant contribution to the pedagogy of Data Structures is the "package" facility, which permits the specification and implementation of abstract data types in a natural and clean fashion. The operations on a defined data type may be encapsulated along with the definition of that type, and the designer may stipulate those operations which are accessible to a user and those which are purely internal. This notion is in accord with current thinking about how programs should be developed for reliability and maintainability, and with the emphasis in some quarters on the development of "re-usable software components," a process sometimes called "capital-intensive software development." It is our firm belief that "package thinking" should be inculcated early in one's programming experience, and that Ada—appropriately taught—can serve as an able helper in this.

Whether Ada's package facility is the *best* way to handle abstract data types is an issue likely to be debated for years to come. For the moment, it provides a feasible way not available in many other (standard) major languages. Our experience and others' is that the facility is easily learned and helps to re-shape one's approach to programming in salutary ways. Many of our students actually code their projects in Pascal, and find that the Ada design helps them to write better Pascal programs.

Compilers for Ada are available for most of the computer systems in wide use in industry and educational institutions, and so many readers will be able to use the packages developed in this book directly. For those not able to do so, we encourage thinking of them as designs to be implemented in whatever programming language is readily at hand.

Though this book *uses* Ada, it is important to realize that it is *not* an "Ada book" in the sense of teaching the language details one at a time or exhaustively. The examples are presented in such a way as to help the student acquire a *reading* knowledge of the language, or large parts of it at least. But Ada is a large multi-purpose language, and there are areas of it never touched by this book, because they do not bear directly on the subject matter.

For the reader needing to learn the langauge details, to *write* rather than just *read* programs, there will be no substitute for investing in a copy of one of the fine textbooks on the language itself. Most of these—in print at the time this book goes to press—are listed in the References. For those needing to steep themselves in Ada, the purchase of the Language Reference Manual is recommended as well, since that volume is the official oracle for answers to questions about the language.

Programs and packages appearing in this book have been tested using the TeleSoft implementation of Ada, operating on the Digital Equipment Corporation VAX/11-780 at the School of Engineering and Applied Science Computer Facility, The George Washington University. The language style used is straightforward and non-esoteric, leading both to easy understanding of the programs and minimum risk of implementation-dependent difficulties.

While many of the programs are given in full, many are purposely incomplete to allow the reader to fill in the missing pieces. Missing pieces are clearly indicated; we tested the programs in full before removing the pieces.

DESIGN SECTIONS

Most chapters include one or two Design sections. Except for those in Chapter 1, which are strongly recommended for all readers, the Design sections are optional and the flow of the body of the book is not disturbed by omitting them. Each Design section is an application of the structure introduced in the current chapter, and is usually presented as an explanation of the application, some diagrams, and *part* of the Ada code for the solution. These sections are, in general, purposely left unfinished so that the reader may complete them, either as self-study or as an assigned problem. Most of the problems are interesting and provocative enough to warrant assignment as programming projects to be coded and tested.

While the Design sections are purposely independent of the "main line" of the book, they do tend to depend upon one or more Design sections in earlier chapters. For example, the simple text-handling package introduced in Chapter 1 is elaborated in the Chapter 4 Design section, then used in the Design sections of Chapters 5, 6, and 7. Similarly, the sparse vector and sparse matrix concepts introduced in Chapter 3 are used in a Design section in Chapter 4, and the very simple state-graph lexical scanner presented in the Chapter 6 Design section is elaborated in a corresponding section of Chapter 7. Finally, the scanner written as a Chapter 5 Design to generate the Reverse Polish Notation form of an arithmetic expression is modified in Chapter 7 to produce an expression tree.

The Design sections show interesting uses of the data structures, and serve to strengthen and reinforce each other. This is appropriate and exemplary of the re-use of application code as well as packages.

STYLE GUIDES

An important feature of this book is the Style Guide section found at the end of most chapters. We believe that a modern Data Structures text should present important structures and algorithms in the most modern and powerful language forms available in a "real-world" language; this explains our choice of Ada.

However, as an aid to those students in courses which do not use Ada as the coding language, or to those in industry needing to code in other languages, we have included the Style Guide sections, where concentrated attention is given to how the ideas expressed in a chapter may be coded in languages where no built-in support is provided. These guides show how one can write powerful programs without powerful languages.

One Style Guide discusses how to code structures which are *logically* records, even though the coding language doesn't support record structures. Another takes up the problem of simulating linked structures using arrays and array indices ("cursors") where no language support is available for pointers and dynamic allocation. These guides will be especially useful to those writing programs in Fortran or Basic.

Even Pascal has its limitations in support of abstract data types, and the Chapter 1 Style Guide shows how Pascal functions can be made to pass record types in and out by the use of pointers. The style used is also applicable to coding in "C," PL/1, or Modula-2.

Finally, the Chapter 7 Style Guide considers the important technique of "threading" binary trees to permit rapid and non-recursive traversal algorithms.

SUMMARY

We hope that this book will make a contribution to the pedagogy of data structures through its early and consistent use of abstract data types *as implemented in real-world packages*. We hope also to contribute to the emergent Ada literature by highlighting its use as a general-purpose programming language in modern, well-structured systems using nontrivial data structures. Since Ada is likely to come into wide use but unlikely ever to come into *universal* use, we hope that the Style Guides will show Ada's utility as a design language as well.

ACKNOWLEDGMENTS

Many people have contributed to this book in many ways. The formal reviewers were Keith Allen, Roie Black, Myron Calhoun, Susan B. Davidson, and Stephen Lowe; their careful reading and annotation were a source of innumerable good ideas. Countless students in Computer Science 159 deserve a vote of thanks for patiently and uncomplainingly learning Data Structures from a manuscript in various stages of completion. Graduate students and colleagues have read parts of the manuscript and offered valuable guidance; especially helpful were Melinda Moran and Lucy Moran. The SEAS Computing Facility provided large quantities of VAX time for testing programs and preparing the manuscript. Several TeleSoft employees, especially Wayne Dunlap, Larry Nixon, and Chris Klein, gave large amounts of behind-the-scenes assistance in getting used to Ada and the TeleSoft implementation. Finally, Ruth, Ben, and Keith Feldman have been incredibly loving and patient through it all.

M.B.F.

Chapter 1

ABSTRACTION AND ABSTRACT DATA TYPES

1.1 GOAL STATEMENT

Abstraction and abstract data types (ADTs) play an important role in modern program design and coding. It is particularly important in a text devoted to data stuctures to understand these concepts fully. In this chapter we shall explore the notions of abstraction and implementation, define abstract data types, and show examples of how the latter can be written as packages in Ada.

Specifically, *rational numbers* or *fractions*, *sets*, and *text strings* will be treated, and packages for them will be sketched out.

At the end of the chapter you will encounter the first of a series of *Style Guides*, where you will be given hints about how to implement concepts explained in the chapter, but using languages which are missing some of the powerful features present in Ada. In this Style Guide an abstract data type for complex numbers will be discussed in the context of languages like Pascal, C, Modula-2, and PL/1.

1.2 ABSTRACTION VS. IMPLEMENTATION

Examples of abstraction abound in everyday programming, although you may not have recognized these as such. Your very ability to use things like "integers" and "real numbers" in programming depends on abstraction, since, in reality, nothing exists in the computer but sequences of bits, operated on by instructions which "understand" the connection between that which you perceive as an integer (written in your program as a base 10 number!) and that group of eight or sixteen or thirty-two bits in the computer's memory.

Usually integer arithmetic is carried out by hardware instructions. To understand the kind of software-level abstraction we will be doing in this book, consider arithmetic on real numbers. In many computers, no real or floating-point instructions are available in the hardware instruction set—or are options the purchaser chose not to pay for. So when you write, say, an assignment statement X := X*Y + 3.0, the compiler not only figures out which hardware memory locations to use to store the variables X and Y, but may also have to generate calls to *subroutines* to do the addition and multiplication operations. The point is that through the use of the *abstraction* "variable name" and the *abstraction* "real number," both provided in any reasonable high-level language, you do not have to worry about the details of the internal storage or actual instructions used to *implement* the calculation you specify when you write an assignment. Abstraction is the way we arrive at a situation called *information hiding*, in which unnecessary details of a data representation or a procedure are hidden from those who have no need (or desire) to see them.

We shall frequently contrast *abstraction* and *implementation*. The abstraction is essentially that which is made visible to the user (in this case the high-level-language (HLL) programmer); the implementation is all the messy details which have been hidden away. In this example, we have used an abstraction we might call RealNumbers, including the operations of *addition*, *multiplication*, and *assignment* of reals. There is also an operation *creation*, which we used by declaring X and Y to be real. The implementation of a real number as an area of memory divided into mantissa and exponent parts, and the operations as subroutines to be called by your machine-language program, have been taken care of by the compiler designer.

Figure 1–1 shows this relationship for what an HLL programmer sees as an integer.

(a) Abstraction of integer assignment as seen by programmer.

(b) Sixteen-bit location (two bytes) with binary equivalent of 735 stored.

Figure 1-1   Abstraction and implementation of integer assignment.

To give another example, you have probably used two-dimensional arrays somewhere in your programming experience. You are probably aware that the computer's memory is not two-dimensional, but is addressed as just a sequence of bytes or words. It is clear, then, that something must be sitting between your high-level-language program and that linear memory which can interpret a statement like A(3,4):=B(4,7)+1.0 correctly. As in the previous example, this "something" is the compiler; abstraction has been used to give you expressive power not present in the machine itself.

The abstraction you have used might be called RectangularArrays, including the operations of *retrieval* (the subscripted reference B(4,7) to the right of a: = sign), *assignment* (the reference A(3,4) to the left of a: = sign), and *creation* (the declaration of the arrays and their sizes at the beginning of your program). As in the previous example, the compiler designer has seen to the implementation of the rectangular arrays as areas of linear memory, and the assignment and retrieval operations as formulas, generated into your machine-language program, which express the correspondence.

Please notice that, without thinking about it in so many words, you've also used the abstraction RealNumbers, since the values stored in the rectangular array are reals. An important aspect of the power of abstraction is the ability to "nest" abstraction many levels deep.

We shall return to arrays in detail in Chapter 3; in the meantime, study Figure 1–2, which shows the abstraction and implementation of a 3x4 integer array.

Yet another example can be drawn from the area of files on magnetic tape. Useful information on tape is recorded at a density, typically, of 1600 characters per running inch of tape (and often more), and a gap of about 3/4 inch is left between groups of useful characters (to allow the tape motors space to accelerate and decelerate before and after reading). Thus a file of, say, personnel records of 200 characters each would waste much more tape than it uses if each record were stored on its own "chunk" of tape, since a record would occupy only 1/8 inch of tape followed by a 3/4-inch gap.

This is one reason why records are "blocked" on tape or disk files. A number of actual records are grouped together on one "chunk" of tape between gaps. If this "blocking factor" were, say, ten, then a block would occupy 1–1/4 inch of tape, with the same 3/4-inch gap.

But tape is relatively cheap, and so this more economical use of storage is a secondary reason for blocking. A more important reason is that there is a fair amount of overhead associated with each tape read or write operation: the time to set up the operation and to start and stop the tape-drive motor is significant compared with the time to transfer the information on the tape to and from main store. Thus time is saved—and motor wear and tear—if more information can be read or written in a single operation, once the drive motor is up to speed.

Let us suppose that you write a program in a high-level language to process this file. Your program is written to process one record at a time, yet in ac-

```
W:  array  (1..3,1..4)  of  integer;
```

(a) Ada declaration.

```
      1   2   3   4
  1  | 0  -1   4   5
  2  | 8   2   0  -3
  3  |-5   1   2   0
```

(b) Programmer's view of filled-in array.

```
 0
-1
 4
 5
 8
 2
 0
-3
-5
 1
 2
 0
```

**(c) Filled-in array as
       stored by compiler.**

Figure 1-2   Abstraction and implementation of two-dimensional array.

tuality a number of records—a block—are being read from your tape file in one I/O operation. Should you be worried about this "mismatch"? Emphatically not! In fact, the operating system or compiler designers have applied abstraction to hide these messy details from you, and your program ends up processing exactly the record it "wants." The abstraction LogicalRecord is implemented as a block of records written as one physical tape record; you use the operations of reading and writing records, which are implemented so that even though your program executes many "write" operations, an actual write to tape is only executed when a block of records has been assembled in an area of main store, usually called a buffer.

In the terminology of operating systems, we refer to *logical* vs. *physical* records, files, devices, etc. You can see that logical and physical bear a close correspondence to abstraction and implementation. The tape example is illustrated in Figure 1–3.

1.3 ABSTRACT DATA TYPES (ADTS)

Once having understood the basic nature of abstraction, we need a more formal way to express situations where it is used. Let us therefore define an *ab-*

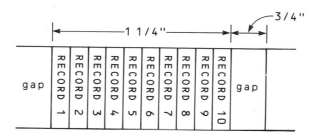

3/4"

1/8"

(a) Magnetic tape with 1600 character/inch storage density, showing storage of un-
blocked, 200-character records. Each input operation reads one physical record, thus
one logical record.

1 1/4"

3/4"

(b) Magnetic tape with same density and record size, but with ten-record blocking factor.
Each input operation reads one physical record, but ten logical records.

Figure 1-3 Abstraction and implementation of magnetic tape file.

stract data type (ADT) as a mathematical object of some sort, together with all
the operations allowing us to create and manipulate instances of that object.

It is unfortunately typical of the computing field that terminology is often
confusing, for example where different concepts have similar sounding names.
This is no doubt because computing is a very new field with many people par-
ticipating, and terminology has not yet become standard.

Be that as it may, we wish to point out, before the reader becomes con-
fused, the difference between the terms *data type*, *abstract data type*, and *data
structure*.

The term *data type* (sometimes just *type*) is used by programming language
designers to mean a set of values that a given variable is permitted to take on. A
variable of type *integer*, for example, is allowed to be assigned integral values
between two extremes, usually the largest positive and negative integers repre-

sentable in the underlying hardware. For a sixteen-bit computer, then, an integer variable typically will be allowed to take on values between –32767 and +32767.

As another example, a variable of type *boolean* (or LOGICAL in Fortran) may have only the values *true* (or .TRUE.) and *false* (or .FALSE.).

Every programming language has a set of basic or *primitive* types for variables. In Fortran these are INTEGER, REAL, and LOGICAL (and often CHARACTER and COMPLEX as well, depending on the version of the language); in Basic they are INTEGER, REAL, and STRING; in Pascal they are integer, real, boolean, and character. Cobol permits character strings, decimal numbers, and several different kinds of binary (or computational) types.

Many recent programming languages, like Pascal and Ada (and PL/1 to a certain extent), permit the definition of new types. These may be restrictions of the primitive types (like an integer between 1 and 10), or as combinations of primitives (such as a *record* consisting of a student name of character-string type and a course average of real type).

An *abstract data type* or *ADT* includes not only a data type definition but a specification of the operations which are valid for the new type. Nothing in the type-definition facilities of Pascal or Ada *requires* such a specification. Ada *permits* it, as we shall see later. But even if one's programming language does not permit the direct definition of an ADT, this concept is extremely useful in designing programs and can thus be thought of as a kind of "pseudo-code" or design language.

What then is a *data structure?* A *data structure* is a way of *representing* or *implementing* an ADT in a program. For example, in a hypothetical language which did not have reals as a primitive data type, we might define an ADT for reals, then decide to represent a real number as a one-dimensional array with two elements, both integers, corresponding to the mantissa and exponent respectively. Alternatively, we could use a record structure if this hypothetical language permitted records. Arrays and records are two commonly-used data structures. We shall see others in the course of this book.

To summarize:

A *data type* is the set of values valid for a variable;

An *abstract data type* is a data type together with a set of operations valid for that type;

A *data structure* is a concrete way of implementing an ADT.

One of the main goals of this book is to illustrate how complexity in programming can be reduced by hiding away detailed information from program segments that have no need to know that information. This is often called *encapsulation* or *packaging*. An important way of encapsulating is through the use of ADTs, since then mathematical concepts like real numbers, sets, graphs, trees, and so on can be treated as such. We can concentrate on the mathematical properties of these entities, their visible structure and the set of operations that can be performed on them, without concern for the details of how they should actually be represented in a program.

This is not to say that we ignore these details entirely, since programs really do need to get written! Rather, we are *postponing* consideration of unnecessary detail, defining our objects first as ADTs for use by higher-level programs, then—later—as concrete data structures which implement those objects and concrete functions and procedures which implement those operations. If we use our programming languages well, we will be able to find ways of then encapsulating those implementations so that the details are hidden from individuals and programs that do not need them.

While this might be relatively easy in Ada, it is still possible in other languages, and searching out ways to do it pays off handsomely in reduced program complexity and enhanced program reliability.

1.4 AN ABSTRACT DATA TYPE FOR FRACTIONS (OR RATIONALS)

Let us take up another example of an abstract data type. Programming languages usually have support for real numbers (decimals) but usually do not have support for fractions. There are certain applications where fractions are useful, e.g. where we want to represent the number 1/3 exactly and not as 0.3333.... This requires that we have a way to remember the numerator and denominator of a fraction.

We now define a Fraction to be an ordered pair <num,denom>, which we understand to be the fraction num/denom. Note first that a fraction cannot have a denominator of 0 (you know that from grade-school work with fractions) and second that a fraction with a denominator of 1 corresponds to an integer ("whole number"). Let us also specify that a fraction will always be stored such that its denominator is *positive*, i.e. that if it is brought into the system as negative, numerator and denominator are multiplied by –1.

We shall not be concerned with whether a fraction is *proper* (numerator less than denominator) or not. So 7/4, for example, is perfectly acceptable. But we shall need to care whether or not a fraction is *reduced*. We want to keep fractions in a standard form, so that we won't have many representations for the same number (e.g. 3/6 = 4/8 = 1/2). In general, then, we shall reduce fractions by dividing numerator and denominator by their greatest common factor.

We now understand the mathematical object Fraction; which operations should be defined for fractions? Clearly we need the ordinary arithmetic operations of sum, difference, product, and quotient; a reduction operation and operations to convert integers to fractions and vice versa would be helpful as well.

Further, we need the relational operators Equal, Less, and GreaterEqual to test the relative magnitudes of two fractions. Note that two fractions are certainly equal if their numerators and denominators are respectively equal, but that they are *also* equal if their *reduced* forms are equal, i.e. $1/2 = 2/4 = 24/48$.

The four arithmetic operations are really *dyadic* (two-operand) functions on fractions which return fractions; the conversion operations are *monadic* and take fractions to integers and integers to fractions.

Let us use the syntax of Ada to specify these functions. In addition to the operations given above, we have included a dyadic function to assign the numerator and denominator values to a fraction, and two monadic operations to retrieve the numerator and denominator values, all in a way which is implementation-independent. Using x and y to denote arbitrary fractions and N and D to denote arbitrary integers, we get the list of operations shown in Figure 1–4. In the figure, we use boldface type to indicate Ada *reserved words*. Sometimes called *keywords*, these are words which have a fixed meaning in the language and are not allowed to be used for other purposes, such as program variables or identifiers.

Let us understand how some of these arithmetic operations work. For example, to multiply two fractions, we multiply their numerators and their denominators; we then reduce the result.

$$3/4 * 5/9 = 15/36 = 5/12$$

$$7/5 * 10/11 = 70/55 = 14/11$$

$$3/4 * 4/3 = 12/12 = 1/1 \ (=1, \text{ but we keep it as } 1/1)$$

```
function MakeFraction(N, D: Integer) return Fraction;
--  "create" operation

function Numer(x: Fraction)            return Integer;
function Denom(x: Fraction)            return Integer;
--  decomposition operations

function Sum (x, y: Fraction)          return Fraction;
function Diff(x, y: Fraction)          return Fraction;
function Prod(x, y: Fraction)          return Fraction;
function Quot(x, y: Fraction)          return Fraction;
--  arithmetic operations

function Equal(x, y: Fraction)         return boolean;
function Less (x, y: Fraction)         return boolean;
function GreaterEqual(x,y: Fraction)   return boolean;
--  comparison operations

function Reduce(x: Fraction)           return Fraction;
function FractionToInt(x: Fraction)    return Integer;
function IntToFraction(N: Integer)     return Fraction;
--  miscellaneous
```

Figure 1-4 Operations on Fractions, in Ada syntax.

```
function MakeFraction(N, D: integer) return Fraction is
   begin
      if D < 0 then
         return (-N,-D);
      else
         return (N,D);
      end if;
   end MakeFraction;



function Sum(x, y: Fraction) return Fraction is
   N: integer;
   D: positive;
   begin
      N := Numer(x)*Denom(y) + Numer(y)*Denom(x);
      D := Denom(x)*Denom(y);
      return Reduce(MakeFraction(N,D));
   end Sum;
```

Figure 1-5   Ada functions for creating a Fraction and finding the sum of two Fractions.

To show an example of what the Ada code for these functions might look like, we choose assignment and addition. Figure 1-5 shows the Ada text for these functions. We use the name Sum for the addition one; later we shall show how Ada allows us to call it by the familiar name "+".

Note the calls to Numer and Denom to keep the addition operation implementation-independent; however fractions are stored, Numer and Denom will "understand" the details. Also note that the result is reduced before being returned.

1.5   ADA AS A DESIGN LANGUAGE FOR ADTS

In this section we introduce some concepts from Ada relating to the specification and implementation of ADTs. Ada provides, through the *package* facility, some powerful tools for this purpose. Many readers of this book will have access to an Ada compiler and so will be able to use this facility directly; but even if you have to use a different language for your actual programming, you will probably find the Ada *package* a convenient way to express your ideas at program *design* time.

1.5.1 The General Structure of an Ada Package

You will recall from above that an abstract data type or ADT consists of two parts: a data type expressing the range of valid values for the ADT, and a set of operations valid for it. A fraction, for example, has a numerator and a denominator which can take on certain integral values; a set of operations valid for fractions was given in the previous section.

A *package* in Ada consists of two parts: a *specification* and a *body*. The former gives a mechanism for describing the ADT to the "outside world"; the latter gives a mechanism for describing the implementation, i.e., all those internal details about which the *user* or *client* of the ADT should need to know little or nothing. (NOTE: Ada packages are in fact rather more general than will be described in this book; since our subject here is data structures and ADTs, we shall concentrate on the use of packages to create ADTs. We shall therefore adopt conventions about the structure of packages which will always be *correct* Ada, understanding very well that we may not always consider *all* ways of expressing things.)

For our purposes here, the specification part of an ADT package will always contain a definition of the data type, and the calling sequences of all those operations accessible to the user of the package. (By calling sequence we mean the form of a call to that operation, just like those given in the previous section for fractions.)

In principle, the only information visible to the outside should be that which is independent of the implementation, so as to hide all of those details. As we shall see, Ada permits a fairly good approximation to this complete hiding, but imposes some syntactic restrictions which preclude perfect application of the principle.

The body of the ADT package will contain the actual code for all the ADT operations; obviously these will be implementation-dependent. The general principle is that the body ought to be able to be separately compiled, so that a change in the implementation imposes no change on the interface with the outside world.

1.5.2 Package Specifications and Package Bodies

An ADT consists of a *data type* and a set of operations. An implementation of that ADT, ideally, should consist, then, of a *data structure* which represents the data type in a program, and the sections of program text, or bodies, of the operations—usually written as functions or procedures—which know the details of the data structure and thus how to manipulate it.

In describing the ADT Fraction, we should ideally need only to mention that it has a Numerator and a Denominator, with integer and natural values respectively, and then list the calling sequences of the operations as above. This should—ideally—suffice for a *specification*. In the *body* of the ADT package—ideally—should reside the *data structure* definintion and the operation bodies. The rules of Ada allow us to approach that ideal fairly closely, but not reach it perfectly.

It is true that in an Ada package the *operations* are handled just as we would like in the ideal; unfortunately Ada requires that the *data structure* implementing a data type appear somewhere in the *specification* part of a package, and not in the "hidden" part of a package, as we would like in the ideal.

Let us represent the data type Fraction by a data structure which is a *record* with numerator and denominator fields; using the facility of Ada which permits initialization of values in a type, we get the type definition shown in Figure 1–6.

Every time we declare a variable to be of type Fraction, as in F1:Fraction, we get one of these records, initialized to the value 0/1. Putting this together with the Ada syntax for a package specification and the operation calling sequences as above, Figure 1–7 shows a complete specification for the package Fractions.

You will note that we have used Ada's facility which permits re-defining (or rather defining additional meanings for) built-in infix operators. Thus we call the Sum function "+," the Less function "<" and so on. This allows us to write *expressions* using fractions like (W*X)+(Q/R) just as we would write expressions using integers or reals. (For reasons beyond the scope of this discussion we cannot use "=," so we must be content with Equal.)

In the jargon of language designers, this definition of additional meanings for operators (and all subprograms, for that matter) is called *overloading*. There is no ambiguity in doing this, since in Ada all variables are explicitly given a type, so the compiler knows which "+" to use because it knows the types of the two operands.

If you have to write programs in a language which doesn't allow overloading of subprogram names and operators (most languages don't!), think of the notation "+" as being an abstraction for a function to which you will give a unique name in your implementation, as we did back in Figure 1–4. An example of this style is given in the Style Guide at the end of the chapter.

Figure 1–8 shows a part of the package body; for the sake of brevity, we have replaced some of the detailed code by one-line comments. You can fill in the missing details in an exercise.

```
type Fraction is
   record
      Numerator: integer := 0;
      Denominator: positive := 1;
   end record;
```

Figure 1-6   Ada type definition for Fraction.

```
package Fractions Is

    type Fraction Is
        record
            Numerator: Integer := 0;
            Denominator: positive := 1;
        end record;


    function MakeFraction(N, D: Integer) return Fraction;
        -- "create"

    function Numer(x: Fraction)          return Integer;
    function Denom(x: Fraction)          return Integer;
        -- decomposition

    function "+"(x, y: Fraction)         return Fraction;
    function "-"(x, y: Fraction)         return Fraction;
    function "*"(x, y: Fraction)         return Fraction;
    function "/"(x, y: Fraction)         return Fraction;
        -- arithmetic

    function Equal(x, y: Fraction)       return boolean;
    function "<"(x, y: Fraction)         return boolean;
    function ">="(x, y: Fraction)        return boolean;
        -- comparison

    function Reduce(x: Fraction)         return Fraction;
    function FractionToInt(x: Fraction)  return Integer;
    function IntToFraction(I: Integer)   return Fraction;
        -- miscellaneous


end Fractions;
```

Figure 1-7   Package specification for Fractions.

1.5.3 Private Types

Since Ada requires the data type declaration to appear in the *specification* or
"visible" part of the package, a client of the package can see, for example, the
record structure we have chosen for Fractions, and thus might be tempted to
write, given x an Integer and y a Fraction, a statement like

$$x := y.\text{Numerator},$$

instead of using the Numer operation we have provided in the package.

This explicit use of knowledge of how a Fraction is implemented—as a
record—is innocent enough in this example, but in other cases might present a
problem. In many circumstances—especially where we are using data types
with alternative implementations, as we shall see later in the book—we would

```
package body Fractions is

   -- code for function body MakeFraction

   function Numer(x: Fraction) return integer is
      begin
         return x.Numerator;
      end Numer;

   -- code for function body Denom
   -- code for function body "+"

   function "-"(x, y: Fraction) return Fraction is
      N: integer;
      D: positive;
      begin
         N := Numer(x)*Denom(y) - Numer(y)*Denom(x);
         D := Denom(x)*Denom(y);
         return Reduce(MakeFraction(N,D));
      end "-";

   -- code for function body "*"
   -- code for function body "/"
   -- code for function body Reduce

   function Equal(x, y: Fraction) return boolean is
      begin
         return Numer(x)*Denom(y)=Numer(y)*Denom(x);
      end Equal;

   -- code for function body "<"
   -- code for function body ">="

   function FractToInt(x: Fraction) return integer is
      begin
         return Numer(x)/Denom(x);
      end FractToInt;

   function IntToFract(I: integer) return Fraction is
      begin
         return(I,1);
      end IntToFract;


end Fractions;
```

Figure 1-8 Partial package body for Fractions.

like to change implementing data structures and operation bodies (for efficiency, say) without forcing a change to a program which only *uses* the ADT. Luckily Ada provides a mechanism for this which gets a bit closer to our ideal. In the package *specification* we can state that a type is *private* without giving its details right away, and then include a second part of the specification called the *private* part where the details of the data structure are given. An example of this for the Fraction case is shown in Figure 1-9, where the new specification is given. Note that no change to the body is required in this case.

What is the advantage of the private part? If a user of the package were to write x.Numerator, directly accessing a component of the record instead of using the package-provided function Numer(x), it would result in a compilation error! Thus, even if we have made the data structure *visible* (to the human eye), and given the user *knowledge* of the internal details, we have restricted him or her from making use of this knowledge and *meddling* with the details.

For reasons having to do with how compilers for the language will be implemented, Ada compels us to write the private part in the package *specification*. Clearly it would be preferable to hide those details away in the *body*, but at least Ada lets us prohibit unauthorized *use* of the details.

```
package Fractions is

    type Fraction is private;

    function MakeFraction(N, D: integer) return Fraction;
        -- "create"

    function Numer(x: Fraction)           return integer;
    function Denom(x: Fraction)           return integer;
        -- decomposition

    function "+"(x, y: Fraction)          return Fraction;
    function "-"(x, y: Fraction)          return Fraction;
    function "*"(x, y: Fraction)          return Fraction;
    function "/"(x, y: Fraction)          return Fraction;
        -- arithmetic

    function Equal(x, y: Fraction)        return boolean;
    function "<"(x, y: Fraction)          return boolean;
    function ">="(x, y: Fraction)         return boolean;
        -- comparison

    function Reduce(x: Fraction)          return Fraction;
    function FractionToInt(x: Fraction)   return integer;
    function IntToFraction(I: integer)    return Fraction;
        -- miscellaneous

 private
    type Fraction is
       record
          Numerator: integer := 0;
          Denominator: positive := 1;
       end record;

 end Fractions;
```

Figure 1-9   Package specification using a private type.

1.5.4 Using an Ada ADT Package

The Ada package is a better mechanism for implementing ADTs than can be found in most widely used languages, even though it is not perfect. An Ada package can be separately compiled and stored in a library for future use by client programs. Indeed, the specification and the body of the package can be compiled *separately from each other*. If something inside the *body* is changed, only the body needs to be re-compiled. If anything in the *specification* is changed, though, then both parts of the package have to be re-compiled. This is because the specification makes a promise to the client about the resources provided by the package. It is the job of the body to deliver on the promise made by the specification, so if the promise is changed, one must re-compile the body to be sure that it makes good on the new promise.

What this means for us, in our study of ADTs, is that the details of an ADT implementation can be changed without changing or even re-compiling any client programs, *as long as only the package body has been changed.* Unfortunately, the specification often needs to be re-compiled, because Ada requires the type definition for an ADT to be there and not in the body, and Ada rules require that if the specification is re-compiled, then client programs must be. As long as the type and operation names are not changed, a client program does not have to be changed, just re-compiled occasionally. The source-code management system intended to be included in Ada-related programming support environments (APSEs) is supposed to take care of demanding re-compilations when necessary, since one of its functions is to keep track of changed modules.

It is time for a concrete example of the use of a package. Assume two previously compiled packages. The first is just Fractions from the previous section; the second is a package we'll call FractionIO, whose details we won't show. This package handles Fraction input and output in a way consistent with Ada I/O style: *get* reads a fraction from the terminal keyboard and *put* writes one to the terminal screen. The **out** parameter in *get* means that *get*'s result is reported *out* to the caller. Similarly, *put* has an **in** parameter. A specification for FractionIO appears in Figure 1–10.

Now in Figure 1–11 we give a program that uses the packages. Notice that a main program is a parameterless procedure in Ada, and that declarations of and arithmetic operations on fractions look just like their counterparts in integer and real arithmetic.

Two unfamiliar Ada keywords appear at the beginning of the program, namely **with** and **use**. The first keyword tells the compiler that Fractions and FractionIO are available in a library and will be used to make their resources (types and operations) available to the client program. The compiler will use the package specifications to make sure that all references to package resources are legal ones, and later the linker will get the object code compiled from the bodies and link it in with the object code for the client.

```
with Fractions; use Fractions;
package FractionIO is

    procedure get(F: out Fraction);
    procedure put(F: in  Fraction);

end FractionIO;
```

Figure 1-10   Specification for FractionIO.

The second keyword, **use**, operates at a somewhat different level. It is a rule in Ada that all references to package resources must, in principle, be *qualified* by the name of the package where they reside. If this rule were followed, then, for example, F1 + F2 would have to be written

Fractions."+"(F1,F2),

and put(F3) would have to be written

FractionIO.put(F3).

This defeats one of the benefits of overloading: the clean and consistent writing style we can use, including infix operators. In cases where no ambiguity results from doing so, we can "factor out" this qualification by putting it at the beginning in a **use** clause.

This "factoring out" could cause trouble where, for example, subprograms *with the same name and parameter lists* are defined in two different packages. Since the compiler uses the parameter lists to distinguish overloaded subprogram names, this creates an ambiguity that can only be resolved by qualification. In the kind of packages dealt with in this book, this ambiguity is unlikely to occur, so the "factoring out" will work satisfactorily.

1.6   DESIGN ONE: AN ABSTRACT DATA TYPE FOR SETS

The mathematical abstraction *set* is very important in the kind of programming we shall be doing in this book. In fact, many of the interesting data structures we shall introduce can be thought of as just implementations of sets. We will come back to this in several sections of the book, but let us now concentrate on the abstraction.

We can think of a *type*, as introduced earlier in this chapter, as a "universe" of permissible values. Integers, natural numbers, characters, fractions, and so on, are all such "universes." For purposes of this discussion, we stipulate that our universes are *finite*, that is, have a finite number of members.

```
with Text_IO, Fractions, FractionIO;
use  Text_IO, Fractions, FractionIO;

procedure TestFractions is


    X, Y, Z: Fraction;

begin
     X := MakeFraction(2,4);
    new_line;
    put_line("please enter one fraction");
     get(Y);
    new_line;
     put("X="); put(X); put("  ; Y="); put(Y);
    new_line;
     If Equal(X,Y) then put("X=Y");
                       else put("x not = Y");  end if;
    new_line;
     If X<Y         then put("X<Y");
                       else put("X not < Y");  end if;
    new_line;
     If X>=Y        then put("X>=Y");
                       else put("X not >= Y"); end if;
    new_line;
     put("X in lowest terms is "); put(Reduce(X));
    new_line;
     put("X+Y="); put(X+Y);
    new_line;
     put("X-Y="); put(X-Y);
    new_line;
     put("X*Y="); put(X*Y);
    new_line;
     put("X/Y="); put(X/Y);
    new_line;
     put("(X+Y)*(X-Y)=");  put((X+Y)*(X-Y));
    new_line;
end TestFractions;
```

Figure 1-11 Example program using Fractions.

Given a universe, a *set* S is just a collection of objects belonging to that universe. Often sets are described just by listing their members between braces, as in the set {a,b} taken from the universe of English alphabet letters. In general, there is no *ordering* associated with a set, so {a,b} and {b,a} usually describe the same set. Two sets are said to be *equal* if they have the same members. A set is said to be *empty* if it has no members. In cases where there is no ordering, it also makes no difference if we name a member twice, so {a,b,a} = {b,a,b} = {a,b}.

What are the important operations associated with sets? Certainly *inserting* a member in a set and *deleting* a member from a set are essential; so are testing a set to see if a given element is a member and testing a set to see if it is empty.

There are several other operations on sets which are very useful. These are analogous to arithmetic operations on integers and reals (and fractions, for that matter). The most important dyadic operations are *union* of two sets S and T (sometimes written S+T, sometimes using other symbols), which produces the set containing all of S's members and all of T's members; *intersection* of S and T (sometimes written S*T), which produces the set containing all elements which are members of *both* S and T; and *difference* S-T, which produces the set containing all elements which are members of S but *not* of T. An often-used monadic operation is the *complement* –S, which returns the set containing all elements in the universe which are *not* members of S.

For example, if S = {a,b,c} and T = {b,c,d,e} and the universe is the letters a-k inclusive, then

$$S+T = \{a,b,c,d,e\}$$

$$S*T = \{b,c\}$$

$$S-T = \{a\} \text{ and } T-S = \{d,e\}$$

$$-S = \{d,e,f,g,h,i,j,k\}$$

For a simple example of an ADT for sets, let us choose as our universe the natural numbers 1 through 100 inclusive, list all the functions above in our specification, then implement a set as a one-dimensional array with subscripts

```
package NaturalSets is

   type NaturalSet is private;

   procedure Insert(S: in out NaturalSet; E: natural);
   procedure Delete(S: in out NaturalSet; E: natural);

   function  IsIn(S: NaturalSet; E: natural)  return boolean;
   function  IsEmpty(S: NaturalSet)            return boolean;
   function  SizeOf(S: NaturalSet)             return integer;
   function  Equal(S,T: NaturalSet)            return boolean;

   function  "+"(S,T: NaturalSet)              return NaturalSet;
   function  "*"(S,T: NaturalSet)              return NaturalSet;
   function  "-"(S,T: NaturalSet)              return NaturalSet;
   function  "-"(S: NaturalSet)                return NaturalSet;

   private
      type NaturalSet is array(1..100) of boolean;
      PHI: constant NaturalSet := (1..100=>false);

end NaturalSets;
```

Figure 1-12 Specification for a Sets package.

1. .100 of *Boolean* values. Given a set S represented in this fashion, we will let S(i)=TRUE if and only if the natural number i happens to be a member of S, and FALSE otherwise. This representation is often called the *characteristic function* or *bit map* of a set. If we were to let the members of the set be members of some arbitrary enumerated universe, we would have a fairly good approximation to the built-in but limited set facility of Pascal.

Now let us devise an Ada package for this ADT. Figure 1–12 gives the desired specification, complete with private part defining the type NaturalSet.

```
package body NaturalSets is

   procedure Insert(S: in out NaturalSet; E: natural) is
      begin
         S(E) := true;
      end Insert;

   -- code for procedure Delete

   function  IsIn(S: NaturalSet; E: natural) return boolean is
      begin
         return S(E);
      end IsIn;

   function  IsEmpty(S: NaturalSet) return boolean is
      begin
         return S = PHI;
      end IsEmpty;

   function  SizeOf(S: NaturalSet) return integer is
      N: integer := 0;
      begin
         for I in S'first..S'last loop
            if S(I) then N := N+1; end if;
         end loop;
         return N;
       end SizeOf;

   function  "+"(S,T: NaturalSet) return NaturalSet is
      R: NaturalSet := PHI;
      begin
         for I in S'first..S'last loop
            R(I) := S(I) or T(I);
         end loop;
         return R;
      end "+";

   -- code for function "*" (intersection of sets)
   -- code for dyadic function "-" (set difference)
   -- code for monadic function "-" (complement of a set)
   -- code for function Equal (set equality)


end NaturalSets;
```

Figure 1-13   Partial body for a Sets package.

In Figure 1–13 we show part of the body, giving the code for Insert, IsIn, IsEmpty, S+T, and SizeOf, which returns the *cardinality* of a set S, or the number of members S has. You can complete the body as an exercise.

In the code for SizeOf we have used an interesting Ada construction: "S'first..S'last." Ada provides a facility called "attributes," which allows a program writer to retrieve certain characteristics of a data structure, such as the dimensions of an array. In this case S'first and S'last will return, respectively, the lowest and highest subscript values for which S is defined. Since S is declared as a NaturalSet, which in turn is an array whose subscripts range from 1 to 100, S'first will return 1 and S'last will return 100. The loop statement in the SizeOf function, then, loops over all integer values between 1 and 100 inclusive.

Array attributes are very useful in writing programs dealing with arrays, since a subprogram does not need to be told explicitly (for example by extra parameters) how large its array parameters are. Attributes such as these will be used frequently in this book.

1.7 DESIGN TWO: AN ABSTRACT DATA TYPE FOR TEXT STRINGS

Ada does not have any built-in support for variable-length character strings. There is a built-in type *string*, but a string object is nothing but a character array and needs to be declared with a fixed length. On the other hand, it is common in applications to use string objects with a fixed *maximum* length but a variable *actual* length. If we just use Ada string objects, there is nothing built into Ada to keep track of how many characters there actually are in the string at any given moment.

Let us design a package for text strings which will provide the desired capability. We'll create an ADT Text which will have a fixed maximum length (say, thirty-two characters) but a variable actual length. This will give approximately the same facility available in PL/1 or UCSD Pascal. Figure 1–14 shows a type definition for Text. As text object is a record with a value part—a string capable of holding Maximum (=32) characters—and a length part—a non-negative integer no larger than Maximum.

What operations should apply to Text objects? A specification giving these operations appears in Figure 1–15. As in the fraction case, we need an operation to create a Text object given a normal Ada string. We call this operation MakeText, and in fact overload it so that Text objects can be made from single characters as well as strings. As before, along with our "create" operation we

```
type Text is
  record
    Pos: Index := 0;
    Value: string(1..Maximum);
  end record;
```

Figure 1-14   Type definition for Text objects.

need some "decomposition" operations, say Length(T) and Value(T), to return the current length and current value parts respectively.

Another operation on Text objects is *concatenation*, represented by the infix operator "&." The concatenation of two text objects T1 and T2 returns a Text object with the characters of T1 followed by those of T2. So Make-Text("ABC") & MakeText("DEF") will return a Text object with length 6 and value "ABCDEF".

For convenience, we define in fact *five* overloaded operators for concatenation, all called "&," so that a client program can, with no difficulty, and without extra calls to MakeText, concatenate normal Ada strings and characters with Text objects. Note that this is a sort of "mixed-mode arithmetic," use of which is often frowned upon in numerical problems. Here we allow mixed operations because they are so convenient and their results are so obvious.

The list of operations includes some comparison operations, needing no explanation except to point out that the comparison assumes "dictionary" or "lexical" order, so that "BCD" < "BCDE" (obvious) but also "BCD" < "CD" (perhaps less obvious).

Also included are Head(T) which returns the first character of its Text argument, and Tail(T), which returns T with its first character removed. Other useful operations are three Locates, which search a target Text object for the presence of another given character, string, or Text object, returning the position in the target where the substring begins, and Substr(T,Start,Size), which returns the Text substring of length Size, counted from position Start of T. So Locate("BC",MakeText("ABCDEF")) returns 2 and Locate('G',Make-Text("AB")) returns 0 because 'G' isn't in "AB". And Substr(Make-Text("ABCDEF",3,4)) returns a Text object with value "CDEF" and length 4.

In Figure 1–16 we show Ada implementations of several of these operations; you can finish the body as an exercise. This package has an important limitation: if any concatenate or MakeText operation results in a Text value longer than thirty-two characters, there is an overflow condition which results in the client program terminating abnormally. We shall just ignore this limitation—it's no worse than the usual arithmetic overflow—and remove it in the more sophisticated TextHandler package given in the Chapter 4 design section.

```
package TextHandler is

   Maximum: constant Integer := 32;
   subtype Index is integer range 0..Maximum;

   type  Text is private;

   function MakeText (S: string)    return Text;
   function MakeText (C: character) return Text;
   function NullText                return Text;
   --       "create" operation"

   function Length (T: Text) return Index;
   function Value (T: Text)  return string;
   function Empty (T: Text)  return boolean;
   --       decomposition operations

   function "&"(T1, T2: Text)             return Text;
   function "&"(T1: Text; C: character)   return Text;
   function "&"(C: character; T1: Text)   return Text;
   function "&"(T1: Text; S: string)      return Text;
   function "&"(S: string; T1: Text)      return Text;
   --       concatenation operations

   function Equal(T1, T2: Text) return boolean;
   function "<"  (T1, T2: Text) return boolean;
   function "<=" (T1, T2: Text) return boolean;
   function ">"  (T1, T2: Text) return boolean;
   function ">=" (T1, T2: Text) return boolean;
   --       lexical comparison

   function Head(T: Text) return character;
   function Tail(T: Text) return Text;
   --       head and tail functions

   function Locate(Sub: Text; Within: Text)      return Index;
   function Locate(Sub: string; Within: Text)    return Index;
   function Locate(Sub: character; Within: Text) return Index;
   --       Find Sub in Text; return 0 if not there

   function Substr(T: Text; Start, Size: Index)  return Text;
   --       return substring of length Size

private
   type Text is
      record
         Pos: Index := 0;
         Value: string(1..Maximum);
      end record;

end TextHandler;
```

Figure 1-15 Specification for Text package.

```
package body TextHandler is

   function MakeText(S: string) return Text is
      T: Text;
      begin
         if S = "" then
            T.Pos := 0;
         else
            T.Pos := S'Last - S'First + 1;
            T.Value(1..T.Pos) := S;
         end if;
         return T;
      end MakeText;

   function Value (T: Text) return string is
      begin
         if T.Pos = 0
            then return "";
            else return T.Value(1..T.Pos);
         end if;
      end Value;

   function "&"(T1, T2: Text) return Text is
      T: Text;
      begin
         if Empty(T1) then return T2; end if;
         if Empty(T2) then return T1; end if;

         T.Pos := T1.Pos + T2.Pos;
         T.Value(1..T.Pos) := T1.Value(1..T1.Pos)
               & T2.Value(1..T2.Pos);
         return T;
      end "&";

   function Equal(T1,T2: Text) return boolean is
      begin
         return T1.Value(1..T1.Pos) = T2.Value(1..T2.Pos);
      end Equal;

end TextHandler;
```

Figure 1-16   Partial Package Body for Text package.

1.8   STYLE GUIDE: AN ADT FOR COMPLEX NUMBERS IN STANDARD PASCAL

For the benefit of students who will be coding programs in a language other than Ada, we give some hints about writing ADTs in standard Pascal. Pascal is typical of languages such as Modula-2, C, and PL/1 which don't allow the use of overloaded operators or procedures. These languages also do not permit functions to have results which are structured types like records.

The syntax of our ADT development in this section is that of standard Pascal; Modula-2 syntax is nearly identical. C or Pl/1 programmers will find that they will need to translate the syntax a bit but that the principles are the same. This Style Guide will be interesting to Ada programmers as well, because it points out some limitations in the other languages which have been remedied in Ada.

In order not to repeat an example already seen above, we shall choose *complex numbers* to implement here. You may recall that a complex number has a "real" part and an "imaginary" part (there is nothing *imaginary* about these numbers; the name is historical), and that both of these are represented as real numbers in the programming language.

Following the requirements given above for an ADT, a complex number package should contain the following parts:

1. a definition of a complex as consisting of a real part and an imaginary part;
2. a method to be used by client programs in creating a new complex given two integers or reals to serve as the real and imaginary components;
3. a set of operations on complex numbers, so that client programs can do arithmetic on complex numbers without needing access to the details of what complex numbers look like internally.

For complex numbers the operations include sum, difference, product, quotient, and absolute value or magnitude operations, plus a small set of comparison operations like equals, less than, greater than, etc. The general idea is that this extended data type "comes with" the same general level of support offered in the base programming language for integers and reals.

1.8.1 Packages in Standard Pascal

Implicit in the notion of a package is that we can somehow physically isolate the package from other packages and from calling programs. Unfortunately, standard Pascal is not much help here, since neither a compile-time facility for copying separate pieces of source text into a source file nor a facility for separate compilation of packages is supported. Many implementations of Pascal provide one or both of these, but this discussion is limited to the possibilities of the standard language.

Another limitation in standard Pascal is that all type definitions must appear in one group following a type keyword, and these must appear before all code for functions and procedures. This certainly hinders our being able to group a type together with all *its* operations, another type with *its* operations, and so on. Once again, there are some implementation-dependent relaxations of this rule.

Yet a third limitation is that structured types, including records, may *not* serve as function results. In Ada we had no problem writing an addition function taking two fractions as its inputs and *returning* a fraction where the fractions were implemented, of course, as records. In Pascal, as in C, Modula-2, and PL/1, a function returning a record is simply an illegal construct.

A fourth problem is that only Ada allows giving several subprograms the same name ("overloading") and letting the types of the arguments help the compiler resolve ambiguities. Also, only Ada allows actually using an infix operator, say "+," to name a newly defined function.

1.8.2 A Pascal Complex-number Package

Let's see how to overcome some of these limitations. First let us define a Pascal type called Complex as a record with real and imaginary components, and declare some variables of type Complex, as in Figure 1–17. Now we can set A, B, and C as follows:

$$A.RealPart := 1.5; \quad A.ImagPart := -3.7;$$

$$B.RealPart := 2.0; \quad B.ImagPart := -5.1;$$

$$C.RealPart := 0.0; \quad C.ImagPart := 4.1$$

Now, how shall we do arithmetic on complex numbers? Given two complex numbers C1 and C2, their complex sum—call it Result—is a complex number such that

$$Result.RealPart := C1.RealPart + C2.RealPart$$

$$Result.ImagPart := C1.ImagPart + C2.ImagPart$$

We can't easily write the sum operation as a function, because Pascal doesn't allow functions to return records. We *could* implement this operation as

```
type Complex =
   record
      RealPart: real;
      ImagPart: real
   end {Complex};


var A, B, C, D, E, F:  Complex:
```

Figure 1-17 Type definition and variable declaration for Complex number.

```
procedure CSum ( var Result: Complex; C1,C2 : Complex);
  begin
    Result.RealPart := C1.RealPart + C2.RealPart;
    Result.ImagPart := C1.ImagPart + C2.ImagPart;
  end {CSum};
```

Figure 1-18   Pascal procedure for Complex sum.

a procedure, then do the equivalent of saying $D := A + B$ by writing CSum(D,A,B). The code for this procedure is shown in Figure 1–18.

Things start looking messier when we try to emulate a more complicated assignment like $D := A + B + C$. We would then need to write something like

$$CSum(Temp,A,B); \ CSum(D,Temp,C)$$

where the temporary complex number is used to hold the intermediate result $A + B$. As the expression got longer, we would need more and more separate calls to the CSum procedure, each doing only a single operation. Here the advantage of using a function for CSum is quite clear, since our assignment could be written

$$D := CSum(A, \ CSum(B,C))$$

which is much cleaner (especially in longer expressions).

As mentioned before, if we try to write CSum and other operations as functions, standard Pascal sets up an obstacle: functions may only return *scalar* types and Complex is a structured type (namely a record). What to do? Enter the pointer.

1.8.3 The Pointer in Pascal

What is a pointer? A pointer is an abstraction of the idea "address of...." Pointers exist in many programming languages; C, Modula-2 and PL/1 all have them; we shall see them later in Ada.

Pointers must be used with care. In fact, it has often been said that "pointers are data what go-to's are to code." But in appropriate situations, pointers in Pascal are extremely useful. In the current situation, pointers are useful because they are scalar types, and thus may be returned as function results!

We can use pointers to advantage in creating our package for complex numbers. The mechanism is to change the name of our complex-number record to CompNum, then define a *pointer* type Complex as a pointer to a record of type CompNum. This is shown in Figure 1–19.

The syntax needs a bit of explanation: the construct @CompNum is read "pointer to something of type CompNum." In the "official" Pascal language, an "up-arrow" symbol is used to represent a pointer; since most practical com-

```
type CompNum =
  record
    RealPart: real;
    ImagPart: real
  end {CompNum};


  Complex = @CompNum


var A, B, C, D, E, F : Complex
```

Figure 1-19   Revised type definitions for Complex numbers.

pilers use the symbol "@" for this, we shall use it here. Declaring the variables A, B, C, D, E, F does not, then, create six *records*, but only six *pointers*. The records will come into being later.

We can give a client program the equivalent of MakeFraction by noticing that the Pascal built-in procedure *new* can be used to "create" instances of a type at execution time. In Chapter 4 detailed consideration will be given to just how this happens; in brief, the space is found in a special storage area called the *heap*, which is automatically provided when a program is compiled.

A call such as new(P), where P is a pointer to some type, will create space for an instance of that type, returning the location of the new instance in P. In Figure 1–20 you will see a Pascal function MakeComplex, which takes two real numbers as arguments and returns something of type Complex. The construct P@ is read "the thing pointed to by P" and is called a *dereferencing* operation. So the statement P@.RealPart := R means "store R in the RealPart of the thing pointed to by P."

MakeComplex then, lets a user write, for example,

$$A := MakeComplex(2.0,-5.5)$$

```
function MakeComplex (R,I : real) : Complex;
  var P:  Complex;
begin
  new(P);
  P@.RealPart := R;
  P@.ImagPart := I;
  MakeComplex := P
end {MakeComplex};
```

Figure 1-20   Pascal "Create" function for Complex numbers.

```
function Re( C:  Complex) : real;
   begin
      Re := C@.RealPart
   end {Re };


function Im( C:  Complex) : real;
   begin
      Im := C@.ImagPart
   end { Im };
```

Figure 1-21   Decomposition functions for Complex numbers.

and, assuming that A has been declared to be of type Complex, never realize what is going on at the lower level.

We can further insulate the user from the "dot" notation of Pascal records and from any concern with pointers by providing two functions Re(C) and Im(C), which access the real and imaginary components of a Complex C and which correspond to the Numer and Denom functions in our Fractions package. These are shown in Figure 1–21.

Given that Y is of type real, then Y := Re(A) looks quite close to the corresponding notation from mathematics. The existence of these functions also helps to insure that a user will not (need to) know or refer to the internal details of a Complex.

At this point we can start writing other functions to do complex arithmetic; all such functions can now be written with arguments and returned values of type Complex, and no further reference need ever be made to lower-level implementation details. For example, we give in Figure 1–22 the code for two functions, both of which are quite brief. The first is CSum which returns a Complex giving the sum of its complex-number arguments; the second is CEqual, which tests to see if its two complex arguments are equal.

```
function CSum ( X,Y : Complex) : Complex;
  begin
    CSum := MakeComplex (Re(X)+Re(Y) , Im(X)+Im(Y) )
  end { CSum} ;


function CEqual ( X,Y : Complex ) : boolean;
   begin
      CEqual := Re(X)=Re(Y) & Im(X)=Im(Y)
   end {CEqual} ;
```

Figure 1-22   Two Pascal functions on Complex numbers.

1.8.4 What Happens to the Allocated Memory?

This would all work very well, except for one problem. If we were to write, for example, a complex-expression equivalent of

$$E := A \times B + C \times D, \text{ i.e.,}$$

$$E := CSum(CProd(A,B), CProd(C,D))$$

our scheme would call *new* to get space for the temporary results CProd(A,B) and CProd(C,D), as well as for the final sum of the two. What happens to the two temporary records we created?

The answer is that they remain allocated, and will not be re-used! Continual use of expressions like this will continually allocate temporary space which will not be recovered. Eventually our program will run out of dynamic memory space (usually called heap space) and bomb, even though we're not actually using all that space.

This is not a happy state of affairs, and suitable solutions exist, but to discuss them now would leap ahead to some material more appropriately considered later in the book. We will return to this subject in Chapter 4, in another Style Guide. In the meantime, all you can do is assume that your Pascal compiler gives you a large enough heap space to absorb the wasted memory.

1.8.5 The Specification Part

Since Pascal, unlike Ada, does not permit writing separate specifications and bodies, we shall have to be content with writing the specification part as a block comment. Figure 1–23 shows this style of specification for the complex number package.

1.9 SUMMARY

This chapter has presented the important concepts of *abstraction, implementation, data type, abstract data type* or *ADT*, and *data structure*.

Abstraction is the practice of viewing computer solutions in terms natural or appropriate to the problem being solved; implementation is the conversion of the abstract solution into a concrete one suitable for coding in a real programming language.

A data type is a set of appropriate values (like fractions, sets, reals, integers, etc.); an ADT is a data type plus a set of operations appropriate for that type; and a data structure is a programming mechanism suitable for the representation of the type in a real program.

```
{ package ComplexNumbers

    type Complex                        details private

    function MakeComplex  ( R,I : real )        : Complex;
        "create" operation

    function Re  ( C : Complex )                : real;
    function Im  ( C : Complex )                : real;
        decomposition operations

    function CSum  ( X,Y : Complex )            : Complex;
    function CDiff ( X,Y : Complex )            : Complex;
    function CProd ( X,Y : Complex )            : Complex;
    function CQuot ( X,Y : ·Complex )           : Complex;
        arithmetic operations

    function CEqual( X,Y : Complex )            : boolean;
    function CLess ( X,Y : Complex )            : boolean;
    function CGtrEq( X,Y : Complex )            : boolean
        comparison operations

    function Conjugate ( X: Complex )           : Complex
    function Magnitude ( X: Complex )           : Complex
        miscellaneous

    end of specification for package ComplexNumbers  }
```

Figure 1-23 Pascal specification for Complex-arithmetic package.

We have introduced the feature of Ada called *packages*, which can be used effectively as a mechanism for implementing ADTs. A package has three parts, the *specification*, the *body*, and, usually, the *private part*, which is physically present as part of the specification but serves a different purpose.

Packages permit the designer to indicate explicitly which parts of the implementation are to be *exported*, or visible to the "outside world," and which parts contain details which are more appropriately hidden away from the user's view.

Designs and (partial) Ada implementations for three ADTs–fractions, very simple sets, and text objects—have shown you the way to get started with ADTs and Ada packages; the Style Guide section gave some ideas on how you might write them in languages other than Ada. The rest of the book will continue in this vein, presenting ADTs and alternative strategies for their implementation.

1.10   EXERCISES

1. Complete the implementation of Fractions as begun in section 1.5.

2. Develop appropriate input ("get") and output ("put") operations for fractions.

3. Complete the implementation of Sets as begun in Section 1.6.

4. Complete the TextHandler begun in Section 1.7.

5. Make a list of other abstractions and implementations you have encountered in your programming experience.

Chapter 2

ALGORITHMS, RECURSION, AND PERFORMANCE PREDICTION

2.1   GOAL STATEMENT

Any pragmatic study of data structures must also include some study of *algorithms*, the methods by which problems are solved on a computer. Data structures without algorithms are useless and empty curiosities.

In this chapter you will study two important aspects of algorithms. The first is the use of *recursion* or *recursive algorithms* to solve certain computing problems. A recursive algorithm moves ahead by applying *itself* to a smaller part of the problem; this is seen in programming terms in the fact that the algorithm, written as a function or procedure, "calls itself." Several useful but easy-to-understand recursive algorithms will be presented, together with Ada programs implementing them.

The second area introduced in this chapter is *performance prediction*. Here you will learn techniques and "rules of thumb" to estimate the computation time of an algorithm, or more specifically the *variation* of the computation time as a function of the *size* of the problem being solved. An important bit of terminology in performance prediction is "big O" notation. This notation is a way of representing the "order of magnitude" or "growth rate" of an algorithm, in other words the variation with problem size we just mentioned.

You will be introduced to the most common variations or "big O's" to be encountered later in the book. These are the *constant, logarithmic, linear, quadratic,* and *N* × *log(N)* growth rates.

2.2 ALGORITHMS AND ALGORITHM DESIGN

If you are reading this book, you probably have some experience in programming. You probably know, intuitively, what an *algorithm* is. Informally, an algorithm is a method used to solve a problem on a computer. Formally,

An algorithm is

a *finite sequence of instructions,* each of which

has a *clear meaning* and can be

performed with a *finite amount of effort*

in a *finite length of time.*

A program is an algorithm if it never goes into an infinite loop, no matter what input we give it.

This is a text devoted to the study of data structures. Why, then, is there a chapter on algorithms? Algorithms are the methods used in systematic problem solving, to move the solution ahead from its starting point to its end. Thus while this book indeed concentrates on data structures, it cannot ignore the study of algorithms, since data structures, by themselves, are useless. Without methods for storing data in the structures, retrieving data from them, and performing computational operations on the data stored there, data structures are nothing but empty curiosities.

Furthermore, the computation time and memory space required by data structures and the algorithms that work on them are important and sometimes scarce resources. Indeed, you will see in this book frequent references to "trade-offs." A trade-off is a situation in which alternative solutions to a problem are considered in terms of their resource requirements: one solution may require more time but less space than another; a third might require more time *and* more space than either of the others but the programs might be simpler and easier to maintain, thus more economical in *human* terms. We thus speak in terms of *trading off* space for time, or performance for clarity, or computer resources for human ones.

No book can give you a "right answer" which will serve in every case. When you are faced with a trade-off situation in deciding on a computer solution to some problem you have, you must base your decision on the specific circumstances in effect at the time. What a book *can* supply is a set of tools for you to use in analyzing all the factors and trade-offs; the analysis itself, and the final decision, is up to you and your colleagues.

You can see that data structures and algorithms are interrelated and cannot be studied completely apart from one another. Since you already have some experience in writing algorithms, in this chapter we will not go back to "first principles." Rather, we will focus your attention on two important concepts in algorithms. One is the important and useful mathematical notion of *recursion*, a tool we shall use frequently in this book. The other is *performance prediction*, a tool to "give us a handle" on the time requirements of a problem solution.

2.3 RECURSIVE ALGORITHMS

In this section, we introduce a concept in algorithm design called *recursion*. A recursive algorithm—an algorithm which uses recursion—is defined in terms of itself; the solutions of many interesting programming problems are stated clearly and elegantly in recursive form, and you will see many recursive algorithms in this book.

A classical simple example of recursion is the definition of the *factorial* of a positive integer N. Written N! and read "N-factorial," this is easily understood as the product $1 \times 2 \times ... \times N$. Thus $3! = 6$, $4! = 24$, $5! = 120$, etc. But we can write a definition without any "dot-dot-dot" as follows:

To find N!:

1. If N=1 then N! = 1;
2. Otherwise N! = N × (N-1)!

We have defined the "!" operation in terms of itself. Notice that the definition is not circular, because the "!" is applied to a smaller and smaller number each time, until it is applied to 1. Figure 2–1 shows the definition applied to

```
5! = 5 x 4!
   = 5 x (4 x 3!)
   = 5 x (4 x (3 x 2!))
   = 5 x (4 x (3 x (2 x 1!)))
   = 5 x (4 x (3 x (2 x 1)))
   = 5 x (4 x (3 x 2))
   = 5 x (4 x 6)
   = 5 x 24
   = 120
```

Figure 2-1 Recursive calculation of 5!.

```
function Factorial(N: in positive) return positive is

    begin

        if N = 1 then return 1;
                 else return N * Factorial(N-1);
                 -- Note recursive call of Factorial!
        end if;

    end Factorial;
```

Figure 2-2   Recursive Ada function to find N!, N>=1.

calculate 5!; try the definition on some other numbers to be sure you understand how the recursion works. You will discover that N! gets very large very quickly: even an innocent-looking calculation like 10! produces a rather big number. In fact, if you were to write a program to calculate N! and run it on a computer using sixteen bits to represent an integer, your program could not calculate factorials larger than 7!, since 8! > 32767.

It is very important to notice that a workable recursive algorithm must always reduce the size of the "data set," or the number that it is working with, each time it is recursively called, and must always provide a terminating condition such as the first line in our factorial algorithm. Otherwise, the algorithm may never terminate, getting itself stuck in an "infinite recursion."

In programming terms, it is nice to know that modern programming languages like Ada permit direct use of recursion in defining functions and procedures. Recursive algorithms seem mysterious to programmers trained only in Fortran, Cobol, or Basic, because those languages don't allow recursion, but recursion is really a very simple and elegant concept directly applicable in Ada, Pascal, Modula-2, PL/1, C, and others. You can see this in Figure 2–2, where a recursive factorial function is given in Ada.

Finding the factorial of a positive integer is only a simple example of what can be a very handy tool in developing algorithms. You will see this in the rest of this section, where attention will be focused on four easily understood but useful recursive solutions. Ada programs are given for three of the four; a program for the fourth will be shown later in the book.

These algorithms are *finding the reversal of a string, finding the permutations of the elements in a set, recursive binary search*, and **recursive merge sort.**

2.3.1 Reversal of a string

There is a certain type of phrase in our natural languages known as a *palindrome*. This is a phrase which reads the same forwards and backwards. Two examples of English palindromes are "RADAR" and "ABLE WAS I ERE I

SAW ELBA." The phrase, "MADAM, I'M ADAM," perhaps spoken by the Biblical first man when he met his wife Eve, is a palindrome if we neglect spaces and punctuation.

One way to discover whether a phrase, or string of characters, is a palindrome, is to find the *reverse* of the string. The string is a palindrome if its reverse is identical to it.

We can find the reverse of a string very easily by the following algorithm:

To find the reverse of a string:

1. If the string contains only one character, its reverse is identical to it and we're finished.

2. Otherwise, remove and save the first character.

3. *Find the reverse* of the remaining string, then concatenate the saved character onto the right-hand end.

Notice that we've *found the reverse* of a string by removing the first character and *finding the reverse* of what's left. This is a *recursive* algorithm: to carry it out on the whole set of data we need to carry it out on a smaller set of data.

Assume we have available a text-string package such as was described in Chapter 1, which gives us the predefined functions Head(S), which returns the first character; Tail(S), which returns the string with the first character removed; and S1 & S2, which returns the concatenation of S1 and S2. Figure 2–3 shows an Ada function StringReverse(S), which returns the reverse of a string (we have to call it StringReverse because "reverse" is a reserved word in Ada). Note the place in which StringReverse is called by StringReverse! This is known as a *recursive call* of a function.

Figure 2–4 shows a function Palindrome(S), which uses Reverse to determine whether its text-string argument S is a palindrome.

```
function StringReverse(S: Text) return Text is

   begin

      if Length(S) <= 1
         then return S;
         else return StringReverse(Tail(S)) & Head(S);
      end if;

   end StringReverse;
```

Figure 2-3   Recursive function to find the reverse of a string S.

```
function Palindrome(S: Text) return boolean is

  begin

    If Equal(S,StringReverse(S))
      then return true;
      else return false;
    end If;

  end Palindrome;
```

Figure 2-4   Boolean function to determine whether a string S is a palindrome.

2.3.2 Permutations of a Set

Consider a well-to-do family of two parents and two college-age children. Each family member has an automobile; their house has a four-car garage. Letting their cars be called A,B,C,D, and the garage stalls 1,2,3,4, what are the different ways in which the cars can be parked in the garages?

Suppose A parks in stall 1. Then we can list all the ways left to B,C, and D. Suppose then that B parks in stall 2. Clearly C and D can park in two different ways: C in stall 3 and D in stall 4, or the other way around.

But suppose C parks in stall 2. Then it is B and D that use stalls 3 and 4 in one of two ways. And if D parks in stall 2, then it is B and C sharing stalls 3 and 4.

Clearly, then, there are six possibilities once A has parked in stall 1. It's easy to see that another six possibilities come from B parking in stall 1, and twelve more from C and D parking there. There are a total of 24 possibilities, all shown in Figure 2–5.

This is an example of finding the *permutations* of the elements of a set, where here the set is the family's automobiles, and a permutation is an assignment to the stalls in the garage. If the set has N members, the number of permutations is N! = 1x2..xN.

Let's try to write an algorithm to print out the permutations of the members of a set. Letting the set be {A,B,C,D}, we can say:

To print all permutations of {A,B,C,D}:

1. Print A, followed by *all permutations* of {B,C,D}.
2. Print B, followed by *all permutations* of {A,C,D}.
3. Print C, followed by *all permutations* of {B,A,D}.
4. Print D, followed by *all permutations* of {B,C,A}.

1	2	3	4
A	B	C	D
A	B	D	C
A	C	B	D
A	C	D	B
A	D	B	C
A	D	C	B
B	A	C	D
B	A	D	C
B	C	A	D
B	C	D	A
B	D	A	C
B	D	C	A
C	A	B	D
C	A	D	B
C	B	A	D
C	B	D	A
C	D	A	B
C	D	B	A
D	A	B	C
D	A	C	B
D	B	A	C
D	B	C	A
D	C	A	B
D	C	B	A

Figure 2-5   Permutations of {A,B,C,D}.

We have interchanged A with B, C, and D in turn (as though B, C, and D had parked, in turn, in stall 1).

Now, to print out all permutations of {B,C,D}, we have a problem just like the larger one, but smaller! And printing out the permutations of {C,D} is just a smaller version of *that* problem! This sort of problem—one where the same algorithm can be applied repeatedly to smaller and smaller sets—lends itself to a recursive solution.

Let's construct a recursive Ada procedure to print the permutations of an ordered set S with members numbered 1 though N. Without being concerned for how a set is implemented, assume we have a predefined procedure Print-Set(S), which prints the entire set S, a function CopySet(S) which returns an exact copy of S, a function SizeOf(S) which returns the cardinality of S, and a procedure Interchange(S,k,i) which interchanges the i-th and k-th members of S. Our recursive procedure is called PrintPermutations(S,k,N), which prints the permutations of the k-th through N-th members of S. The detailed Ada text is shown in Figure 2–6. Be certain you understand how it works!

```
procedure PrintPermutations(S: in set; k: in positive) is

      N: positive := SizeOf(S);
      S1: set(1..N) := CopySet(S);
      -- The local variable is used here so the input set
      -- S doesn't get changed.

  begin

    if k = N
       then PrintSet(S1);
    else
       for i in k..N loop

          Interchange(S1,i,k);
          PrintPermutations(S1,k+1);
          -- this recursive call prints all permutations of
          -- the set with the 1st through k-th members held
          -- constant and the k+1st through N-th varying.

       end loop;
    end if;

end PrintPermutations;
```

Figure 2-6   Recursive procedure to print permutations of a set S.

To give a more complete example of an Ada program, let's implement a set as just an array whose elements are the members of the set. Really we should think of this as an ADT implemented by a package, but to keep the example uncomplicated, we just show the type definitions and the few operations needed by the permutations program.

Figure 2–7 shows a program TestPerms which gives these definitions and operations, and incorporates the PrintPermutations procedure.

2.3.3 Recursive Binary Search

Imagine that you've written up a list of your friends, giving their names in alphabetical order, together with their telephone numbers. Because you're very popular, you have many friends and this list is quite long, running over a number of pages.

Let's consider a clever way to look up a friend's phone number in this long list (actually, it's a way better suited to a computer than a person, but that's because people "look things up" intuitively instead of using algorithms!).

To look up a name:

1. Divide your list in half, then look at the name right in the middle. If it's the one whose number you're searching for, you're done.

```
with TextIO; use TextIO;
procedure TestPerms is

  type set is array (integer range <>) of character;
  P: set(1..5) := ('A','B','C','D','E');

  function SizeOf(S: set) return positive is
    begin
      return S'length;
    end SizeOf;

  function CopySet(S: set) return set is
      S1: set(S'first..S'last);
    begin
      S1(S1'first..S1'last) := S(S'first..S'last);
      return S1;
    end CopySet;

  procedure PrintSet(S: set) is
    begin
      for i in S'first..S'last loop
        put(S(i)); put(" ");
      end loop;
      new_line;
    end PrintSet;

  procedure Interchange(S: in out set; i,k: positive) is
      temp: character;
    begin
      temp := S(i);
      S(i) := S(k);
      S(k) := temp;
    end Interchange;

  -- insert the code for PrintPermutations right here.


begin
  PrintPermutations(P,1);
end TestPerms;
```

Figure 2-7   Program illustrating PrintPermutations.

2. If your friend's name is *earlier* in the alphabet than the middle one, ignore all the names from this middle one to the end, and *look up the name* only in the first half. Divide *it* in half, then look at the middle item, etc.

3. If your friend's name is *later* in the alphabet than the middle one, ignore the first half of the list, and *look up the name* in the second half as above.

Eventually one of two things will happen: you'll find your friend in the list, or you'll divide the list in half so many times that only one name will remain and it's not the one you wanted! This means that the friend you were looking for isn't in your list.

Like the reversal and permutation algorithms, this method is recursive: the same method applied to the full list is applied to half the list, then to half of the half, etc. Let's construct an Ada function for this. We'll let the list be implemented as an array with subscripts 1..N. The function will be called LookUp-Name(L,Name), which looks up Name in the array L. LookUpName will return the location of Name if it can find it, and zero if it can't.

Since our list is implemented as an array, we can use two interesting features of Ada: the *array slice* and *array attributes.* If L is an array, then the attribute *L'first* gives the value of its *lowest* subscript and *L'last* gives the value of its *highest* subscript. Furthermore, the *slice* L(k..m) refers to the *subarray* L(k) through L(m). Thus the function call LookUpName(L(k..m),Name) will search only in the subarray L(k) through L(m); the call LookUp-Name(L('first..L 'last),Name) will search the entire array (as will just Look-UpName(L,Name), by the way).

The Ada text for this function appears in Figure 2–8. Try finding the locations of some names in the table given in Figure 2–9.

```
function LookUpName(L: list; Name: NameType) return natural is

        Lower: positive := L'first;
        Upper: positive := L'last;
        Middle: positive := (Lower + Upper) / 2;
        -- integer division gives middle item if number of items
        -- is odd, item just below middle otherwise.

    begin

        if      Name = L(Middle) then return Middle;
                -- we found it!

        elsif   Lower = Upper    then return 0;
                -- subarray only has one name and it's
                -- not the one we were looking for!

        elsif   Name < L(middle) then
                return LookUpName(L(Lower..Middle-1),Name);
                -- just look in the first half -
                -- recursive call!

        else    return LookUpName(L(Middle+1..Upper),Name);
                -- just look in the second half -
                -- recursive call!

        end if;

    end LookUpName;
```

Figure 2-8   Recursive function to find a name in an alphebetized list.

```
 1  ALAN
 2  ALEX
 3  BEN
 4  BILL
 5  BRAD
 6  EUGENE
 7  JENNY
 8  JESSICA
 9  JONATHAN
10  JUSTIN
11  KEITH
12  KEVIN
13  KRISTIN
14  MARTHA
15  SHARON
16  SHERRY
```

Figure 2-9   Table of names in alphabetical sequence.

We call this algorithm *recursive binary search*. It is an example of a whole class of algorithms known as "divide-and-conquer," which work, as does this one, by dividing and subdividing the set of data into two parts.

2.3.4 Recursive Merge Sort

Our last example of recursion in this section involves sorting the elements of a list into ascending sequence. We will just sketch out an algorithm, *Recursive merge sort*, leaving the details until our chapter on sorting later in the book.

The algorithm depends upon our knowing how to *merge* two sorted lists into a single sorted list. Informally, the two sorted lists {B,G,H,P} and {A,F,K,L,R,Z} can be merged into a single list {A,B,F,G,H,K,L,P,R,Z}, much as you might merge two sorted decks of 3x5 cards into a single deck.

Without being concerned with the details of the merge operation, consider how the two original sorted lists came to be sorted: why not by the very same process? In other words, if we start with a single unsorted list, we can write an informal algorithm as follows:

To sort a list:

1. If the list contains only one item, it is sorted already.

2. Otherwise, divide the list in half, *sort* the two halves, then merge them.

Aha! Another recursive algorithm! Our sorting method moves forward by dividing its problem in half, then applying itself to the two halves of the list.

```
Original     (Z A C F Q B G K P N D E M H R T)
Divide       (Z A C F Q B G K) (P N D E M H R T)
Divide       (Z A C F)(Q B G K)  (P N D E)(M H R T)
Divide       (ZA)(CF)  (QB)(GK)  (PN)(DE)  (MH)(RT)
Sort pairs   (AZ)(CF)  (BQ)(GK)  (NP)(DE)  (HM)(RT)
merge        (A C F Z)  (B G K Q)  (D E N P)  (H M R T)
merge        (A B C F G K Q Z) (D E H M N P R T)
merge        (A B C D E FG H K M N Q P R T Z)
                                      sorted!
```

Figure 2-10 Recursive ("top-down") merge sort.

Recursive merge sort is thus another divide-and-conquer algorithm. An example of its use is shown in Figure 2–10.

You have seen five recursive algorithms in this section, and will see many more throughout this book. Recursion is not a mysterious or magical concept, rather just another tool in the algorithm designer's tool kit. It is time now to move to another important topic in algorithms, namely *performance prediction*.

2.4 PERFORMANCE PREDICTION AND THE "BIG O" NOTATION

In considering the trade-offs among alternative problem solutions, an important factor is the expected computation time of each of the alternatives. It is difficult to predict the *actual* computation time of an algorithm without knowing the intimate details of the underlying computer, the object code generated by the compiler, and other related factors. The actual time must really be *measured* for a given algorithm, language, compiler, and computer system by means of some carefully-designed performance tests, usually called "benchmarks."

On the other hand, it is very helpful to know the way the running time will *vary* or *grow* as a function of the "problem size": the number of elements in an array, the number of records in a file, and so forth. Programmers sometimes discover that programs that have run in perfectly reasonable time for the small test sets they have used, take extraordinarily long when run with real-world size data sets or files. These programmers were deceived by the "growth rate" of the computation.

To take an example, it is common to write programs whose running time varies with, for example, the *square* of the problem size. A program taking, say, one second to complete a file-handling problem with ten records in the file, will require not two but four seconds for twenty records. Increasing the file size by a factor of ten, to 100 records, will multiply the run time by 100 to 100 seconds.

One thousand records will need 10,000 seconds or about three hours to complete! And 10,000 records (the number of accounts in a fair-sized bank or students in a fair-sized university) will need almost two weeks! This is a long time compared to the one second taken by the ten-record test.

This example shows that it makes sense to know something about growth rates, lest program running time grow in disturbing ways when problems grow to meaningful size. Sometimes there is no choice: there may be no alternative solution to that program running in "squared" or *quadratic* time. But a programmer with some experience in performance estimation is at least in a position not to be surprised!

2.4.1 Algorithm Growth Rates

Getting a precise estimate of the computation time of an algorithm is often difficult, but as you have seen, it helps to "get a handle on it." We do this by trying to write a formula for the computation time in terms of the problem size N. This will have a factor in it that depends upon the programming language, compiler, and underlying computer. It is often a good assumption that this "system dependent" factor is reasonably constant, not varying with the problem size, and so we can "factor it out." (Obviously it's nice to have a small "system dependent" constant as well as a small growth rate, but reducing the size of the constant is hard to do in a general way precisely because it's system dependent!)

We give the name *growth rate* to that part of the formula that *does* vary with problem size. In discussing the growth rates of algorithms, it is fashionable to use the notation O() (read "growth rate," "big O," or "order of magnitude"). The most common growth rates encountered in data structures work are the following:

1. $O(1)$ or *constant*;
2. $O(\log(N))$ or *logarithmic* (the logarithm is usually taken to the base 2);
3. $O(N)$ or *linear* (directly proportional to N);
4. $O(N \times \log(N))$ (usually just called N log N);
5. $O(N^2)$ or *quadratic* (proportional to the square of N).

To give you an idea of the computation time of typical file sizes, Figure 2–11 shows the values of each of these functions for a number of different values of N. The values happen to be powers of 2, but this is just to make the computation of logarithms convenient.

From this table you can see that as N grows, $\log(N)$ remains quite small with respect to N, and $N \times \log(N)$ grows fairly large, but not nearly as large as N^2. In studying sorting in Chapter 8, you'll discover that most sorting methods have growth rates of $N \times \log(N)$ or N^2. In the next section we'll look at some common algorithmic structures and discuss how to estimate their growth rates.

N	1	Log(N)	N x Log(N)	N**2
1	1	0	0	1
2	2	1	2	4
4	1	2	8	16
8	1	3	24	64
16	1	4	64	256
32	1	5	160	1024
64	1	6	384	4096
126	1	7	896	16384
256	1	8	2048	65536
512	1	9	4608	262144
1024	1	10	10240	1048576
2048	1	11	22528	4194304
4096	1	12	49152	16777216
8192	1	13	106496	67108864
16384	1	14	229376	268435456
32768	1	15	491520	1073741824

Figure 2-11 Table of common algorithm growth rates.

2.4.2 Estimating the Growth Rate of an Algorithm

While there are no absolute "cookbook" rules that will always work to estimate performance, we can "get a handle on it" by taking advantage of the fact that algorithms are developed in a "structured" way. Structured algorithms combine statements into usefully complex blocks in four ways:

1. *sequence*, or writing one statement below another;
2. *decision*, or the well-known *if-then* or *if-then-else*;
3. *loop*, including counting loops, *while* loops, *until* loops, and the general *loop-exit-end loop* structure;
4. *subprogram call.*

In Figure 2–12 you can see the Ada notation for a number of different variations on these structures. Now let's take a look at some typical algorithm structures and estimate their "big Os." We'll always denote by N the "problem size."

Simple Statement

A simple statement is, for example, an assignment statement. If we assume that the statement contains no function calls (whose execution time may, of course, vary with problem size), the statement takes a fixed amount of time to execute. This we denote by O(1), because if we factor out the constant execution time we're left with 1.

```
Temp := A;
A    := B;
B    := Temp;
```

(a) Sequence.

```
If x > Max
    then Max := x;
end If;
```

(b) Decision.

```
If x > y
    then Max := x;
    else Max := y;
end If;
```

(c) if-then-else

```
If x >= y and x >= z
    then Max := x;
elsif y >= x and y >= z
    then Max := y;
else
    Max := z;
end If;
```

(d) if-then-elsif-else

```
for i in p..q loop
    x := x + i;
end loop;
```

(e) counting loop

```
while x > 0 loop
    y := y + 3;
    x := x/2;
end loop;
```

(f) while loop

```
loop
    x := x + k;
    exit when x >= 100;
    y := y - z;
end loop;
```

(g) loop-exit-end loop

Figure 2-12   Some Ada control structures.

Sequence of Simple Statements

A sequence of simple statements takes, obviously, time equal to the sum of the individual statement times. If the individual statements are O(1), then so is the sum.

Decision

For purposes of estimating performance we rely on the fact that both the *then* part and the *else* part can be arbitrary structures in their own right. To estimate conservatively, then, we take the larger of the two individual "big Os" as the "big O" of the decision.

There are variations of the decision structure. For example, the *case* structure is really a multi-way *if-then-else*, so in estimating a *case* we just take the largest "big O" of all of the case alternatives.

Similarly, Ada and many other languages provide a structure like *if-then-elsif-else*, as was shown in Figure 2–12. This is also just a multi-way decision.

That performance estimation can get very complicated and "tricky" can be seen by realizing that the condition tested in a decision may involve a function call, and that the timing of the function call may itself vary with problem size!

Counting Loop

A *counting loop* is a loop in which the loop counter is incremented (or decremented) each time the loop is executed. This is different from some loops we will consider a bit later, where the counter is multiplied or divided by a value.

What is the performance of a simple counting loop? Suppose the body of the loop contains only a sequence of simple statements. Then the performance of the loop is just the number of times the loop executes. Let us use the term *trip count* to mean "the number of times a loop executes." If the trip count is constant—independent of problem size—then the whole loop is O(1). On the other hand, if the loop is something like

for counter **in** 1..N **loop**

the trip count does depend on N, so the performance is O(N). These two loop structures, where the body contains only simple statements, are shown in Figure 2–13.

```
for counter in 1..5 loop
    ...
        something with O(1)
    ...
end loop;
```

(a) Trip count is constant.

```
for counter in 1..N loop
    ...
        something with O(1)
    ...
end loop;
```

(b) Trip count depends on N.

Figure 2-13 Two simple counting loops in Ada.

Now suppose that the loop body is more complex. Real algorithms have this sort of complexity, so let's consider a number of possibilities. Remember that we can't cover every case; we'll look at some common ones to be encountered in this book, so that you can recognize these when you see them.

Figure 2–14 shows a double counting loop. The outer loop's trip count is clearly N. But the inner loop executes N times for each time the outer loop executes, so the body of the inner loop will be executed N*N times, and the performance of the entire structure is $O(N^2)$.

In Figure 2–15, a structure is shown that looks deceptively similar to the last one. The outer loop surely has a trip count of N. But the trip count of the inner loop depends not only on N but also on the value of OuterCounter! If OuterCounter = 1, the inner loop has a trip count of 1. If OuterCounter = 2, the inner loop trip count is 2; if OuterCounter = 3, the inner loop trip count is 3. Finally, if OuterCounter = N, the inner loop trip count is N.

How many times will the body of the inner loop be executed? It will be the *sum*

$$1 + 2 + 3 + ... + N\text{-}1 + N.$$

This summation, as you probably learned somewhere in an algebra course, is $N\times(N+1)/2 = ((N^2)+N)/2$. We will say that the performance of this structure is $O(N^2)$, since for large N the contribution of the N/2 term is negligible.

It is interesting that making the inner loop trip count depend on Outer-Counter does not alter the "big O," since we neglect the term in N.

The structure in Figure 2–16 is similar, but the trip count of the inner loop *decreases* rather than increases as above. If OuterCounter = 1, the inner loop has a trip count of N. If OuterCounter = 2, the inner loop trip count is N-1; if OuterCounter = 3, the inner loop trip count is N-2. Finally, if Outer-Counter = N, the inner loop trip count is 1.

The number of times the body of the inner loop is executed is the sum

$$N + N\text{-}1 + N\text{-}2 + ... + 1$$

which is really the same sum as before, i.e. $N\times(N+1)/2 = ((N^2)+N)/2$. This structure also has performance $O(N^2)$.

```
for OuterCounter In 1..N loop
    for InnerCounter In 1..N loop

        ...
          something with O(1)
        ...

    end loop;
end loop;
```

Figure 2-14   A double counting loop in Ada.

```
for OuterCounter In 1..N loop
    for InnerCounter In 1..OuterCounter loop

    ...
        something with O(1)
    ...

    end loop;
end loop;
```

Figure 2-15   Another double counting loop.

Look at the loop structures in Figure 2–17 and convince yourself that in all cases the performance is $O(N^3)$.

From these examples we can generalize as follows: a structure with k nested counting loops—loops where the counter is just incremented or decremented by 1—has performance $O(N^k)$ if the trip count of each loop depends on the problem size. A growth rate $O(N^k)$ is called *polynomial*.

Multiplicatively-controlled Loop

By a *multiplicatively-controlled loop* we mean one in which the variable controlling the loop is multiplied or divided by a constant each time the loop is executed. Multiplicatively-controlled loops arise often in the kinds of algorithms you will see in this book.

While most programming languages have a special structure for counting loops, they don't usually have a structure designed specifically to accommodate multiplicative control; generally we just use a *while* or *until* loop.

Recall that whatever the specific structure used, every loop needs

- an *initialization* step which gives the starting value(s) of the control variable(s);
- a *termination* condition which is tested during each iteration and which indicates the circumstances under which the loop stops executing; and

```
for OuterCounter In 1..N loop
    for InnerCounter In OuterCounter..N loop

    ...
        something with O(1)
    ...

    end loop;
end loop;
```

Figure 2-16   Yet another double counting loop.

```
for OuterCounter in 1..N loop
    for Middle Counter in 1..N loop
        for InnerCounter in 1..N loop

            ...
            something with O(1)
            ...

        end loop;
    end loop;
end loop;
```

(a)

```
for OuterCounter in 1..N loop
    for Middle Counter in 1..OuterCounter loop
        for InnerCounter in 1..MiddleCounter loop

            ...
            something with O(1)
            ...

        end loop;
    end loop;
end loop;
```

(b)

```
for OuterCounter in 1..N loop
    for Middle Counter in 1..OuterCounter loop
        for InnerCounter in MiddleCounter..N loop

            ...
            something with O(1)
            ...

        end loop;
    end loop;
end loop;
```

(c)

Figure 2-17   Some triple counting loops.

- a *modification* step indicating how the control variable(s) should be changed to move the loop along from its starting point to its ending point.

The difference between a *while* structure and an *until* structure is that in the former the termination condition is tested before each iteration, and in the latter the condition is tested at the end of each iteration.

```
Control := 1;

while Control <= N loop
   ...
     something with O(1)
   ...

   Control := 2 * Control;
end loop;
```

Figure 2-18   A multiplicatively-controlled loop.

Consider the structure in Figure 2–18. In this loop, whose performance clearly depends on the problem size N, the variable Control is multiplied by the constant 2 until Control gets to be larger than N.

Since Control's starting value is 1, after k iterations

$$\text{Control} = 2^k$$

The number of iterations k can be found just by taking logarithms of both sides so that we get

$$\log(\text{Control}) = k \text{ (log is taken to the base 2)}$$

Since the loop stops when Control >= N, the performance of this algorithm is O(log(N)) (log taken to base 2).

Looking at the structure a bit more generally, suppose we multiply Control by some other constant. Giving this constant the name *Factor*, we can see that after k iterations

$$\text{Control} = \text{Factor}^k$$

and so, by the argument above, the performance is O(log(N)) (log taken to base Factor). It turns out that in considering the "big O" of an algorithm, it doesn't matter what base we use for logarithms. This is because the logarithm of a number to one base is just a constant times the logarithm of the same number to a different base. Since constant factors are "factored out" of a "big O," the base doesn't matter. You can fill in the details of this in an exercise.

Now look at Figure 2–19, where the control variable is divided by a factor (2 in this case) instead of multiplied. This is very similar to the previous example: there Control was started at a small value and multiplied repetitively until it reached some maximum; here Control is started at a large value and divided repetitively until it reaches a minimum.

What is the "big O" of this structure? Instead of repeating the analysis above, we just say that it is O(log(N)), and leave the details to an exercise.

Now look at the two structures in Figure 2–20. Here we have analogies to the nested counting loops considered earlier. The performance of these structures is O(N × log(N)); you can do the analysis as an exercise.

```
Control := N;

while Control /= 0 loop
   ...
      something with O(1)
   ...

   Control := Control / 2;
end loop;
```

Figure 2-19   Another Multiplicatively-Controlled Loop.

```
for Counter in 1..N loop

   Control := 1;
   while Control <= N loop
      ...
         something with O(1)
      ...

      Control := 2 * Control;
   end loop;

end loop;
```

(a)

```
Control := N;
while Control /= 0 loop
   for Counter in 1..N loop
      ...
         something with O(1)
      ...
   end loop;

   Control := Control / 2;
end loop;
```

(b)

Figure 2-20   Two N x log(N) loop structures.

Subprogram Call

We can handle a subprogram call by realizing that the subprogram is also an algorithm with its own "big O," then imagining that this algorithm appears "in line" with the calling program.

In this way we can deal with it as we dealt with other complex algorithms above. If the subprogram call appears inside a decision statement, its "big O" is used in determining the maximum of the "big Os" of the different branches of the decision. If the subprogram call appears inside a loop, its "big O" is, essentially, multiplied by the trip count of the loop.

If the subprogram (call it A) in turn calls another subprogram (call it B), then we use B's "big O" in calculating A's, and then A's in calculating the calling program's "big O," and so on for deeper nesting of subprograms.

Things get tricky if A and B are the same subprogram, that is if a recursive call is involved. In calculating A's "big O," then, the depth of recursion—the number of times that A is called recursively—is usually, itself, a function of the problem size, so we need to do the same sort of analysis we've been doing with other structures, to get a handle on the depth of recursion.

The structures you have seen in this section show examples of the most common "big O" performances: constant, linear, quadratic, log(N), and N × log(N). They also show how to think through the "big O" analysis for composite program control structures.

In the next section we will return to the algorithms discussed in section 2.3 and some others, and estimate their performance.

2.4.3 Some Examples of Performance Prediction

Let's return to the algorithms from section 2.3 and estimate their performance. This experience will give you some ideas about how to do a "big O" analysis on recursive programs.

Factorial

In calculating N!, 1 is subtracted from the argument to Factorial each time a recursive call is done. Since multiplying one number by another is O(1), the result is very similar to a one-level counting loop: its performance is O(N).

String Reversal

Each time StringReverse is called, its argument—the string—is shortened by one character. Thus the number of recursive calls is determined by the length of the string, in fact directly proportional to it. So the performance seems to be O(N).

In fact there's a subprogram call involved: concatenation of a character to the end of a string. If that operation doesn't depend on the string length, the performance of StringReverse is indeed O(N). On the other hand, if for some reason the concatenation operation had to "walk across" the whole string to add the new character onto the end—a linear operation—then we'd have an overall result of $O(N^2)$ because a linear operation would be done a linear number of times. Without knowing more about concatenation, we can't go any further.

Permutations of a Set

In section 2.3.2 when we introduced the idea of permutations, we calculated that a set of size N has N! permutations. The program PrintPermutations in fact has growth rate $O(N!)$, much larger than any of the other growth rates we've seen. Since algorithms with factorial growth rate are almost impossibly slow for interestingly large values of N, we try to avoid them.

On the other hand, sometimes we can't avoid factorial growth. Whichever algorithm we choose for printing all permutations, we cannot escape the mathematical fact that a set of size N has N! permutations. Anyone claiming an algorithm which can print N! values with performance better than $O(N!)$ is claiming something magic, not mathematical!

Recursive Binary Search

Recall that in Binary Search we divide our sorted list in half, then in half again, etc., until we either find what we're looking for or are left with only one element which isn't the one we want. This is just a recursive version of the loop structure in Figure 2–19, for which we already discovered a performance of $O(\log(N))$.

Recursive Merge Sort

Recursive merge sort, as we saw before, is another divide-and-conquer algorithm, involving repeated halving of the list to be sorted. The number of times we divide the list in half is $\log(N)$, so the performance seems to be $\log(N)$. But here again there is a lower-level subprogram called, namely "merge," whose implementation is unknown to us.

To give a hint, the merge operation is usually linear in performance: all items in both lists are copied once. The topmost level will then merge two lists of length N/2, requiring the copying of N values; the second level will do *two* merges, but each list is of length N/4, and so on. So if we add up all the merging done at a given level of recursion, we always get exactly N operations. But since there are $\log(N)$ levels of recursion, we arrive at a growth rate of $O(N \times \log(N))$. This is a recursive version of a loop structure in Figure 2–20.

2.5 DESIGN: MAINTAINING A DYNAMIC TABLE AS AN ARRAY

Let's consider a bit more fully the problem of maintaining a table like the phone list discussed earlier. Let us assume that each item to be stored in the table contains a *key* part and a *value* part. The key part is the field we shall use to look items up in the table; the value part is everything else. (In the phone list case, the keys are your friends' names; the values are their phone numbers.)

Now if we consider the table to be an ADT, then five operations apply:

Create, or set up a new table with no items in it;

Update, or add a new item to the table;

Search, or look up an item in the table (as in the phone list example given earlier), returning the value part corresponding to a given key;

Delete, or remove from the table the item with a given key;

Report, or print out or display all the entries currently in the table, presumably in the order of their keys.

Figure 2–21 shows a sketch of an Ada package specification for this ADT. We leave out the details of the type definitions for the keys and values, because they're not really relevant to the discussion.

Let's discuss two possible implementations of this table, both using an array, then consider the performance of the various operations. We won't bother to give detailed programs for them, since we're just interested in "reasoning out" the performance issues. We assume that the array can hold up to MaxItems items, and that the actual number of items in the array at a given moment is given by ActualItems. The Create operation in both implementations just involves declaring the array, which takes at most a constant amount of execution time, and setting ActualItems to indicate that the table is empty, also a constant-time operation. Completing the package specification then involves only filling in the array type definition as shown in Figure 2–22.

```
package TableHandler is

   type KeyType is ...
   type ValueType is ...
   type TableType is ...

   procedure Create(T: in out TableType);
   procedure Update(T: in out TableType; K: KeyType; V: ValueType);
   function  Search(T: TableType; K: KeyType) return ValueType;
   procedure Delete(T: in out TableType; K: KeyType);
   procedure Report(T: TableType);

end TableHandler;
```

Figure 2-21 Sketch of TableHandler package specification. (many details missing!)

```
package TableHandler is

   type KeyType is ...
   type ValueType is ...
   type TableType is private;

   procedure Create(T: in out TableType);
   procedure Update(T: in out TableType; K: KeyType; V: ValueType);
   function  Search(T: TableType; K: KeyType) return ValueType;
   procedure Delete(T: in out TableType; K: KeyType);
   procedure Report(T: TableType);

private

   MaxItems: constant := ...; -- pick a number

   type Item is
      record
         Key: KeyType;
         Val: ValueType;
      end record;

   type List is
      array(1..MaxItems) of Item;

   type TableType is
      record
         TableArray: List;
         ActualItems: integer range 0..MaxItems;
      end record;

end TableHandler;
```

Figure 2-22   A more complete TableHandler specification.

2.5.1 Implementation One: Unordered Array

In Implementation One we leave the array unordered, updating it just by
keeping track of the number of positions currently occupied, then inserting a
newly-arriving item in the next available position. An Update operation thus
has performance $O(1)$ (constant), since the number of operations required to
store an item in the next available position in an array doesn't depend on either
the size of the array or on how many items are already there.

How about a Search operation? Since the items are not in any particular
order in the table, we need to start at one end of the (occupied portion of the)
table and check the key of every item, until either we find the one we wanted or
we reach the other end of the occupied portion. Sometimes we find our item on
the first attempt; sometimes we need to search the entire table; on the average,
we check half the items. Since both the worst and average situations depend

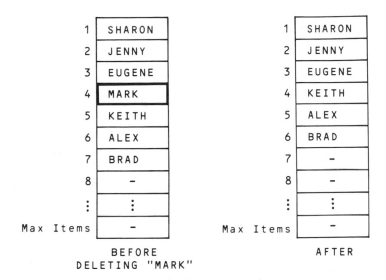

(a)   Deletion by moving all items up.

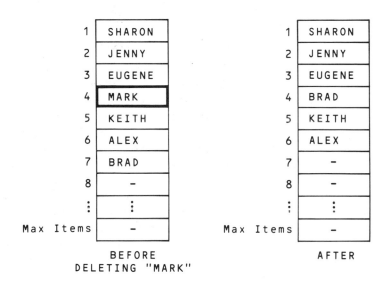

(b)   Deletion by moving last item up.

Figure 2-23   Deletion from unordered table.

directly on the number of items in the table, we can say that a Search operation is linear or O(N) (actually O(ActualItems)).

A Delete operation also has linear performance. We delete an item corresponding to a given key by searching for it as in a Search, then removing it by moving all items below it up one position, as shown in Figure 2–23a. Since the number of operations for both the search and the move depend directly on ActualItems, we have a linear operation.

We can speed up the Delete by recognizing that since the items in the table are not in order, we lose nothing by just copying the latest item into the position occupied by the one to be deleted, as shown in Figure 2–23b, then recovering the vacated space by decrementing ActualItems. While the average time for a Delete is surely reduced by this optimization, the growth rate is unchanged because the search part of the operation is still linear. This is a very good example of the two parts of the actual performance of an algorithm: the average time per operation and the growth rate.

A Report operation involves sorting the table in some way, since we want the table to be printed out in key order. The details of the sorting process will be left for Chapter 8, where many sorting algorithms are presented and compared. For completeness here, we just mention that the growth rate of a sorting algorithm is, in most cases, either O(N × log(N)) or O(N²).

2.5.2 Implementation Two: Array Ordered by Key

This implementation corresponds to the kind of table discussed in the phone list example, where we discovered the Binary Search algorithm, which carries out a Search with O(log(N)) performance.

Update and Delete operations turn out to have linear performance in this implementation. In an Update, we need to insert the newly arriving item in its proper place in the array, to preserve the ordering. To do this, we find this place by a modified Search operation: since the item is not yet in the table, the search will always fail, but instead of just reporting that fact, we will make the search report the last location it tested, which will tell us exactly where the new item needs to go. This will work correctly except where the new key is smaller than the previously smallest key or greater than the previously greater one, so we can just test those two possibilities as special cases before beginning the binary search.

Once the proper location has been found, we need to make room for the new item by moving the ones with greater keys *forward* one position. So the performance has a logarithmic component and a linear one; as ActualItems increases, it is so much greater than its logarithm that the logarithmic component can be ignored. Thus Update has linear performance.

Delete is really just like Search except that we remove the item to be deleted by moving all items with greater keys *back* one position in the array.

	UNORDERED	ORDERED
Create	O(1)	O(1)
Update	O(1)	O(N)
Search	O(N)	O(Log(N))
Delete	O(N)	O(N)
Report	O(N x Log(N))	O(N)

Figure 2-24 Comparative performance of table operations for unordered and ordered array storage.

Since we can't use the speed-up from Implementation One (why?), the move is linear, so the whole Delete operation is linear.

The last operation to consider is *Report*. Since the table is already ordered, Report can just start at the beginning and step through the array, printing each item as it encounters that item. So Report is a linear operation.

Figure 2–24 gives a tabular summary of the growth rates of the operations in both implementations.

2.6 SUMMARY

In this chapter we have discussed *algorithms*, and in particular the two important areas of *recursion* and *performance prediction.*

An algorithm is a method used to solve a problem in a systematic way: it consists of a finite number of steps which will complete its work, regardless of the input given to it, in a finite amount of time with a finite effort.

A recursive algorithm is one which "invokes itself," whose own name appears in its definition. Infinite recursion is avoided by making certain that the algorithm has in its definition a specific step indicating the conditions for stopping the recursion, and that each recursive call operates on a "data set" smaller than the previous one.

Five recursive algorithms were presented: factorial, string reversal, permutations, binary search, and merge sort. The Ada versions of these algorithms made clear that recursive programs can be written straightforwardly in the Ada language.

Performance prediction is the process of estimating how the computation or running time of an algorithm or program varies with the "problem size." The currently accepted way of expressing this variation, often called "growth rate," is the O(...) or "big O" notation.

While there is no easy, guaranteed way to calculate the performance, there are certain techniques and "rules of thumb" that are helpful in "getting a handle on it." Performance prediction is facilitated when programs are written according to "structured coding" conventions, because such programs have a well-defined loop and decision structure.

In the section on performance prediction, examples were given of various program structures and their "big O" formulas. The most common growth rates in our data structures work are, in order of steepness, constant or O(1), logarithmic or O(log(N)), linear or O(N), O(N × log(N)), and quadratic or O(N**2).

The design section introduced you to two different implementations of a table as an array. Although few program details were given, the growth rates of the various operations were "reasoned out" and compared for both implementations.

This concludes the "preliminaries" part of the book. Equipped with an introduction to abstract data types, recursion, and performance prediction, you are ready to see how these concepts play important roles in the study of data structures.

2.7   EXERCISES

1. Give a recursive definition of the integer addition operation. Write and test a recursive function to produce the sum of two integers (HINT: Use the built-in "+" operation *only* to add 1 to a number).

2. Give a recursive definition of the integer multiplication operation. Write and test a recursive function to carry out the definition (HINT: Multiplication is repeated addition).

3. Give a recursive definition of the integer exponentiation operation. Write and test a recursive function to carry out the definition (HINT: Exponentiation is repeated multiplication).

4. The Fibonacci numbers of order 1 are a sequence of positive integer starting with 1,2,3,5,8, . . . , in other words, each number except the first two is the sum of the two previous numbers. Give a recursive definition of this sequence; write a recursive procedure to print out the first twenty-five numbers.

5. What is the "big O" of the usual algorithm to set to zero all the elements of a 2-dimensional square array with N rows and N columns?

6. Show that in computing a "big O" which turns out to have a logarithmic component, i.e. something of the form log(. . .), the base we use to represent the logarithm does not matter.

7. Show that the growth rate of the algorithmic structure given in Figure 2–19 is O(log(N)).

8. Show that the growth rates of the structures in Figure 2–20 is $O(N \times \log(N))$.

9. Estimate the performance of the concatenation and substring search algorithms from section 1.7.

10. Consider the problem of searching for a key k in an unordered array where duplicate keys are permitted. Discuss the performance of each of the following cases:

    a. k does not appear in the array;

    b. k appears once in the array;

    c. k appears several times in the array (not necessarily in adjacent locations!) but only the location of the first appearance is desired;

    d. k appears several times in the array and it is desired to report the locations of all appearances.

11. Repeat the previous problem for an ordered array.

Chapter 3

ARRAYS, VECTORS, MATRICES, AND LISTS

3.1 GOAL STATEMENT

In this chapter we continue our study of abstraction and implementation by taking up the various ways in which the familiar mathematical abstractions of vectors and matrices can be represented in programs.

We begin with a discussion of how these abstractions are handled in "classical" programming languages like Fortran and Pascal. Later sections then consider how vectors and matrices can be more efficiently represented in a number of special cases. Specifically, we shall be interested in how vectors or matrices with a majority of zero or empty elements can be stored. Such vectors or matrices are usually called "sparse"; their study provides the context for the introduction of linked data structures.

The design section of this chapter focuses on the array types and operations in Ada, and on how vector and matrix arithmetic can be done using these. In the Style Guide some hints are presented on how to simulate arrays of records in languages that don't have record types.

3.2 "CLASSICAL" REPRESENTATION OF VECTORS AND MATRICES

The "first generation" of computers, developed in the 1950s, were intended chiefly for the solution of scientific and engineering—that is, *mathematical*—problems. (Indeed, the first devices resembling what we would call digital computers—built in the mid-1940s—were designed mainly to do calculations resulting in the tables used for artillery control). Later it was realized that computers could be very powerful in data processing and other less mathematical applications like language translation, large-scale information systems, and so on.

In the mid-1950s, when an alternative was sought to coding mathematical problems in machine language, Fortran was developed by John Backus and his team at IBM. Given the predominance of vectors and matrices in mathematical problems, it is not surprising that the Formula Translator—Fortran—embodied support for these in the form of what were (and still are) called *arrays*. The single- and multi-dimensional arrays of Fortran are *implementations* of the mathematical abstractions of vectors, matrices, and tensors (three-dimensional matrices), and serve as the model for similar implementations in Fortran's successor languages: Algol, PL/1, Basic, Pascal, and even Ada.

3.2.1 Vectors or One-Dimensional Arrays

A *vector* of N components is a set of N values which is ordered in the sense that each value is assigned a specific "position" in the set. For example, the vector $V1 = <3,5,-1>$ is different from the vector $V2 = <5,-1,3>$: they both have the same set of values, but they appear in different orders.

If we number the components 1,2,...,N, then it makes sense to talk about the i-th component of this vector. For example, if $i = 2$, then the i-th component of V2 is -1. In everyday mathematical notation we would write this with a *subscript*; in programming, there is not usually the ability to write actual subscripts and so brackets [] or parentheses () are generally used, as in V2[i] or V2(i). In this discussion we will use the () form exclusively, since this is the form used by both Fortran (the original) and Ada (the language of the programs in this book).

In everyday programming we implement vectors through the use of one-dimensional arrays. The high-level language we are using generally allows us to indicate to the compiler what size array we need: this is done using a *declaration* like

INTEGER A(10) (in Fortran), or

A: **array**(1..10) **of** integer (in Ada).

Both of these declarations indicate that the compiler is to set aside space for ten integer values, and that the valid range of subscripts into the resulting array is 1,2,...,10.

Having instructed the compiler to *create* the array (without storing any particular values into its elements!), we can now carry out two operations on array elements: we can *store* a value, as in the Fortran assignment A(2) = 3, or we can *retrieve* a previously stored value, as in the Ada assignment Y := A(2). We could just as well have stored or retrieved using a variable as the subscript, as in A(I) = 3, as long as we made certain that at the time the statement was executed I had a value in the range 1 thru 10.

The point here is that there are really two separate operations involved: a storage operation and a retrieval operation, even though most programming languages permit the same array-element-referencing syntax to be used on either side of the assignment operator. These two abstract operations have been implemented in a way which is syntactically convenient and intuitively comfortable.

It is important to realize that the *type* of a vector's elements need not be numerical, though integers and reals are the types seen frequently in engineering problems and programming texts. For example, we shall have frequent occasion to think of vectors of *records* of one sort or another, like student records. Many examples use numbers as the elements of a vector because they are easily written and because support for vectors in early programming languages was motivated by numerical problems; bear in mind, though, that nearly everything we say in this chapter generalizes very nicely to many other types.

We shall return to these abstractions later, when we consider matrices, which are implemented as two-dimensional arrays. In the meantime, let us discuss what sort of machine instructions a compiler would have to produce in order to support subscripting. When an array is declared, space is reserved for as many elements as are requested by the declaration. How much is this? It depends, in fact, on the *type* of the thing to be stored in each element. For example, in many sixteen-bit computers (like the PDP-11), an integer in Fortran is deemed to occupy one sixteen-bit word, but a real (or floating-point) number occupies two words, or thirty-two bits. So an array of 100 floating-point numbers, declared, say, by REAL T(100) in Fortran-66, will require 200 words of PDP-11 memory.

On the other hand, in machines like the IBM System/370, where space is allocated in eight-bit bytes rather than sixteen-bit words, the same array requires 400 bytes, because floating-point numbers in that machine occupy four bytes each.

Similarly, one could envision an array of 200-character student records with name, address, course grades, etc., and thus 200 bytes per element might be necessary. A total of 20,000 bytes would then be required for the entire array.

Once the space is allocated, the compiler must generate certain instructions which "understand" the relationship between a subscript reference like T(i) and the internal storage on the particular computer involved. This relationship is usually called the *storage mapping*, or sometimes the *storage mapping function*.

Letting add(T) be the machine address of the first storage unit (byte, word, etc.) of the array, and NUNITS be the number of storage units per array element, what is the storage mapping for an array whose lowest subscript value is 1 (as in Fortran-66)? We need a formula which tells us how many elements to "skip over" in order to reach the i-th one. Clearly we need to skip over i − 1 of them. So the address of T(i) is in fact

$$add(T) + (i − 1)*NUNITS$$

Is this formula correct? Consider a 4-byte real as in the System/370. Here addressing is done byte-by-byte, so NUNITS = 4. The address of T(1) is in fact just add(T) because the second term drops out; the address of T(2) is add(T) + 4, and so on.

The array-declaration scheme in Fortran-66 is really a special case, since the lowest subscript value must always be 1. In the more general situation, as implemented in most other languages including Ada, the lowest value may be any integer, the only restriction being that it must be less than the highest subscript value. These two values are usually called the *range* of the subscripts.

Under the more general scheme, what should the storage mapping look like? Call the lowest subscript value First, and the highest Last. Then assuming we declare

$$T: \textbf{array}(First..Last) \textbf{ of } real$$

we will need (Last-First + 1)*NUNITS of space, such that T(First) maps to add(T). To get to an arbitrary T(i), how many elements do we need to skip over? It is i-First elements.

To see this, suppose that First = 3 and Last = 10, as in

$$T: \textbf{array}(3..10) \textbf{ of } integer$$

Clearly there will be eight elements required, each NUNITS long; to get to T(5), say, we need to skip elements 3 and 4, which is 5 − 3 = 2 elements. To get to the first element T(3), we skip no elements (3 − 3 = 0). So our storage mapping becomes

$$T(i) \text{ maps to } add(T) + (i-First)*NUNITS$$

Notice, by the way, that this is perfectly consistent with the special case used in Fortran-66: in that language, First = 1 *always*. It also works even if First and/or Last are negative. Let us try finding the storage mapping for NUNITS = 4 and the declaration

$$T: \textbf{array}(−5..7) \textbf{ of } real$$

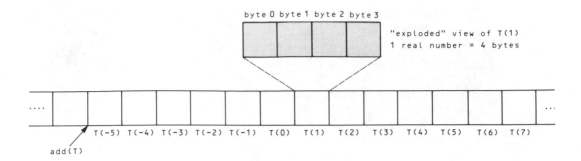

Figure 3-1   Storage allocation in linear memory for T: array(−5 . . 7) of real.

This will require $7 - (-5) + 1$ 4-byte elements, or 52 bytes; T(i) maps to add(T) + (i − (− 5))*4 or add(T) + (1 + 5)*4. Then T(-5) maps to add(T); T(0) maps to add(T) + 20 (we've skipped over five elements!) and so on. This arrangement is shown in Figure 3–1.

A brief aside: there is nothing sacred about mapping the *lowest-subscripted* element to add(T); indeed, in some computers, such as the Hewlett-Packard HP-3000, the hardware design is such that add(T) maps most conveniently to the "zero-th" element, so elements with negative and positive subscripts are deemed to lie below and above the "zero" point, respectively. Even if there is *no* zero-th element, add(T) is mapped to where it would be located if there were one. For uniformity in this book, we shall retain the convention that the lowest-subscripted element maps to add(T).

3.2.2 Matrices and Two-Dimensional Arrays

Let us now take up the question of matrices. We define an $R \times C$ *matrix* M as a rectangular array of elements, having *R rows* and *C columns*, and then refer to any particular element in the matrix by using two subscripts r and c in an expression M(r,c). Note that if we were to view M pictorially, as in Figure 3–2, the rows would be oriented horizontally, the columns vertically, and the subscript reference would give the *row* subscript first. (Once again there is nothing sacred about this view; it is just a convention.)

As in the one-dimensional case, we have an abstraction Matrix, implemented in most programming languages by the feature allowing us to declare two-dimensional arrays and to store and retrieve elements in them in the form M(r,c). How do compilers implement this abstraction?

It should come as no surprise to you that memory in most computers is organized logically in *linear* fashion, with the addresses of the storage units (words or bytes) running in a single increasing sequence. So a structure with two dimensions has to be mapped onto a structure with only one dimension.

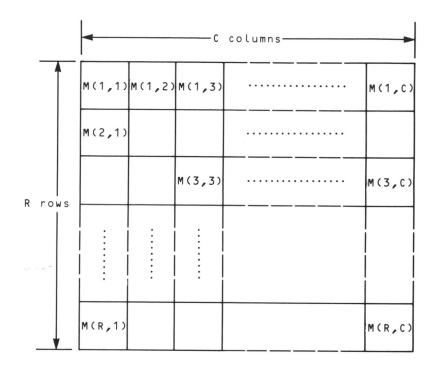

Figure 3-2 Abstract (programmer's) view of an R x C rectangular array or matrix.

Most programming languages implement the abstraction Matrix in a form called *row-major*, where the two-dimensional array is stored *row by row* in linear memory, as shown in Figure 3–3.

That this is not the only way to do it is evidenced by the *column-major* scheme in Fortran, in which a two-dimensional array is stored *column by column*. This is shown for the same array in Figure 3–4.

What is the storage mapping function for a two-dimensional array stored in row-major form? As before, let us begin with the familiar case where the rows and columns are numbered 1..R and 1..C respectively. Since the array is stored row by row, to reach any element in the r-th row we need to "skip over" r-1 rows; then to reach the c-th element in the r-th row, we need to "skip over" c-1 elements. Each row has C elements; each element requires NUNITS of storage. So the mapping function is

M(r,c) maps to add(M) + (r − 1)*C*NUNITS + (c − 1)*NUNITS

Letting NUNITS = 4 as above (for, say, a four-byte real in the System/370), for the 5 × 6 array in Figure 3–5, 120 bytes of storage are needed.

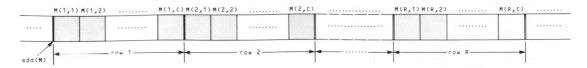

Figure 3-3 Row-major implementation of an R x C array in linear memory.

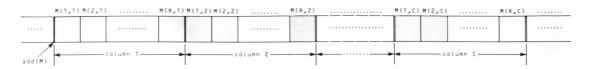

Figure 3-4 Column-major implementation of an R x C array in linear memory.

$$M: \text{array} \ (1..5,1..6) \ \text{of real}$$

(a) Declaration.

1.0	-3.5	7.4	2.0	-4.5	0.0
-4.6	0.0	1.0	2.3	-1.5	1.0
-2.2	-1.0	2.0	0.0	-5.72	0.0
-5.0	1.0	-2.1	3.0	2.3	-4.0
0.0	4.35	3.6	1.0	0.0	1.0

(b) Abstract (programmer's view).

(c) Row-major implementation in linear memory (note real numbers are stored as four-byte floating point).

Figure 3-5 Abstraction and implementation of a 5 x 6 array of real numbers.

$$M(1,1) \text{ maps to add}(M) + 0;$$

$$M(5,6) \text{ maps to add}(M) + 4*6*4 + 5*4 = \text{add}(M) + 116;$$

$$M(3,2) \text{ maps to add}(M) + 2*6*4 + 1*4 = \text{add}(M) + 52.$$

As in the one-dimensional case, we can generalize this idea to permit subscripts to have an arbitrary integer range, as in Pascal or Ada (or Fortran-77, for that matter). Consider then the declaration in Ada

M: **array**(FirstR..LastR,FirstC..LastC) **of** real

The details of the row-major storage mapping function are left as an exercise, as is the question of developing a storage mapping for two-dimensional arrays implemented, as in Fortran, in column-major form.

3.2.3 Higher-Dimensional Structures

There is often a need in programming problems to work with arrays of higher dimension than two, and most programming languages support a feature to permit up to some fairly large number of subscripts.

How is this facility implemented? It is a generalization of the two-dimensional case. Considering three-dimensional arrays, for example, the third dimension is conventionally called a *plane*, and the new subscript is conventionally added *before* the one for a row. So an Ada declaration

A: **array**(1..4,1..5,1..6) **of** real

would be interpreted as an array with four planes, each having five rows and six columns. A reference A(p,r,c) would then be interpreted as that element at the intersection of the p-th plane, r-th row, and c-th column.

As in the two-dimensional case, this abstract structure is then mapped onto linear storage in either row-major or column-major fashion. In row-major form, we reach the element A(p,r,c) by skipping over p-1 planes to reach the p-th plane, then r-1 rows to reach the r-th row, then c-1 elements (each in a column) to reach the c-th element. In column-major form, we imagine first skipping over c-1 columns to reach the c-th column, then r-1 rows to reach the r-th row, then p-1 elements (each in a plane) to reach the p-th element. These schemes are illustrated in Figure 3-6, for the case of an array A(- 1..1,0..3, 5..6).

Obtaining storage mapping functions for this case and for higher dimensionality is left as a set of exercises. The general idea is that in any row-major scheme, of whatever dimension, the *leftmost* subscript varies most slowly; in any column-major scheme the *rightmost* subscript varies most slowly.

```
M: array (-1..1,0..3,5..6) of ...
```

(a)   Declaration.

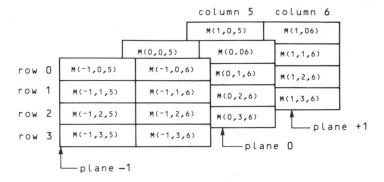

(b)   Abstract view.

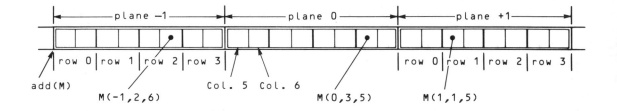

(c)   Row-major implementation.

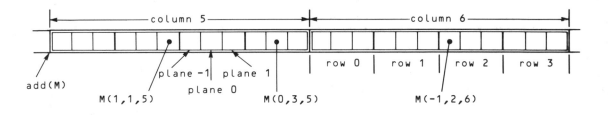

(d)   Column-major implementation.

Figure 3-6   Abstraction and implementation of a three-dimensional array in linear memory.

3.3 DENSELY-PACKED STRUCTURES WITH MANY "ZERO" ELEMENTS

In this section and the next we consider how to handle vectors and matrices with the special property that many of their elements are "zero." We have written "zero" in quotation marks to suggest that we are using "zero" as an abstraction for whatever value is appropriate given the type of the element.

If we are dealing with integers or reals, 0 (the number) is perfectly appropriate. If the elements are *Booleans*, "zero" is interpreted as *false*. If the elements are strings of characters, then "zero" means the null or empty string, or the string with no characters in it. On the other hand, if we are dealing with records which we store or retrieve by some *key* (such as student records stored by student ID number), then perhaps "zero" simply means the record is missing or that no student exists with that number.

From here on, we shall just write zero (no quotation marks) or 0, and will usually show numerical examples, but you understand that the ideas generalize, as usual, to many other types.

Structures with a high proportion of zeroes—sometimes as high as 95 percent—are common in real-world applications, and the number of elements is often *very* large, sometimes too large to fit in main memory if all elements are stored. It is thus important to think about how to store such structures economically. The idea is to devise a way to store only those elements which are *not* zero, keeping track of which elements they are either by some nice storage mapping function or by some bookkeeping scheme.

There are two cases to consider: structures where the non-zero elements are *concentrated* in a predictable part of the structure, and those where the non-zero elements are *randomly* (and, we will assume, uniformly) distributed throughout. The first case is the subject of this section; the second case is taken up in the next section.

3.3.1 Lower Triangular Matrices

A common structure in many computational problems representing physical systems is a square matrix (the number of rows equals the number of columns) in which all the elements above the main diagonal are zero, and thus all the non-zero elements are concentrated on and below the diagonal. This structure is called a *lower triangular* matrix. It is so common, in fact, that one is led to wonder why "scientific" programming languages like Fortran and PL/1 do not support it as a built-in type.

If the number of rows and columns is very large, we could reduce the memory required to store it by just under 50 percent by keeping only the non-zero elements, since the zeroes are predictably located. Specifically, in a matrix

M: **array**(1..R,1..R) **of** element

with elements designated M(r,c), any element located such that c > r is zero; all the others are (most likely) non-zero. This configuration is illustrated in Figure 3–7.

We can obtain a storage structure for a lower-triangular matrix by remembering how two-dimensional arrays are mapped onto linear storage. Recall that we developed a row-major and a column-major arrangement. Let us consider the matrix M from Figure 3–7 and map it onto a one-dimensional array M′ in row-major fashion: first all the non-zero elements in row 1 (there is exactly one of these: M(1,1)), then all those in row 2 (there are two of these: M(2,1) and M(2,2)), then all those in row 3, and so on until row R (all R elements in this row are non-zero!) is located. Figure 3–8 illustrates this mapping.

Now what is the total number of elements required? There are $1 + 2 + \ldots + R = (R + 1){*}R/2$ elements. Secondly, how can we find an arbitrary element M(r,c) in this array? If c > r, we know that M(r,c) was zero and so was not stored in M′. Otherwise, we can find the beginning of row r by "skipping over" r − 1 rows, in other words $1 + 2 + \ldots + r − 1 = r{*}(r − 1)/2$ elements. Then we find the right element M(r,c) by skipping over c − 1 more elements. If we number elements in M′ starting at 1, the storage mapping for $c \leqq r$ is

$$M(r,c) \text{ maps to } M'(1 + r{*}(r − 1)/2 + c − 1)$$

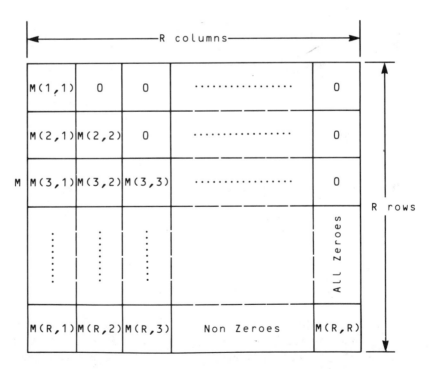

Figure 3-7 Lower-triangular array M (zeroes "above" diagonal").

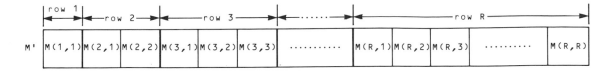

Figure 3-8 Row-major implementation M' of lower-triangular array M.

We can check this by taking the end points and typical points in between:

$$M(1,1) \text{ maps to } M'(1 + 1*(1-1)/2 + 1-1) = M(1)$$

$$M(2,1) \text{ maps to } M'(1 + 2*(2-1)/2 + 1-1) = M(2)$$

$$M(3,3) \text{ maps to } M'(1 + 3*(3-1)/2 + 3-1) = M(6)$$

$$M(R,R) \text{ maps to } M'(1 + R*(R-1)/2 + R-1) = M'((R+1)*R/2)$$

Sometimes it is convenient to represent a physical system in the form of an *upper-triangular* matrix; the storage structure for this is similar to that just given. We leave it as an exercise to show that the storage mapping function is "cleaner" if the mapping is column-major rather than row-major.

3.3.2 Symmetric Matrices

Many physical systems can be represented as a *symmetric matrix*, i.e. a square matrix M such that $M(r,c) = M(c,r)$ for every r and c. In such a situation, we can economize on storage in a way very similar to that used in a triangular matrix. We use just the storage structure for the lower-triangular case, but a slightly different storage mapping function.

Since for $c > r$ we are in the upper region of the matrix (above the diagonal) we can deduce the value of $M(r,c)$ by looking at its "mirror element" $M(c,r)$ below the diagonal. So we use just the storage mapping function from the previous section if $c \leqq r$, and for $c > r$ we use that mapping with r and c interchanged! This is shown in Figure 3–9.

3.3.3 "Band" Matrices

In many computational problems the underlying physical system can be modelled as a "band" matrix, where the non-zero elements are concentrated on the diagonal and within a fixed distance above and below. The total width of this "band" of non-zero elements is called the *bandwidth*.

Figure 3–10 shows some band matrices. We leave it as an exercise to obtain storage mappings for these. A hint would be to think in terms of a "diagonal-major" structure, where each diagonal is stored as a contiguous block in the one-dimensional array. This might lead to a "cleaner" storage mapping function.

	1	2	3	4
1	1	3	-2	7
2	3	-5	2	5
3	-2	2	0	0
4	7	5	0	4

(a) Symmetric Matrix M.

1	2	3	4	5	6	7	8	9	10
1	3	-5	-2	2	0	7	5	0	4

(b) Mapping onto one-dimensional array M′.

$$M(r,c) = \begin{cases} M'(1 + r*(r-1)/2 + c-1) & \text{if } r \geq c \\ M'(1 + c*(c-1)/2 + r-1) & \text{if } r < c \end{cases}$$

(c) Storage mapping function.

Figure 3-9 Economical storage of symmetric matrix.

3.4 SPARSE VECTORS AND MATRICES

The second case of vectors and matrices with many zeroes is the one where the zeroes are distributed unpredictably but (we assume) uniformly through the structure. We call such structures *sparse* vectors or matrices.

The study of sparse vectors and matrices is useful for two reasons. First, sparse systems of *numerical* values occur very frequently in mathematical programming problems such as arise in engineering, physics, and economics. Second, many other common structures can be viewed as sparse structures, specifically files of data which need to be structured according to one or more keys. The methods for handling such files are generalizations of the things we are studying at the moment.

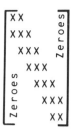

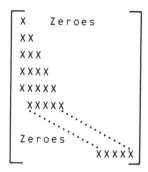

Figure 3-10 Band matrices.

3.4.1 Sparse Vectors

Consider the case of a vector of, say, 1,000 integers, where at any given time a large number of the values —perhaps 75 percent or more— are zero. Instead of storing this vector as a 1,000-element array, let us try to save some space by doing a little bookkeeping.

Implement each *non-zero* element of the vector as a *record* containing the *index* of the element and the *value* of the element as its two fields, and store the entire vector as an array of these records. The size of this array is determined by the number of non-zero elements. Ada declarations for this structure are given in Figure 3–11; in Figure 3–12 we show an example where only seven elements are non-zero.

The only problem with this structure is that it is too static. In most real applications, the number of non-zero elements is not fixed for the duration of the program. Rather, non-zero elements sometimes become zero, and zero elements sometimes become non-zero. So our structure really needs to have some "empty space" built in, to accommodate changing values.

Let us assume that we can make a pretty good guess at the *maximum* number of non-zero elements, and then let MaxNonZero be that number. We can

```
MaxElements: constant Integer := 1000;
MaxNonZeroes: constant Integer := 15;

subtype VectorRange Is Integer range 1..MaxElements;
subtype ArrayRange  Is Integer range 1..MaxNonZeroes;
subtype ValueType Is Integer;  -- or whatever other type

type SparseVectorElement Is
  record
     Index: VectorRange;
     value: ValueType;
  end record;

type SparseVector Is
  array(ArrayRange) of
     SparseVectorElement;
```

Figure 3-11 Declarations for Sparse Vector (number of non-zeroes is fixed)

also keep track of the *actual* number of non-zero elements using a "header" containing ActualNonZero as a value. All of this depends on our being pretty sure that ActualNonZero will never be more than MaxNonZero; in many real situations we can judge well enough to make a good choice of MaxNonZero which neither wastes too much space nor overflows. A declaration for this revised structure is shown in Figure 3–13; Figure 3–14 shows our example again in the revised structure, where we choose MaxNonZero to be fifteen.

Since we've assumed that elements are frequently changing value, it makes sense to consider the performance of operations to make this happen. An element changing from zero to non-zero means we have to add a new item to our structure; a change from non-zero to zero means we have to eliminate

V	Index	Value
1	3	49
2	9	19
3	22	92
4	43	-123
5	52	-27
6	178	34
7	241	-7

Figure 3-12 Sparse vector, stored as array of ordered pairs.

```
MaxElements: constant Integer := 1000;
MaxNonZero: constant Integer := 15;

subtype VectorRange Is Integer range 1..MaxElements;
subtype ArrayRange Is Integer range 1..MaxNonZero;
subtype NonZeroes   Is Integer range 0..MaxNonZero;
subtype ValueType Is Integer;   -- or whatever other type

type SparseVectorElement Is
   record
      Index: VectorRange;
      value: ValueType;
   end record;

type SparseVectorArray Is
   array(ArrayRange) of
      SparseVectorElement;

type SparseVector Is
   record
      ActualNonZero: NonZeroes := 0;
      A: SparseVectorArray;
   end record;
```

Figure 3-13 Declarations for Sparse Vector (number of non-zeroes is variable up to a maximum of MaxNonZero)

that item, to make space for a posible new non-zero one later on. Furthermore, in any interesting application we will need to retrieve the value of the element with a given index, and occasionally to print out the entire sparse vector in order by index.

In the two examples, we showed the vector elements stored in sorted form, that is with their indices in numerical order. We might also imagine storing them without regard to the order of the indices.

All this looks similar to something we have seen before. At the end of Chapter 2 we considered maintaining a dynamically changing table using an array, and calculated the "big Os" for four important operations: Update, Search, Delete, and Report. If we think of the index of a vector element as a key, and the number associated with that element as a value, then our sparse-vector problem just becomes a special case of this general table-maintenance problem.

Whether we choose the ordered-array or unordered-array scheme, the sparse-vector Store and Retrieve operations can be written in terms of the Search, Update, and Delete operations for table handling:

To Retrieve a Sparse Vector Element by Index:

1. Search the table for an element with the desired index.

2. If the search is successful, return the associated value.

3. If the search is unsuccessful, return 0.

```
MaxNonZero=15
ActualNonZero=7
```

V	Index	Value
1	3	49
2	9	19
3	22	92
4	43	-123
5	52	-27
6	178	34
7	241	-7
8		
9		
10		
11		
12		
13		
14		
15		

Figure 3-14   Sparse vector with "extra space".

To Store a Sparse Vector Element by Index:

1. If the element value is 0, Delete it from the table (we assume that Delete does nothing if the element is not in the table).
2. If the element value is non-zero, Search the table for an element with the desired index.
3. If the search is successful, change the value part of the element found.
4. If the search is unsuccessful, Update the table with the new element.

You can write programs to do these operations as an exercise. A bit of discussion is in order: first, thinking of a sparse vector as just a special case of a dynamic table has greatly simplified our problem. Second, we need to consider what happens to performance if we *oversimplify*: in the Store operation, for example, if the table operation Search only returns a value from the table, and not a location, how can we just change the value part? If an unsuccessful Search doesn't return the location where the new item should go, then we need to do a Search followed by an Update. This doubles the time to do the Store operation!

This oversimplification leads us to conclude that if really good performance is desired, either a fairly large set of table operations must be provided—not just the four we developed in Chapter 2—or we must be content to think in generalities only at the conceptual level and write all our operations anew for each application. This is a good example of the tradeoffs we often face between performance and abstraction.

3.4.2 Linking the Elements Together

We can save a fair amount of time in adding and deleting elements, while maintaining the ability to Report—traverse the array—in linear time, by storing the elements *physically* in the order in which they arrive—we assume this order is unpredictable—but keeping them *logically* in order by their indices.

How is this done? Let us add another field to the record describing each element. We call this new field *next*. Recall that elements are stored in an array V with indices in the range 1..MaxNonZero; we shall declare *next* to have values in the same range. Figure 3–15 shows these declarations.

```
MaxElements: constant Integer := 1000;
MaxNonZero: constant Integer := 15;

subtype VectorRange Is Integer range 1..MaxElements;
subtype ArrayRange  Is Integer range 1..MaxNonZero;
subtype NonZeroes   Is Integer range 0..MaxNonZero;
subtype ValueType   Is Integer;  -- or whatever other type

type SparseVectorElement Is
   record
      index: VectorRange;
      value: ValueType;
      next:  NonZeroes;
   end record;

type SparseVectorArray Is
   array(ArrayRange) of
      SparseVectorElement;

type SparseVector Is
   record
      ActualNonZero: NonZeroes := 0;
      First: NonZeroes := 0;
      A: SparseVectorArray;
   end record;
```

Figure 3-15   Declarations for Sparse Vector (number of non-zeroes is variable)

Assume the array starts out empty, with no non-zero elements. As each element arrives, we store it in the next empty physical position in V. But then we connect it *logically* to the previous elements by using *next*. The *next* field of each element indicates the position of V containing the element with the next higher index. A new field *first* added to the header will indicate the position of V containing the element with *lowest* index.

Figure 3-16 shows an array V similar to that in the previous examples, with four elements already in place; they arrived in the index order 52,9,178,22. Notice that we use a *next* value of zero to indicate that no more elements follow, i.e. that the element with highest index has been reached.

Now let the element with index 43 arrive. Figure 3-17 shows V with the new element added physically to V(5) and logically connected in its right place.

MaxElements=1000
MaxNonZero=15
First=2
ActualNonZero=4

V

	Index	Value	Next
1	52	-27	3
2	9	19	4
3	178	34	0
4	22	92	1
5			
6			
7			
8			
9			
10			
11			
12			
13			
14			
15			

Figure 3-16 Sparse vector stored with "next" links.

```
MaxElements=1000
MaxNonZero=15
First=2
ActualNonZero=5
```

V

	Index	Value	Next
1	52	-27	3
2	9	19	4
3	178	34	0
4	22	92	5
5	43	-123	1
6			
7			
8			
9			
10			
11			
12			
13			
14			
15			

Figure 3-17   Vector of Figure 3-16, with $V(43) = -123$.

Finding the right place is done by sequential search, but instead of sequencing according to the *physical* order, as we would ordinarily do, we search in *logical* order, following the "daisy chain" of *next* indicators until we find an element with higher index than that of the new arrival, then reconnecting the indicators accordingly.

Note that the performance of this insertion is again linear; reconnecting the *next* indicators, and placing the new arrival *physically* are both done in constant time, while finding the right logical position, being a sequential search, performs in linear time.

In Figure 3–18 we have shown how V would look with new arrivals 3 (new lowest index) and 241 (new highest index) inserted. You can try to figure out the logic of a routine to carry out such an insertion; we will not give any program text yet, since we'll take up the subject in a much more thorough way in the next chapter.

In the meantime, let's take a quick look at the Delete and Report operations. If a non-zero element goes to zero, we can delete it very easily just by searching in logical order until we find the right element, then connecting the *next* indicator of the logically *preceding* element to "jump around" the one we want to delete. The vector V with the element with index 52 deleted is shown in Figure 3–19. We'll leave until the next chapter a discussion of how to reuse the space formerly occupied by that element; you can think about that for a while.

```
MaxElements=1000
MaxNonZero=15
First=6
ActualNonZero=7
```

V

	Index	Value	Next
1	52	-27	3
2	9	19	4
3	178	34	7
4	22	92	5
5	43	-123	1
6	3	49	2
7	241	-7	0
8			
9			
10			
11			
12			
13			
14			
15			

Figure 3-18   Insertion of V(3) and V(241).

```
        MaxElements=1000
        MaxNonZero=15
        First=6
V       ActualNonZero=6
```

	Index	Value	Next
1	(52)	(-27)	(3)
2	9	19	4
3	178	34	7
4	22	92	5
5	43	-123	3
6	3	49	2
7	241	-7	0
8			
9			
10			
11			
12			
13			
14			
15			

Figure 3-19 Removal of V(52) (note link from V(43) to V(178), "jumping around" V(52)).

Traversing the sparse vector is easy: we just start at the position of V indicated by *first*, then follow the daisy chain, printing out all the elements in logical order.

The structure we have just designed is a special case of a *linked list*. Linked lists are very commonly used for the implementation of many abstractions in computing, and warrant a chapter of their own. But we have motivated the need for a linked structure by considering how sparse vectors might be implemented in a space-saving way.

We can generalize the sparse-vector idea to handle two-dimensional sparse structures: sparse matrices. We shall not go into detail on this yet; rather, we'll wait until the next chapter, after you're more familiar with linked lists.

3.5   DESIGN: VECTOR AND MATRIX OPERATIONS IN ADA

Let's return to the case of "normal" (non-sparse) vectors and martices, and examine some of the nice structures provided in Ada for doing operations on these. The three most important features in this discussion are *unconstrained array types*, *attribute enquiries*, and *operator overloading*.

In this section we shall treat vectors and matrices as ADTs—that is, as mathematical entities with well-defined operations on them like addition and multiplication. We shall see how the Ada features just listed make it quite convenient to write packages for these ADTs whose operations closely model their mathematical originals.

3.5.1 Vector Arithmetic and Ada Arrays

Given two vectors U and V whose components are all of type ValueType, both with dimensions (Rmin..Rmax), as well as a scalar (single value) K of type ValueType, we can list the following the mathematical definitions:

- The *vector sum* of U and V, written U + V, is a vector T with components of the same type and with dimensions (Rmin..Rmax) such that, for each r between Rmin and Rmax inclusive

  $$T(r) := U(r) + V(r)$$

  i.e. the components of the two vectors are added pairwise;

- The *inner product* of U and V, written U * V and sometimes called the *scalar product* or *dot product*, is a *scalar* of type ValueType, whose value is the *sum* of all the pairwise products

  $$U(r) * V(r)$$

  taken over all the components;

- The *sum* of V with a scalar K, written K + V, is a vector T, of the same type and dimensions as M, whose components have values

  $$T(r) := K + V(r)$$

  for every r between Rmin and Rmax;

- The product of V by a scalar K, written K * V, is a vector T, of the same type and dimensions as V, whose components have values

  $$T(r) := K * V(r)$$

  for every r between Rmin and Rmax.

In Figure 3–20 we show examples of these calculations for two six-element vectors.

```
          Given
    U = [1, -3, 2, 0, -1, 4]
    Y = [0, -2, 1, -3, 2, 0]
    K = 2
          then
U + V = [1, -5, 3, -3, 1, 4]
U * V = 0 + 6 + 2 + 0 - 2 + 0 = 6
K + V = [2, 0, 3, -1, 4, 2]
K * V = [0, -4, 2, -6, 4, 0]
```

Figure 3-20   Vector operations.

What we'd really like to do is design an Ada package for vector arithmetic, defining appropriate types and then writing Ada functions to implement these operations, just as we did in the Fraction, Set, Complex and Text packages back in Chapter 1.

Consider the problem of an appropriate type definition for Vectors. Simple array declarations like those earlier in the chapter, such as

V: **array** (1..5) **of** ValueType

are legal but not the best way to work with arrays. There are two difficulties: First, types in Ada are deemed to be equivalent only if they have the same type names, not just if they have the same structure. This is called named type equivalence, and leads to a surprising situation where V and a second array, say U, declared with exactly the same dimensions and value type, are treated as having different types.

This would make it difficult to write an operation to compute, for example, the vector sum of these two arrays, because Ada's "strong typing" philosophy would make it very difficult to "mix" U and V in the same expression like U + V

The second difficulty is that we'd like to make our vector operations general enough to handle vectors of any reasonable size, so the type of the vector arguments to our functions has to be more general than just a single-size array.

The solution is found in the Ada unconstrained array type idea, where an array type is defined as having dimensions which are "as yet unknown," to be filled in at the same time an array object is declared. Such an unconstrained type definition might be:

type Vector **is array** (integer **range** <>) of ValueType;

The construct

integer **range**<>

means that the subscripts of any object of type Vector must be integers; the symbol "<>" is read "box," and means "we'll fill in the missing values when we declare Vector objects."

Now we can declare Vector objects like

$$V: Vector(1..5); \quad Q: Vector(-5..6);$$

and they'll have the proper dimensions.

This all pays off when we write subprograms. If a function, for example, has an argument of type Vector, the dimensions of this argument are determined when the function is called and the argument is passed. So the function can work equally well with any size Vector.

The function can find out what the actual dimensions of its argument are by using attribute enquiries. If V is a vector, then *V'first* gives the low bound, *V'last* gives the high bound, and *V'length* gives the number of components. So for the Vector Q above, $Q'first = -5$, $Q'last = 6$, and $Q'length = 12$.

Figure 3–21 shows a function MaxValue which accepts a Vector as input and returns the largest value stored there; Figure 3–22 shows a complete program which calls MaxValue and will print "25" for the vector shown. For convenience, we have declared ValueType to be a subtype of integers, which makes everything work for arbitrary integers. Be sure you understand how the attribute enquiries work.

A word about the strange-looking construction after the opening *procedure* line of the program. This line and the next are used to "instantiate" the standard input/output package to work with arbitrary integers and make the instantiation available to this program. These may look like "magic words" to you; just use them. A full discussion of input/output instantiation is beyond our scope here, but you should read about it in the input/output chapter of your Ada textbook.

```
function MaxValue(V: Vector) return ValueType is

   CurrentMax: ValueType := V(V'first);

begin

   for R in V'first..V'last loop
      if V(R) > CurrentMax
         then CurrentMax := V(R);
      end if;
   end loop;

   return CurrentMax;

end MaxValue;
```

Figure 3-21   Function to compute maximum value in a Vector.

```
with Text_IO; use Text_IO;
procedure TestMaxValue is

  package MyIntIO is new Integer_IO (integer); use MyIntIO;

  subtype ValueType is integer;
  type Vector is array(integer range <>) of ValueType;

  X: ValueType;
  W: Vector(1..6) := (3,-17,20,0,4,18);

      -- define MaxValue as a local function here

        function MaxValue(V: Vector) return ValueType is
           CurrentMax: ValueType := V(V'first);
        begin
          for R in V'first..V'last loop
            if V(R) > CurrentMax
                then CurrentMax := V(R);
            end if;
          end loop;
          return CurrentMax;
        end MaxValue;

begin -- body of main program

  X := MaxValue(W);
  put("Maximum Value is "); put(X);

end TestMaxValue;
```

Figure 3-22   Program using MaxValue function.

This is a good time to define a package for vector handling. As in the packages in Chapter 1, we'll do the specification first, then fill in pieces of the body, leaving the rest for you to do in the exercises. Figure 3–23 gives such a specification. Notice that there is a new construction referring to an "exception." That will be explained a bit further on.

Why is the Vector type not defined as private? Because we wish to allow client programs access to the individual vector components in the usual array-referencing way, and if the type were private that access would be forbidden!

Let's write the code for two of the vector arithmetic functions. First let's add a scalar to a vector. This function is shown in Figure 3–24. Of course we can use the name "+" for this function, because of overloading. Notice how a vector is created to hold the result; this is an example of Ada's dynamic array creation. When the result vector is returned to the calling program, there needs to be a vector there of the proper size to hold it. (Ada doesn't require that the actual dimensions be the same, only that the length attributes match.) A complete program for this is shown in Figure 3–25.

Now let's write the inner-product program. In order for this to make sense mathematically, the vectors need to have the same dimensions. This property is

```
package Vectors is

    subtype ValueType is Integer;
    type Vector is
        array (Integer range <>) of ValueType;

    ConformabilityError: exception;

    function "+"(U,V: Vector)              return Vector;
    function "*"(U,V: Vector)              return ValueType;
    function "+"(K: ValueType; V: Vector)  return Vector;
    function "*"(K: ValueType; V: Vector)  return Vector;

end Vectors;
```

Figure 3-23   Specification for Vector package.

```
function "+"(K: ValueType; V: Vector) return Vector is
    W: Vector(V'first..V'last);

begin

    for R in V'first..V'last loop
        W(R) := K + V(R);
    end loop;

    return W;

end "+";
```

Figure 3-24   Addition of Scalar to Vector.

```
with Text_IO; use Text_IO;
with Vectors; use Vectors;
procedure TestVectorScalarAddition is

    package MyIntIO is new Integer_IO (Integer); use MyIntIO;

    subtype ValueType is Integer;
    type Vector is array(Integer range <>) of ValueType;

    X: ValueType := -3;
    W: Vector(1..6) := (3,-17,20,0,4,18);
    T: Vector(1..6);   -- "blank" vector to hold result

    begin -- body of main program

        T := X + W;              -- add scalar and vector

        for I in T'first..T'last loop -- print result
            put(T(I));
            new_line;
        end loop;

end TestVectorScalarAddition;
```

Figure 3-25   Program using Scalar-Vector addition.

```
function "*"(U,V: Vector) return ValueType is

   Sum: ValueType;

begin

   -- first check for conformability
   if    U'first /= V'first
      or U'last  /= V'last
   then raise ConformabilityError;
   end if;

   -- if conformable, go on to compute
   Sum := Zero;
   for R in U'first..U'last loop
      Sum := Sum + U(R) * V(R);
   end loop;

   return Sum;

end "*";
```

Figure 3-26   Inner product of two Vectors.

called conformability: two vectors are conformable if they have the same dimensions.

This gives us the opportunity to introduce the Ada *exception* idea. An exception is used to indicate an unusual or erroneous condition in a program. There are certain built-in exceptions for things like out-of-range subscripts or arithmetic overflow. But Ada also lets us define our own exceptions, to handle application-dependent errors. One way to define our own exception is to put its name in the package specification, which exports the exception and thus lets client programs have exception-handling sections which reference it.

In our case, the exception is called ConformabilityError; as you can see from the function code in Figure 3–26, if the dimensions of the two vectors don't match, ConformabilityError is signalled to the calling program by a *raise* statement. Assuming this function were built into our package, Figure 3–27 gives a sample of how the exception might be handled.

Your understanding of these two functions gives you the tools to fill in the missing ones in the package; you can do this as an exercise.

3.5.2 Matrix Arithmetic

Higher-dimensional arrays are handled in Ada just as one-dimensional arrays are; it is best to declare array types without constraints, then fill in the actual dimensions when objects are declared. Figure 3–28 shows the specification for a package to handle objects of type Matrix. Note the *two* occurrences of the

```
with Text_IO; use Text_IO;
with Vectors; use Vectors;
procedure TestExceptionHandling is

   package MyIntIO is new Integer_IO (integer); use MyIntIO;

   subtype ValueType is Integer;
   type Vector is array(Integer range <>) of ValueType;

   X: ValueType;      -- to hold Inner Product Result
   W: Vector(1..6) := (3,-17,20,0, 4,18);   -- these vectors
   T: Vector(1..7) := (1,  5,-6,8,17, 2,0); -- aren't conformable

begin -- body of main program

   X := W * T;    -- inner product; exception will
                  -- be raised because arguments aren't
                  -- conformable.

   put("Inner Product is "); put(X); -- program would get here
                                     -- if no exception raised

exception       -- any block can have an exception handler
                     -- it goes after main code, before end

   when ConformabilityError =>
      put("Cannot do operation; arguments don't match");

end TestExceptionHandling;
```

Figure 3-27   Example of exception handling.


```
package Matrices is

   subtype ValueType is Integer;
   type Matrix is
       array (Integer range <>, Integer range <>) of ValueType;

   ConformabilityError: exception

   function "+"(K: ValueType; M: Matrix) return Matrix;
   function "*"(K: ValueType; M: Matrix) return Matrix;
   function "+"(M,N: Matrix)             return Matrix;
   function "*"(M,N: Matrix)             return Matrix;
   function Transpose(M: Matrix)         return Matrix;

end Matrices;
```

Figure 3-28   Specification for Matrix package.

"box" in the type definition; this allows both the first and second set of dimensions to be fixed at object declaration time.

Mathematically, the matrix sum M + N, and addition and multiplication of matrices with scalars K + M and K * M respectively, are similar to their counterparts in the vector case. In the matrix-addition case, each component in the result is the sum of the corresponding components in the arguments. As in the vector situation, conformability dictates that the two matrices have the same dimensions.

We give in Figure 3–29 the code for K + M. Notice how the attribute enquiries are formed: M′first(1) means "the low bound of the first dimension;" M′last(2) means "the high bound of the second dimension." If the dimension number is left out, as in the vector programs above, Ada assumes we mean the first dimension. As an exercise you can write K * M and the matrix addition function M + N. Be sure in the latter case to check for conformability!

Mathematically, the *transpose* of a matrix Transpose(M) returns a matrix whose second dimension is the same as M's first dimension, and whose first dimension is the same as M's second dimension. Figure 3–30 shows a diagram of this; you can write the Ada function as an exercise.

The last operation is matrix multiplication M * N. Conformability of M and N for multiplication means that the *second* dimension of M must be the same as the *first* dimension of N. The product is a matrix P, which has a *first* dimension equal to the *first* dimension of M and a *second* dimension equal to the *second* dimension of N. So if M is (1..5,−3..0) and N is (−3..0,6..8) then M * N has dimensions (1..5,6..8). Note that order counts here: M * N is *not* the same as N * M; in fact M and N cannot be conformable for both operations unless they're square!

As shown in Figure 3–31, where the Ada function for M * N appears, a component P(r,c) has a value found by taking the inner product of the r-th row

```
function "+"(K: ValueType; M: Matrix) return Matrix is
   P: Matrix(M'first(1)..M'last(1),
             M'first(2)..M'last(2));

begin

   for R in M'first(1)..M'last(1) loop
     for C in M'first(2)..M'last(2) loop
        P(R,C) := K + M(R,C);
     end loop;
   end loop;

   return P;

end "+";
```

Figure 3-29   Addition of Scalar to Matrix.

$$\begin{bmatrix} 1 & -3 & 2 & 0 \\ 6 & -1 & 4 & 5 \\ -2 & 0 & 0 & 7 \end{bmatrix}$$

(a)   A 3 x 4 matrix M.

$$\begin{bmatrix} 1 & 6 & -2 \\ -3 & -1 & 0 \\ 2 & 4 & 0 \\ 0 & 5 & 7 \end{bmatrix}$$

(b) $M^1 =$ Transpose(M).

Figure 3-30   Matrix transposition.

```
function "*"(M,N:  Matrix) return Matrix is

   P: Matrix(M'first(1)..M'last(1),
             N'first(2)..N'last(2));
begin

   -- first check for conformability
   if    M'first(2) /= N'first(1)
      or M'last(2)  /= N'last(1)
   then raise ConformabilityError;
   end if;

   -- if conformable, go on to compute
   for R in M'first(1)..M'last(1) loop
      for C in N'first(2)..M'last(2) loop

         -- find inner product of row of M
         -- with column of N
         P(R,C) := Zero;
         for K in M'first(2)..M'last(2) loop
           P(R,C) := P(R,C) + (M(R,K) * N(K,C));
         end loop;

      end loop;
   end loop;

   return P;

 end "*";
```

Figure 3-31   Function for product of two Matrices.

$$\begin{bmatrix} 1 & 2 \\ -1 & 4 \\ 0 & 3 \end{bmatrix}$$

M

(3 X 2)

$$\begin{bmatrix} 3 & -1 & 2 & 0 \\ 1 & -2 & 0 & 4 \end{bmatrix}$$

N

(2 X 4)

$$\begin{bmatrix} 5 & -5 & 2 & 8 \\ 1 & -7 & -2 & 16 \\ 3 & -6 & 0 & 12 \end{bmatrix}$$

M X N

(3 X 4)

Figure 3-32 *Matrix multiplication.*

of M and the c-th column of N. Go through the code and be sure you understand the computation; check your understanding against the example in Figure 3–32.

This rather long design example shows how vectors and matrices can be dealt with very conveniently in Ada, using unconstrained array types, overloading, and attributes. The Style Guide in the next section involves a shift of context to the problem of working with records, and specifically arrays of records, in languages like Fortran and Basic that lack record types.

3.6 STYLE GUIDE: WORKING IN LANGUAGES WITHOUT RECORD TYPES

The examples in this book will often be presented so as to assume that you understand what "record types" are all about. We have mentioned, for example, that arrays of numeric types like integers and reals can be thought of as just special cases which can be generalized, say, to arrays of student records of 200 characters each. Languages like PL/1, Pascal, Modula-2, C, and of course Ada permit such arrays to be declared and used directly.

Suppose you need to code and debug real programs in a language like Fortran or Basic, both of which are sometimes called "data-structure-poor" and do not permit the *direct* use of record types? You should then view arrays of records as an *abstraction*, useful for program *design*, which then requires your intervention to *implement* them in a way acceptable to your compiler or interpreter.

In the case of Fortran and Basic, this means that each field of the record (or in some cases groups of fields, as we shall soon see), needs to be declared as a separate array of the appropriate type, since the language permits only scalar types to be values in an array. In Figure 3–33 we show how this might be done by giving Ada, Fortran-77, and Basic declarations for the abstraction consisting of a 100-record array of records containing some student information.

A program which *uses* these records should be implemented as directly as possible from the abstract design, using, for example, a *single* index variable to

```
subtype HWRange   Is Integer range 0..10;
subtype TestRange Is Integer range 0..100;

type StudentRecord Is
   record
      Name:           string(1..20);
      HomeworkGrades: array(1..5) of HWRange;
      TestScores:     array(1..2) of TestRange;
      TermAverage:    float;
   end record;

ClassGrades: array(1..100) of StudentRecord;
```

         (a). Declaration in Ada.

```
CHARACTER NAMES (1:100)          * 20
INTEGER   HWGRDE (1:100,1:5)
INTEGER   TESTS  (1:100,1:2)
REAL      AVERGE (1:100)
```

           (b). Declaration in Fortran-77.

```
DIM      N$(1:100)       :REM "$" declares string array
DIM      G%(1:100,1:5)   :REM "%" declares Integer array
DIM      T%(1:100,1:2)
DIM      A (1:100,1:2)   :REM real by default
```

         (c). Declaration in Basic.

Figure 3-33. Declaration of "Arrays of Records"
          in Ada, Fortran-77, and Basic.

select a given record from the array. This leads to a clear and readable result.

This example shows once more the benefits of thinking in terms of an abstract design which expresses the solution of a problem in a natural way, then implementing use of whatever features are available in the given coding language.

3.7 SUMMARY

This chapter covered a number of important issues, pertaining mainly to vectors and matrices, which are mathematical structures, and to arrays, which are programming structures, and their relationships.

Arrays of one or more dimensions are allocated on most computers to one-dimensional storage; the formula showing the relationship between a subscripted array reference in a high-level language, and the physical storage to which it is allocated, is called the storage mapping function. One way to store multi-dimensional arrays is in row-major form, in which the rightmost subscript varies fastest; another is in column-major form, in which the leftmost subscript varies fastest.

Several different kinds of special matrices were presented, specifically those with a large number of zero elements distributed in a predictable fashion. Upper-triangular, lower-triangular, symmetric and band matrices can be stored more efficiently if their zero values are not stored; the storage mapping function then is responsible for carrying out the subscripted reference for the efficient storage scheme. Since high-level languages do not provide built-in facilities for handling these special matrices, building the right package and storage mapping function is up to the programmer.

In this chapter we considered several different strategies for storing sparse vectors, or those with a large number of zeroes in unpredictable locations. Two of these were very similar to the ordered-array and unordered-array table-handling schemes discussed in Chapter 2. A third scheme involves linking together the non-zero elements so that their logical order does not have to match their physical order. This is a special case of a linked-list method, a more general study of which follows in Chapter 4.

The Design section covered the array-handling facilities of Ada, showing the ease with which vector and matrix operations can be written. Most important are the Ada notions of unconstrained array types, attributes, and operator overloading.

Finally, as you learned in the Style Guide section, there is great virtue in thinking of records and arrays of records at the abstract level even if these cannot be written directly in a coding language. The Style Guide presented some hints for simulating record structures in Fortran and Basic.

3.8   EXERCISES

1. Obtain a detailed storage mapping function for a two-dimensional array stored in row-major form.

2. Obtain a detailed storage mapping function for a two-dimensional array stored in column-major form.

3. Obtain a detailed storage mapping function for a three-dimensional array stored in row-major form.

4. Obtain a detailed storage mapping function for a three-dimensional array stored in column-major form.

5. Obtain a general storage mapping function for an array of D dimensions stored in row-major form.

6. Obtain a general storage mapping function for an array of D dimensions stored in column-major form.

7. Language P (perhaps Pascal) stores its multi-dimensional arrays in row-major form; language F (perhaps Fortran) stores them in column-major form. Suppose a program in language P creates a 3-dimensional array, then needs to pass it to a subroutine written in language F. To save time in passing arrays, most subroutine linkage arrangements just pass the address of the array, thus the same physical copy of the array is used by both programs. A reference to, say M(1,5,-4) in the language P program refers to a *different* physical location than the same reference in the language F program. What has to be done to make the two languages communicate better? Write whatever programs you need.

8. Obtain a column-major storage mapping function for a lower-triangular matrix and explain why the row-major form is simpler.

9. Obtain both row-major and column-major storage mapping functions for an upper-triangular matrix and explain why the column-major form is simpler.

10. Obtain storage mapping functions for the band matrices given in section 3.3.3. There are many different possible storage mappings, thus many correct answers.

11. Write a function "*"(K: Valuetype; V: Vector) which finds and returns the product of a scalar K by a vector V, and which is suitable for inclusion in the package described in Section 3.5. Given that, mathematically, K * V and V * K give the same result, explain how you could allow a client program to write either expression.

12. Write a function "+"(U, V: Vector), which finds and returns the sum of its two vector arguments, and which is suitable for inclusion in the

package described in Section 3.5. Do not forget to check for conformability!

13. Write a function "*"(K: Valuetype; M: Matrix) which finds and returns the product of a scalar K by a matrix M, and which is suitable for inclusion in the package described in Section 3.5. Given that, mathematically, K * M and M * K give the same result, explain how you could allow a client program to write either expression.

14. Write a function "+"(M, N: Matrix), which finds and returns the sum of its two matrix arguments, and which is suitable for inclusion in the package described in Section 3.5. Do not forget to check for conformability!

15. Write a function Transpose(M: Matrix), which finds and returns the transpose of a matrix, and which is suitable for inclusion in the package described in Section 3.5.

Chapter 4

LINEAR LINKED LISTS, POINTERS, AND CURSORS

4.1   GOAL STATEMENT

In Section 3.4 we saw an example of the use of *links* or pointers to control storage of items in an array. These links connected the array items together in such a way that their logical order did not have to match their physical order. In this chapter we shall take up in a general way the idea of linked storage.

First we shall see how linked storage is manipulated in languages in which the compiler provides built-in facilities for this. An ADT will be shown for linked lists, and you will see several ways of implementing this ADT using Ada's *recursive data structures*. A recursive structure is something like a recursive program: the type definition for the structure has, embedded within it, a reference to another structure of the same type. Thus in a sense the type definition "calls itself."

In this chapter and the next we shall be focusing on a type of linked or recursive structure called a *linear* structure, that is, a structure all of whose items are connected "in a straight line." This is distinguished from the graph and tree structures to be encountered in Chapters 6 and 7.

This chapter contains two Design sections. The first one reconsiders the subject of sparse vectors and matrices, showing how these can be implemented in a general linked structure and giving the linked version of the arithmetic operations introduced in Section 3.5.

In the second Design section we return to the application of text handling. The text-handler package introduced in Chapter 1 is revised and improved, in order to limit the inconvenience to client programs caused by the fact that strings have a fixed maximum length. A linked-list organization of strings is used to allow strings to have essentially unlimited length with very little wasted storage.

There are also two Style Guides in this chapter. The first Style Guide considers the question of "cursor-oriented" linked allocation, as an aid to the many people needing to write programs using linked lists, but constrained to use languages like Fortran and Basic which lack built-in support.

In the second Style Guide we shall give a strategy for reclaiming the storage used by linked structures, in languages such as Pascal which do not provide automatic "garbage collection." The principles discussed in the Style Guide are also applicable to cursor-oriented memory management.

4.2   LINKED STRUCTURES

The last few examples in Section 3.4 showed some of the advantages of storing information in a structure with *links* or *pointers* so that the *logical* sequence of the items did not have to correspond with their *physical* sequence in an array structure.

In those examples, we created a record-like structure, storing instances of that structure in a one-dimensional array; in that scheme, the links were positive integers taken from the index range of the array. This is often the way linked structures must be handled, specifically in languages like Fortran, Basic, and Cobol where no better mechanism is provided by the language design. Indeed, one of this chapter's Style Guides will show you in greater detail just how this is done.

On the other hand, linked structures are very useful in many areas of programming, and serve as an implementation mechanism for many of the abstract structures to be taken up later in this book. It is precisely because of their usefulness in so many applications that modern languages like PL/1, C, Pascal, Modula-2 and Ada provide a better way to work with linked structures. This is the subject of the next section.

4.3   POINTERS AND DYNAMIC MEMORY MANAGEMENT

In languages providing built-in support for linked structures, the compiler associates with an object program a special storage area, which it leaves initially unassigned to any program variable. The area is usually called the *heap* or *dynamic storage pool*. A module in the run-time support for the language, which we shall call the *heap manager*, is given responsibility for the allocation of sections of storage from the heap *at execution time*.

A special kind of variable is provided in these languages for referencing space allocated dynamically from the heap. In Ada these are called *access variables*; in other languages they are referred to as *pointer variables*. In the Style Guide section of Chapter 1 you saw how to use these variables in Pascal to create new arithmetic systems; here we will see pointer or access variables used to link together a number of objects whose space is allocated from the heap. Since Ada is our chosen programming language in this book, it is Ada's syntax we shall use; the other languages use different syntax but the idea and the semantics are the same.

As was pointed out in Chapter 1, a pointer is just an abstraction for a machine address. Each language has a way of declaring variables which can hold pointers. The mechanism in Ada is through the use of Ada's *access types*. Suppose we had already defined a record type called RecType, something like

type RecType **is**

record

. . . fields . . .

end record;

A type definition such as

type RecPointer **is access** RecType;

would give us the ability to declare variables of type RecPointer—that is, variables which can hold pointers to things of type RecType. For example, a declaration

P1, P2, P3: RecPointer;

would bring into existence three such variables.

When an object of an access type is created in Ada, its value is pre-set (or "initialized by default") to a special, unique internal value known as *null*. This indicates that the pointer doesn't point to anything (yet).

It is important to realize that declaring such variables does *not* cause any *records* to be allocated; only enough space to hold the *address of* (a pointer to) a record is given to each variable!

How then do the records themselves come into being? An Ada operator *new* exists for just that purpose. An assignment statement like

P1 := **new** RecType;

causes the heap manager to search the heap, looking for a block of space large enough to hold a record of type RecType. When such a block is found, its address is stored in the variable P1.

Suppose we now write

P2 := **new** RecType;

what happens? A *second* block of space is allocated from the heap and *its* address is stored in P2. Now suppose that we have found a way to store values in all the fields of the record pointed to by P1, then write

P3 := P1;

P3 is made to point at the same record P1 points to! Note well: an assignment statement using an access variable copies only the pointer to (the address of) the structure involved, *not* the structure itself!

If we write, a second time,

P1 := **new** Rectype;

then space for yet a third record is found in the heap, its address is stored in P1, and P3 is left pointing to the "old" record. If, yet again, we write

P1 := **new** RecType;

the record previously created is left with nothing pointing to it, thus *inaccessible*.

In Ada systems, this space, previously in use but inaccessible, will be returned to the heap whenever the heap manager thinks the space in the heap is running out; a system procedure usually called, picturesquely, a *garbage collector* will wander through the heap, looking for inaccessible blocks of space and "recycling" them for future use. In other languages, the inaccessible space is not usually recycled automatically; the programmer must do it explicitly. We will return to this subject in the second Style Guide.

Figure 4–1 shows diagrammatically how dynamic allocation works. The "cloudlike" shape represents the heap; pointers are represented using arrows to do the "pointing."

4.4 USING DYNAMIC ALLOCATION FOR LINKED STRUCTURES

Dynamic allocation and pointers can be used to great advantage in working with the kind of linked structures introduced in section 3.4. The secret here is to define a type which we shall call a *node* (some other authors refer instead to a *cell*). Such a node will contain an information part, and a pointer part. We make the pointer part be of type "pointer to another node," then proceed to link nodes together into a chain or *linked list*.

Figure 4–2 shows the Ada definitions for such a node. Notice that Ada requires us to have "mentioned" type and variable names before we use them in further definitions. We satisfy this rule by "mentioning" the access type Node-

```
INITIAL   CONDITION
P1,  P2,  P3:  RecPointer
```

HEAP

P1 ∅

P2 ∅

P3 ∅

```
P1 := new RecType:
```

P1 •

P2 ∅

P3 ∅

```
P3   :=   P1;
```

P1 •

P2 ∅

P3 •

```
P1 := new RecType:
```

P1 •

P2 ∅

P3 •

```
P1 := new RecType:
```

P1 •

P2 ∅·

P3 •

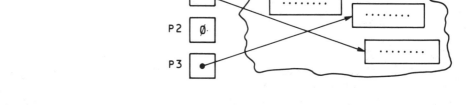

Figure 4-1   Run-time allocation from the heap (statements are executed in sequence)

```
type OneWayListNode;  -- incomplete type definition
                      -- required for recursive type

type NodePointer is access OneWayListNode;

type OneWayListNode is
   record
      Info: InfoType;
      Next: NodePointer := null;
   end record;
```

Figure 4-2 Type definitions for linked-list node.

Pointer in an "incomplete" type definition first, then defining the node type OneWayListNode, then giving the full definition of the access type.

Clearly InfoType can be any type at all. For definiteness in the examples, we will assume that InfoType has been defined somewhere as a *character* type. Also, it will become obvious later on why we have called the node a one-way list node.

The type OneWayListNode is a special case of things called *recursive types*, which are called "recursive" because each node's pointer part points to another node of the same type. In this respect recursive types are similar to recursive programs.

4.4.1 Creating a One-Way Linked List

Recall that the Ada operator *new* causes the "creation" or allocation of space in the heap. Suppose we declare two variables L1,L2: NodePointer in a program, then later write

L1 := **new** OneWayListNode;

L1.Info := 'E';

we will have set up a chain or list with one node in it. The variable L1 is known as the *head* of the list. Since L1 is *outside* the heap—that is, in our program as a declared variable—it serves as our "doorway" into the dynamically allocated list.

Now suppose we write

L2 := **new** OneWayListNode;

L2.Info := 'A';

L1.Next := L2;

then we shall have *linked* or connected the two nodes together into a chain or list. In Figure 4–3 you can see the results of a sequence of such list operations.

```
1    L1,L2:    NodePointer;
2    L1 := new OneWayListNode;
3    L1.Info   :=   'E';
```

```
4    L2 := new OneWayListNode;
5    L2.Info   :=   'A';
6    L1.Next   :=   L2;
```

```
7    L2 := new OneWayListNode;
8    L2.Info   :=   'C';
9    L1.Next.Next   :=   L2;
```

```
10   L1 :=   L1.Next;
11   L2 := new OneWayListNode;
12   L2.Info   :=   'X';
```

```
13   L1.Next.Next
              := new OneWayListNode:
14   L1.Next.Next.Info   :=   'P';
15   L1.Next.Next.Next   :=   L2;
```

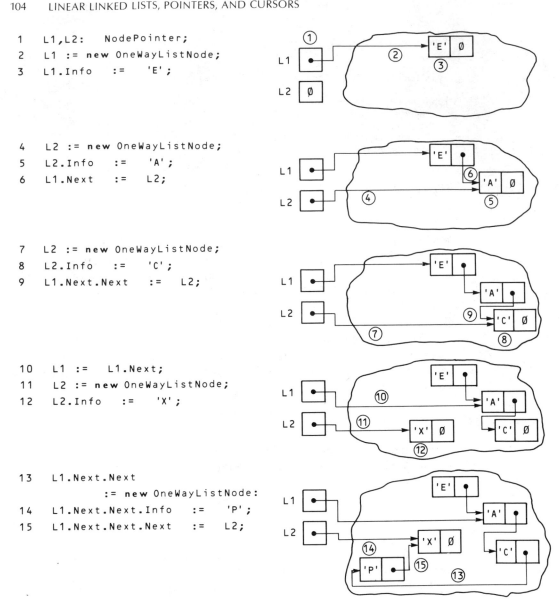

Figure 4-3   Building one-way lists.

Be sure you follow each operation through and make certain you understand the dynamic changes going on in the heap. Notice that the node containing 'E' becomes inaccessible, since even though its pointer is left pointing at something, nothing points to *it*!

4.4.2 An ADT for One-Way Linked Lists

What are the appropriate operations on one-way lists? To create an ADT that will be generally useful for many applications, it makes sense not to make any assumptions about the type of thing stored in the Info part of a list node. Accordingly, the ADT we describe here will deal mostly with keeping track of the connections in the list, working with list nodes in which the Info part has been pre-stored.

Instead of starting a list just by declaring a variable of type OneWayList-Node, let us define a type List as a record containing just one field, namely a NodePointer, and then create empty lists by declaring variables of this type.

Figure 4–4 shows all the relevant type definitions. Also shown are two functions: a "create" function MakeNode, which accepts an object of type InfoType and returns a node with that object stored in it, and the decomposition function InfoPart. Figure 4–5 shows the declaration of L1 and L2 as Lists, and a few calls of the functions, together with diagrams showing the results of these declarations and calls.

```
type OneWayListNode;
type NodePointer is access OneWayListNode;
type OneWayListNode is
   record
      Info: InfoType;
      Next: NodePointer := null;
   end record;

type List is
   record
      Next: NodePointer := null;
   end record;


function MakeNode(Item: InfoType) return NodePointer is
      p: NodePointer;
begin
      p := new OneWayListNode;
      p.Info := Item;
      return p;
end MakeNode;


function InfoPart(P: NodePointer) return InfoType is
begin
      return P.Info;
end InfoPart;
```

Figure 4-4 Some declarations for one-way lists.

```
1   L1,L2:   List;
2   C:   InfoType;
3   L1   :=   MakeNode('A');




4   L2   :=   MakeNode(InfoPart(L1))
5   L1.Next   :=   L2;




6   L1.Next.Next   :=   MakeNode('B');
7   C   :=   InfoPart(L1.Next.Next);
```

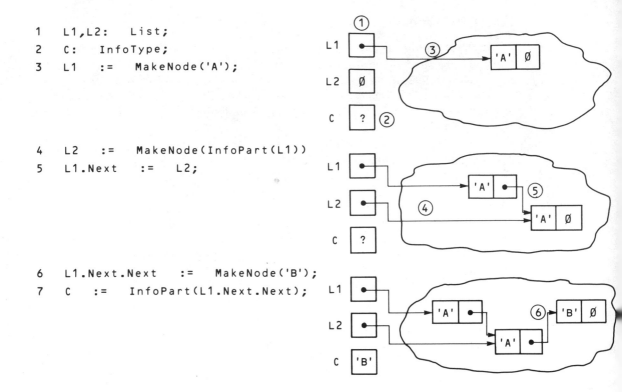

Figure 4-5   Using MakeNode and InfoPart

An important list operation connects a node to the *front* of the list. If L1 is a List, and P1 a pointer to a list node, then the procedure in Figure 4–6 carries out this operation. Notice that L1 must be declared as an **in out** parameter, because we need to modify its contents. Figure 4–7 shows the results of a number of calls to MakeNode and AddToFront.

Another important operation connects a node to the *rear* of a list. Notice the difference here: since the variable L1 points to the *front* of the list, the only

```
procedure AddToFront(L1: in out List; P1: NodePointer) is

begin

    P1.Next := L1.Next;
    L1.Next := P1;

end AddToFront;
```

Figure 4-6   Procedure to add a node to the front of a list.

```
1   M:    List;
2   Q:    NodePointer;
3   AddToFront(M,MakeNode('A'));
```

```
4   Q   :=   MakeNode('C');
5   AddToFront(M,Q);
6   AddToFront(M,MakeNode
    (InfoPart(M.Next.Next)));
```

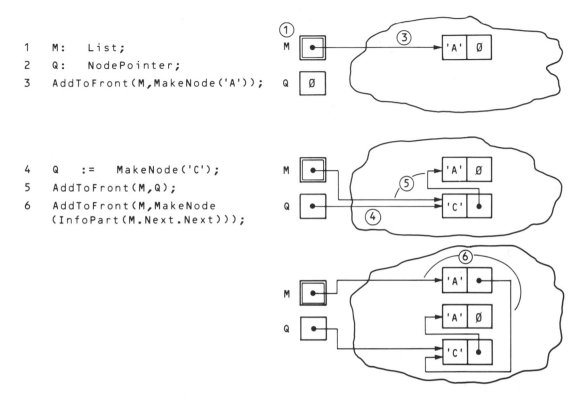

Figure 4-7   Using AddToFront.

way we can find the end is to search the whole list until we find a node whose pointer field is null. This requires a special case if the list L1 is empty when we try to find the end of the list. This function is shown in Figure 4–8: pay careful attention to the way the loop operates, particularly the statement p := p.next. Try "walking through" the code for this procedure as you follow the diagrams in Figure 4–9.

Two more useful functions are Successor(L1,P1), which returns a pointer to the node which *follows* P1 in the list L1, and Predecessor(L1,P1), which returns a pointer to the node *preceding* P1. Because we have no *immediate* way of finding the predecessor node, this function must search the list in the manner of AddToRear. Note that the predecessor of the first node in the list is deemed to be null, just like the successor of the last node in the list. The Successor and Predecessor functions are shown in Figure 4–10.

Now it is time to give a specification for an ADT to deal with one-way lists. This appears in Figure 4–11. The specification shows a function Front, which returns a pointer to the first node in a list, and three more procedures:

```
procedure AddToRear(L1: in out List; P1: NodePointer) is

   p: NodePointer := L1.Next;  -- p will "walk through" list
   q: NodePointer;

begin

   while p /= null loop
      q := p;        -- set q to trail p by one node
      p := p.next;
   end loop;         -- at this point we've found the last node

   q.next := P1;
   P1.next := null;

end AddToRear;
```

Figure 4-8   Procedure to add a node to the rear of a list.

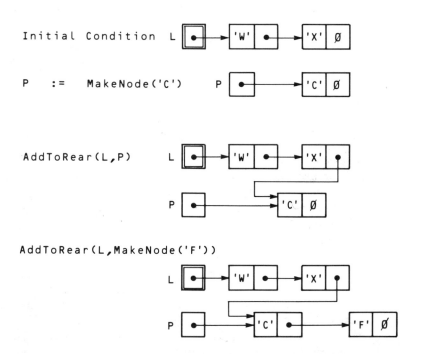

Figure 4-9   Using AddToRear.

```
function Successor(L1: List; P1: NodePointer)
                return NodePointer is
begin

   return P1.Next;

end Successor;



function Predecessor(L1: List; P1: NodePointer)
                return NodePointer is
   p: NodePointer := L1.Next; -- p starts at beginning
   q: NodePointer;            -- q will trail p by 1 node

begin

   if p = P1 then     -- P1 is first node in list
      return null;
   end if;

   while p /= null and then p /= P1 loop
      q := p;         -- q points to p's predecessor
      p := p.next;
   end loop;

   if p = null then  -- P1 is not in the list!
      return null;
   else
      return q;
   end if;

end Predecessor;
```

Figure 4-10 Successor and Predecessor functions.

Delete, InsertBefore, and InsertAfter. You can write the code for these as an exercise.

4.4.3 One-Way Lists with Head and Tail Pointers

Recall that the procedure AddToRear required a search through the entire list to find the end. This takes time proportional to the existing length of the list. We can speed the process up in a classic example of a time/space tradeoff: we just change our definition of List so that the record contains *two* pointers: one to the first or head node in the list, one to the last or tail node in the list. This uses a bit of extra space, but is well worth it, because now a node can immediately be added to the end of the list without a search, that is in *constant* time. Figure 4–12 gives the procedure AddToRear modified to take the two-pointer list head into account; we leave it to you to discover whether modifications are required to any other operations in the ADT.

```
package OneWayLists is

   type OneWayListNode;
   type NodePointer is access OneWayListNode;
   type OneWayListNode is
      record
         Info: InfoType;
         Next: NodePointer := null;
      end record;

   type List is
      record
         Next: NodePointer := null;
      end record;


   function  MakeNode(Item: InfoType) return NodePointer;
   -- create

   function  InfoPart(P1: NodePointer) return InfoType;
   function  Front(L1: List) return NodePointer;
   -- decomposition

   function  Empty(L1: List) return boolean;
   -- true iff L1 is empty

   function  Successor(L1: List; P1: NodePointer)
                  return NodePointer;
   function  Predecessor(L1: List; P1: NodePointer)
                  return NodePointer;
   -- Successor, Predecessor

   procedure AddToFront(L1 : in out List; P1: NodePointer);
   procedure AddToRear(L1: in out List; P1: NodePointer);
   procedure InsertBefore(L1: in out List; P1,P2: NodePointer);
   procedure InsertAfter(L1: in out List; P1,P2: NodePointer);
   -- various update routines

   procedure Delete(L1: in out List; P1: NodePointer);
   -- remove node pointed to by P1 from L1


end OneWayLists;
```

Figure 4-11 Specification for linked-list package.

   This ADT gives a rather minimal set of operations. Many other operations
can be written in terms of these, using the fact that new lists are created just by
declaring variables and that Ada (like other languages supporting pointers)
allows two pointer values to be tested for equality or inequality. The writer of
these other operations needs no knowledge of the internal structure of lists or
list nodes.

```
type List is
   record
      Next: NodePointer := null;
      Tail: NodePointer := null;
   end record;


procedure AddToRear(L1: in out List; P1: NodePointer) is
begin

   If Empty(L1) then
      L1.Next := P1;
      L1.Tail := P1;
   else
      L1.Tail.Next := P1;
      L1.Tail := P1;
   end If;

end AddToRear;
```

Figure 4-12   Type and AddToRear procedure for one-way lists with head and tail pointers.

Some of these operations are: finding the number of nodes in a list; making a copy of a list; attaching one list onto the end of another; destroying an entire list, and more. As an example, Figure 4–13 gives a function which returns a copy of a list L1. Writing the others is left as an exercise.

```
function CopyList(L1: List) return List is
   L2: List;
   p: NodePointer;
begin

   p := Front(L1);

   while p /= null loop

      AddToRear(L2,MakeNode(InfoPart(p)));
      p := Successor(L1,p);

   end loop;

   return L2;

end CopyList;
```

Figure 4-13   Procedure to copy a one-way list.

4.4.4 Building an Ordered List

The linked-list ADT operations were designed to have no knowledge of the structure of the Info part of the nodes. Some applications require building a list in such a way that the nodes are ordered in some way, for instance in ascending order based on a field in the InfoPart. Programs to do this kind of list building obviously require some knowledge of the details of the InfoPart, so that it can find the field on which the list is sorted, and know what "less than" and "greater than" mean for the type of that field. Let us call that field the *key* field, and the rest of the InfoPart the *value* field, and define a list node accordingly, as in Figure 4–14. We will assume that the functions Key(P1) and Value(P1) are available to return the fields of a node pointed to by P1.

Now let us write a procedure InsertInOrder which inserts a node pointed to by P1 into a list L1, in ascending order according to the key field. The insertion process has four separate cases:

1. an inserted node is the first one to be added to an empty list;
2. the inserted node's key is less than those of all others in the list, thus the node goes at the beginning of a nonempty list;
3. the key is greater than all the others, thus the node goes at the end of the list;
4. the key lies between two others, thus the node goes in the middle of the list somewhere.

```
type OneWayListNode;   -- Incomplete type definition
                       -- required for recursive type

type NodePointer is access OneWayListNode;

type InfoType is
   record
      Key:   KeyType;
      Value: ValueType;
   end record;

type OneWayListNode is
   record
      Info: InfoType;
      Next: NodePointer := null;
   end record;

type List is
   record
      Next: NodePointer := null;
      Tail: NodePointer := null;
   end record;
```

Figure 4-14   Type definitions for ordered list.

The procedure InsertInOrder is shown in Figure 4–15. Notice that it uses operations from the linked-list ADT, and needs no deeper knowledge of the linked-list organization. Notice how the four cases are handled, and the fact that a so-called "trailing pointer" is used to keep track of the predecessor of a node, so we can avoid the linear searching required to use the Predecessor function. Make sure you understand exactly how the procedure operates by tracing its actions on the example cases shown in Figure 4–16.

A similar procedure can be written to delete from a list the node containing a given key from a list. That is left as an exercise.

The algorithm for InsertInOrder and Delete can be greatly simplified if we use a "dummy" or "wasted" node at the beginning of a list. We do this by writing a "create" routine for ordered lists which sets up the dummy node. A list which is *logically* empty, then, actually has one node in it *physically*. The procedure MakeList is shown in Figure 4–17; a sample initialized list is given in Figure 4–18. The "dummy node" technique allows the four cases of the

```
procedure InsertInOrder(L1: in out List; P1: NodePointer) is
        p:      NodePointer := Front(L1);
        q:      NodePointer;   -- trailing pointer
        found: boolean := false;
        k:      KeyType := Key(P1);
    begin

        if    Empty(L1) then                 -- case (1)
           AddToFront(L1, P1);

        elsif k < Key(p) then                -- case (2)
           AddToFront(L1, P1);

        else
           while (p /= null) and (not found) loop
              if k < Key(p) then
                 found := true;
              else
                 q := p;
                 p := Successor(p);
              end if;
           end loop;

           if p = null then                  -- case (3)
              AddToRear(L1,P1);
           else
              InsertAfter(L1,P1,q);           -- case (4)
           end if;

        end if;

end InsertInOrder;
```

Figure 4-15 InsertInOrder for one-way list.

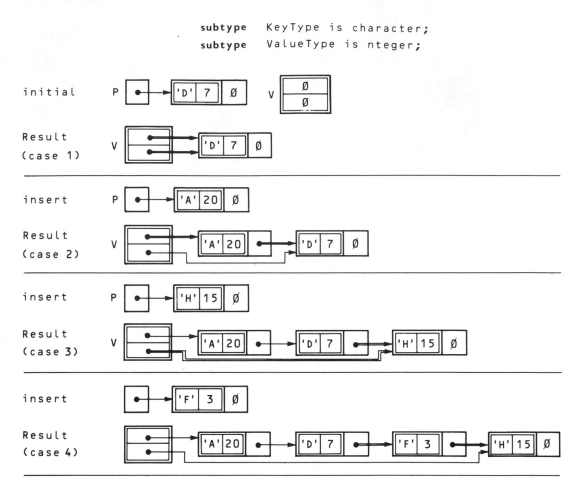

Figure 4-16   Building an order list (changed pointers indicated by double lines).

```
function MakeList return List is
    L: List;
begin
    L.Next := new OneWayListNode;
    L.Tail := L.Next;
end MakeList;
```

Figure 4-17   Function to initialize list with "dummy node."

```
V:    List;
V   :=    MakeList;
```

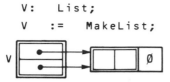

Figure 4-18   Initialized one-way list with "dummy node."

InsertInOrder procedure to be collapsed into two cases, as can be seen in Figure 4–19. Be sure you understand how this new procedure works.

As an exercise, you can write a Delete procedure for this new "dummy node" implementation, and also a Search function. It makes sense to define the Search function as returning a pointer to the node containing a given key, rather than the value, so that Search can easily return **null** if the desired node is not in the list. Thinking about these operations reveals that an ordered list can really be viewed as just another implementation of a dynamic table as developed in Chapter 2.

```
procedure InsertInOrder(L1: in out List; P1: NodePointer) is
        p:      NodePointer := Successor(Front(L1));
                            -- remember the dummy node!
        q:      NodePointer;   -- trailing pointer
        found: boolean := false;
        k:      KeyType := Key(P1);
  begin

      while (p /= null) and (not found) loop
        if k < Key(p) then
           found := true;
        else
           q := p;
           p := Successor(p);
        end if;
      end loop;

      if p = null then                      -- cases (1,3)
         AddToRear(V,P1);
      else
         InsertAfter(V,P1,q);               -- cases (2,4)
      end if;

  end InsertInOrder;
```

Figure 4-19   InsertInOrder for one-way list, using dummy node.

4.4.5 Two-Way Linked Lists

Recall that finding the predecessor of a node in a one-way list requires a linear search. We can trade time and space again by adding, *to each node*, a pointer to its predecessor. This is rather space consuming, but since it allows finding the predecessor in *constant* time, it might be a price worth paying if the application requires finding predecessor nodes frequently.

Figure 4–20 shows a type definition for a node with forward and backward pointers. Figure 4–21 shows the code for Predecessor and Delete; you can have the job of making the necessary changes to other ADT operations to accommodate the new structure. Note that we assume, as in the one-way case, that the Next pointer of the last node in a list is null, and the Previous pointer of the first node in a list is null.

4.5 DESIGN ONE: SPARSE VECTORS AND MATRICES REVISITED

Armed with an understanding of linked lists, let's return to the example of sparse vectors discussed in Chapter 3, and consider how these should be represented as lists.

Let a vector be a one-way ordered list as in the previous section. A node in the list represents an ordered pair <index,value>; in this application the *key* is a vector index.

Using the ordered-list node type from the previous section, Figure 4–22 shows a type SparseVector which serves as the list head and contains fields giving the minimum and maximum indices allowable for the vector. Through-

```
type TwoWayListNode;

type TwoWayNodePtr is access TwoWayListNode;

type TwoWayListNode is
   record
      Info:    .InfoType;
      Next:     TwoWayNodePtr := null;
      Previous: TwoWayNodePtr := null;
   end record;

type TwoWayList is
   record
      Next:    TwoWayNodePtr := null;
      Tail:    TwoWayNodePtr := null;
   end record;
```

Figure 4-20 Type definitions for two-way lists.

```
function Predecessor(L1: TwoWayList; P1: TwoWayNodePtr)
              return TwoWayNodePtr is

begin

    return P1.Previous; -- null if P1 is first node in L1

end Predecessor;


procedure Delete(L1: in out TwoWayList; P1: TwoWayNodePtr) is

begin

    P1.Previous.Next := P1.Next;        -- skip P1 going forward
    P1.Next.Previous := P1.Previous;    -- skip P1 going backward

    if P1 = L1.Next then                -- P1 was first node
       L1.Next := P1.Next;
    end if;

    if P1 = L1.Tail then                -- P1 was last node
       L1.Tail := P1.Previous;
    end if;

end Delete;
```

Figure 4-21   Predecessor and Delete operations for two-way lists.

out the following discussion, let us denote by MaxNonZero the maximum number of non-zero items in a vector, that is, MaxIndex – MinIndex + 1.

4.5.1 Vector Arithmetic

In Chapter 3 we presented arithmetic packages for vectors and matrices. Here we will show the implementation of two of the operations presented there—multiplication by a scalar and vector addition—for the case of sparse vectors. The other operations are left as an exercise.


```
subtype VectorIndexRange is Integer range  .. whatever

type SparseVector is
  record
    MinIndex: VectorIndexRange := VectorIndexRange'first;
    MaxIndex: VectorIndexRange := VectorIndexRange'last;
    VectorBody: List;
  end record;
```

Figure 4-22   Declaration for sparse vector (implemented as one-way list).

```
function Retrieve(V1: SparseVector; i: KeyType)
                   return ValueType is
    p: NodePointer := Successor(First(V1.VectorBody));
                             -- dummy node is used!
begin

    while p /= null loop

        if    Key(p) = i then
            return Value(p);

        elsif Key(p) > i then
            return Zero;        -- it wasn't there!

        else
            p := Successor(p);
        end if;

    end loop;

    return Zero;                -- we got to the end
end Retrieve;
```

Figure 4-23   Retrieve function for sparse vector.

In Figure 4–23 we give the code for a function Retrieve(V,i), which searches the list for a node containing a given key, returns its value if it was there, and 0 otherwise. This corresponds to the Retrieve operation sketched out in section 3.4. We leave as an exercise the procedure Store(V,i,x), which stores the value x in the location of V with index i. Recall that this was also sketched in section 3.4 and is a bit more involved than it first looks.

Now in Figure 4–24 we show a function for multiplying a sparse vector by a scalar. Notice that it looks very similar to the corresponding function in section 3.5 that just worked with "normal" vectors, except that the array references are replaced by calls to Store and Retrieve. Figure 4–25 shows a vector addition function built on the same principle.


```
function "*"(V: SparseVector; X: ValueType)
                   return SparseVector is
    W: SparseVector;
begin

    for k in V.MinIndex..V.MaxIndex loop
        Store(W,k,(Retrieve(V,k) * X));
    end loop;

    return Temp;

end "*";
```

Figure 4-24   Multiplication of sparse vector by scalar (the naive way).

```
function "+"(U,V: SparseVector) return SparseVector is
   W: SparseVector;
begin

   if U.MinIndex /= V.MinIndex or
      U.MaxIndex /= V.MaxIndex then
      raise ConformabilityError;
   end if;

   for k in U.MinIndex..U.MaxIndex loop
      Store(W,k,(Retrieve(U,k) + Retrieve(V,k)));
   end loop;

   return W;

end "+";
```

Figure 4-25   Addition of two sparse vectors (the naive way).

Let's look at the performance of vector addition using this scheme. Assume that each vector has ActualNonZero nonzero components (i.e. the list has ActualNonZero nodes not counting the dummy). Then each Retrieve operation is O(ActualNonZero), since on the average half the list must be searched.

Now, since the vector is defined for MaxNonZero components, MaxNonZero calls to Retrieve must be executed for each of the two vectors, and—in the worst case—MaxNonZero insertions must be done. Since each insertion is also O(ActualNonZero), the overall addition operation is O(MaxNonZero * ActualNonZero)! But vector addition as done in Chapter 3 is O(MaxNonZero), since the two arrays are traversed only once. Thus we have paid a price in time performance in return for the economy of space achieved by storing vectors in sparse form.

Actually, the tradeoff is between abstraction and performance: the slow performance came from our unwillingness to let the addition function know the details of a sparse vector. We required the addition function to use calls to Store and Retrieve. If we are willing to let that function use knowledge of the fact that sparse vectors are stored as *lists*, we can speed it up considerably. Only one pass through the two lists is required; since the lists are stored in order on the index, we use a very simple "merge" algorithm.

Begin at the beginning of both vectors U and V. If the index of the first node of U is less than that of V, we know the corresponding element of V is zero. So we just add the element of U onto the end of the sum vector W. Then we find the successor node in U and try again.

On the other hand, if the V index is less, then we add the node from V onto the end of the W list, moving to *its* successor.

If the two indices are ever equal, then both U and V have nonzero values in that position, and we add the values together before adding a node for that index onto the end of W.

Eventually, we reach the end of one of the vectors. Suppose we reach U's end first. At that point, we just copy the rest of V onto W, since all remaining components of U are zero!

Figure 4–26 shows the function to carry out this addition. It is somewhat more complicated than the naive version, but it is a lot faster, since its performance is O(ActualNonZero) instead of O(MaxNonZero × ActualNonZero)! If

```
function "+"(U,V: SparseVector) return SparseVector is
    W: SparseVector;
    k1, k2: KeyType;
    p1 : NodePointer := Successor(Front(U));
    p2 : NodePointer := Successor(Front(V));
begin

    while p1 /= null and p2 /= null loop
        k1 := KeyPart(p1);
        k2 := KeyPart(p2);

        if    k1 < k2 then    -- corresponding V element = 0
            AddToEnd(W,MakeVectorElement(k1,ValuePart(p1)));
            p1  := Successor(p1);
        elsif k1 > k2 then    -- corresponding U element = 0
            AddToEnd(W,MakeVectorElement(k2,ValuePart(p2)));
            p2  := Successor(p2);
        else                  -- indices equal; add together
            AddToEnd(W, MakeVectorElement(k2,
                            ValuePart(p1) + ValuePart(p1)));
            p1  := Successor(p1);
            p2  := Successor(p2);
        end if;

    end loop;          -- finished walking 1 vector;

    if p1 = null then
        while p2 /= null loop       -- copy tail of V
            k2 := KeyPart(p2);
            AddToEnd(W,MakeVectorElement(k2,ValuePart(p2)));
            p2 := Successor(p2);
        end loop;

    else
        while p1 /= null loop       -- copy tail of U
            k1 := KeyPart(p1);
            AddToEnd(W,MakeVectorElement(k1,ValuePart(p1)));
            p1 := Successor(p1);
        end loop;
    end if;

    return W;

end "+";
```

Figure 4-26 A faster addition of sparse vectors.

MaxNonZero is much larger than ActualNonZero—a good assumption, of course, in the case of sparse vectors—then the speedup is really significant.

We shall return to merge algorithms later in the book, in our study of sorting external files.

4.5.2 Sparse Matrices

The linked-list implementation of sparse vectors can be extended to two dimensions to handle sparse matrices. First consider the classical array case, as we did for vectors. For two matrices M and N, both with Rmax rows and Cmax columns, their matrix sum is a matrix P such that for each r and c, P(r,c) = M(r,c) + N(r,c). The sum operation is O(Rmax × Cmax).

Remember too that for two matrices M and N, if the number of rows Rmax2 of N is the same as the number of columns Cmax1 of M, then they are multiplication-conformable and their matrix product is a matrix P, with Rmax1 rows and Cmax2 columns. As a reminder, an Ada fragment for finding the matrix product is shown in Figure 4 27. Its performance is O(Rmax1 × Cmax2 × Cmax1), or cubic.

Finding the product of matrices is an important application, so if our sparse matrix implementation is to be realistic, we shall need to be able to scan rows or columns with equal ease. We thus define a node of a sparse matrix as having row and column indices and row and column pointers. Type definitions for such a node are found in Figure 4–28, as is the definition of a sparse matrix.

The "header" of a sparse matrix contains two arrays, one with Rmax elements, one with Cmax elements, to serve as heads of the respective row and column lists. Each node is thus on two lists, a row list and a column list. To scan a row we follow its row list; to scan a column, we follow its column list.

```
...
for R In 1..Rmax1 loop
    for C In 1..Cmax2 loop
        --
        M3(R,C) := 0;
        for K In 1..Cmax1 loop
            M3(R,C) := M1(R,K) * M2(K,C) + M3(R,C);
        end loop;
        --
    end loop;
end loop;
--
...
```

Figure 4-27 Fragment for matrix product.

```
subtype RowRange Is Integer range 1..MaxRows;
subtype ColRange Is Integer range 1..MaxCols;
subtype ValueType Is Integer;   -- or whatever other type

type InfoType Is
   record
      RowIndex: RowRange;
      ColIndex: ColRange;
      value: ValueType;
   end record;


type SparseMatrixElement;
type NodePointer Is access SparseMatrixElement;
type SparseMatrixElement Is
   record
      Info: InfoType;
      NextRow: NodePointer := null;
      NextCol: NodePointer := null;
   end record;

type List Is
   record
      Next: NodePointer := null;
      Tail: NodePointer := null;
   end record;


type SparseMatrix Is
   record
      MinRow: RowRange := RowRange'first;
      MaxRow: RowRange := RowRange'last;
      MinCol: ColRange := ColRange'first;
      MaxCol: ColRange := ColRange'last;
      RowBody: array(MinRow..MaxRow) of List;
      ColBody: array(MinCol..MaxCol) of List;
   end record;
```

Figure 4-28   Declarations for sparse matrix (implemented as cross lists).

Filling in the details of a package for sparse-matrix arithmetic is left as an exercise. As a hint to the structure of a matrix, an example is given in Figure 4–29 of the "normal" and sparse forms of a 5 × 5 matrix of integers.

This sparse matrix implementation is often called *cross lists* or *orthogonal lists*. It is a special case of a more general one in which each node has N indices or *keys* and N pointers, and the values may be, for example, information records of some sort. In the general situation, the structure is often called a *multi-list* structure, and appears in discussions of data base organization.

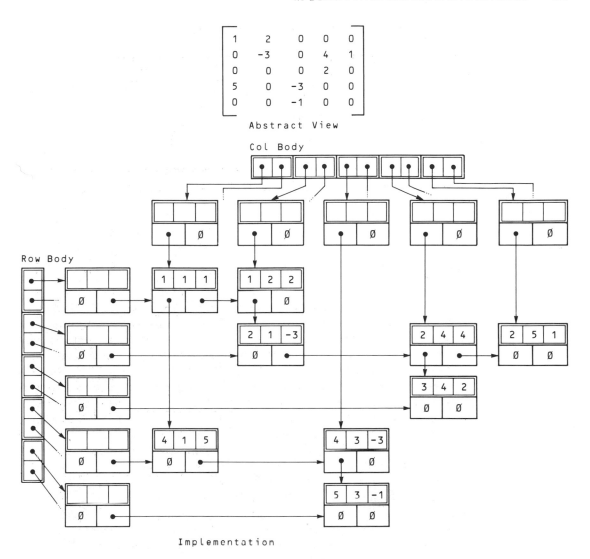

Figure 4-29 Sparse matrix implemented as multi-list structure (tail pointers are omitted to avoid clutter).

4.6 DESIGN TWO: TEXT HANDLING REVISITED

In this section we return to the package for text handling designed back in Chapter 1. You may recall that in that design a Text object consisted of a thirty-two-character array and a current-length field. The design is seriously

T: Text := MakeText("ABCDEFGHIJ");

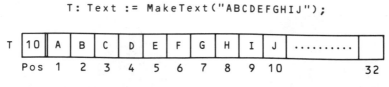

(a) **Original scheme from Chapter 1.**

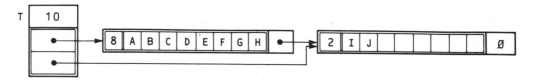

(b) **New scheme using one-way list.**

Figure 4-30 Old and new structures for Text objects.

limited for general text-handling work by the fact that every text object contains exactly thirty-two characters' worth of space. This wastes a lot of space, especially if many of the objects have only a few characters. Furthermore, if a concatenation is done of two Text objects with a total length of more than thirty-two, an overflow condition results.

We can solve both problems with an alternative design, namely letting a Text object consist of a linked list of smaller objects, for example with a length of eight characters. If the actual length of the string is not a multiple of eight, then some space is wasted at the end, but it is probably less than in the other design. A comparison of how a particular ten-character string would be stored in both schemes is shown in Figure 4-30.

We can, in fact, re-use most of our work from the previous package if we just change Maximum to, say, eight, and change the name of the Text object to ShortText, to avoid confusion with our new Text object. Figure 4-31 shows the specification for the revised package, called ShortTextHandler, and Figure 4-32 shows the type definitions for the new scheme, which assumes that both ShortTextHandler and OneWayLists are available.

In Figure 4-33 we show the code for MakeText in this new implementation; Figure 4-34 gives a function Equal that works for the new Text structure.

Concatenating one Text object to another is now a matter of copying the first object to a result list, then copying the second Text object, character-by-character, onto the end of the result. The character-by-character copy is necessary in order to fill in the empty space at the end of the first list. This makes substring searching and equality checking much easier.

A diagram showing the concatenation of two of these new Text objects is given in Figure 4-35; writing this function and completing the package is left as an exercise.

```
package ShortTextHandler is

   Maximum: constant integer := 8;
   subtype Index is integer range 0..Maximum;

   type ShortText is private;

   function MakeShortText (S: string)    return ShortText;
   function MakeShortText (C: character) return ShortText;
   function NullShortText                return ShortText;
   --      "create" operation"

   function Length (T: ShortText) return Index;
   function Value (T: ShortText)  return string;
   function Empty (T: ShortText)  return boolean;
   --      decomposition operations

   function "&"(T1, T2: ShortText)  return ShortText;
   --      and other overloaded concatenation operations

   function Equal(T1, T2: ShortText) return boolean;
   function "<"  (T1, T2: ShortText) return boolean;
   function "<=" (T1, T2: ShortText) return boolean;
   function ">"  (T1, T2: ShortText) return boolean;
   function ">=" (T1, T2: ShortText) return boolean;
   --      lexical comparison

   function Head(T: ShortText) return character;
   function Tail(T: ShortText) return ShortText;
   --      head and tail functions

   function Locate(Sub: ShortText; Within: ShortText) return Index;
   --      and othe overloaded Locate operations

   function Substr(T: ShortText; Start, Size: Index)
                   return ShortText;
   --      return substring of length Size

private
   type ShortText is
      record
         Pos: Index := 0;
         Value: string(1..Maximum);
      end record;

end ShortTextHandler;
```

Figure 4-31   ShortTextHandler package specification.

```
type InfoType is ShortText;


type Text is
   record
      Length: natural;    -- total length now unlimited!
      Value:  List;       -- list header: has 2 pointers!
   end record;
```

Figure 4-32   Type Definitions for Text objects constructed as one-way lists.

```
function MakeText(S: string) return Text is

    Lgth:   natural := S'length;
    T:      Text;
    L:      List;
    start:  natural;
    finish: natural;

begin

    if S = "" then
        return T;
    end if;

    start := 1;

    while start <= Lgth loop

        if start + Maximum - 1 <= Lgth then
            finish := start + Maximum - 1; -- AT LEAST  8 CHARS. LEFT
        else
            finish := Lgth;               -- LESS THAN 8 CHARS. LEFT
        end if;

        AddToRear(L,                      -- GET CURRENT GROUP OF CHARS.
            MakeNode(MakeShortText(S(start..finish))));

        start := start + Maximum;         -- ADVANCE TO NEXT GROUP

    end loop;

    T.Length := Lgth;
    T.value  := L;
    return T;

end MakeText;
```

Figure 4-33   Revised MakeText for unlimited-length Text objects.

4.7   STYLE GUIDE ONE: SIMULATING DYNAMIC MEMORY MANAGEMENT

Recall from Chapter 3 the example of sparse vectors using arrays to store the vector elements and integers in the range of the array subscripts to represent links or "pointers." In this Style Guide we will combine that example with the Style Guide from Chapter 3, to show how a sparse vector system (or other system using linked lists) might be set up in a language—Fortran, for example—supporting neither pointers nor record types.

We are pretending that our implementation language has no heap or dynamic storage allocation built in, and no record types either. We shall thus *sim-*

```
function Equal(T1, T2: Text) return boolean is

    p1: NodePointer := Front(T1.value);
    p2: NodePointer := Front(T2.value);

begin

    if T1.length /= T2.length then
        return false;
    end if;

    while p1 /= null loop

        if not Equal(InfoPart(p1), InfoPart(p2)) then
            return false;  -- mismatch at this node
        else
            p1 := Successor(p1);
            p2 := Successor(p2);
        end if;

    end loop;

    return true;          -- if we ever get to this point
```

Figure 4-34   Equality test for unlimited-length Text objects.

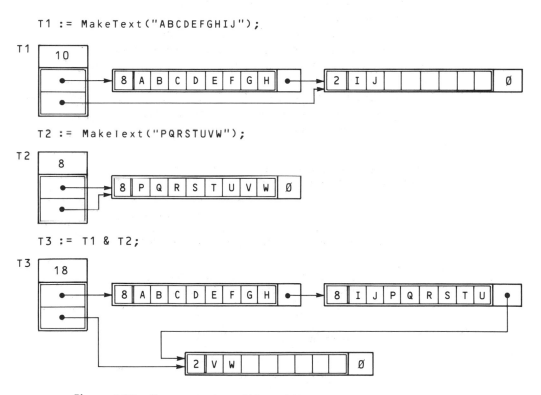

```
T1 := MakeText("ABCDEFGHIJ");
```

```
T2 := MakeText("PQRSTUVW");
```

```
T3 := T1 & T2;
```

Figure 4-35   Concatenation of Text objects.

127

ulate these by using subscripts to represent pointers, and a separate one-dimensional array to represent each field of a record type. Our basic routines for handling list and vector elements can then be easily recoded to suit the new implementation.

In this example we assume that the application requires storage of *many* vectors at one time, so that operations may be done on them. Let the vector range be 1..1,000 as before; assume that no more than 500 vector *elements* will be non-zero at any one time, independent of the number of *vectors* currently active. Remembering the terminology of Chapter 3, and using the type Node-Pointer now to designate an integer link, we show in Figure 4–36 the declarations for a number of structures. Make certain you understand why there are three arrays and why the dimensions and types are what they are! A sparse vector is, now, just a one-dimensional array of two elements, namely a head "pointer" and a tail "pointer," as shown in the figure.

To handle allocation of nodes in this simulated heap structure, let's declare another vector, called Avail, which will let us know the location of the next available node in the array, and initialize the whole array by calling a routine StoragePoolInit which just sets the link of each node to point at the next physical node. The Ada code for StoragePoolInit is given in Figure 4–37; a diagram of the initialized space is shown in Figure 4–38.

This scheme is a miniature version of the *new* operation in Ada and its equivalents in other languages. As new nodes are required to store values in any of the vectors, they are allocated from this "list of available space," as it is usually called. If a node is deleted, it is just returned to the list of available space by adding it to the front of the list. This return serves to keep track of all the "garbage" as we go along, so no separate "garbage collection" is needed. This is analogous to the Pascal *dispose* operation.

```
MaxElements: constant Integer := 1000;
MaxNonZero:  constant Integer := 500;


subtype VectorRange Is Integer range 1..MaxElements;
subtype NodePointer Is Integer range 0..MaxNonZero;
subtype ValueType   Is Integer; -- (or whatever)


Indices:  array(1..MaxNonZero) of VectorRange;
Values:   array(1..MaxNonZero) of ValueType;
Links:    array(1..MaxNonZero) of NodePointer;


Avail:    NodePointer;


type SparseVector Is array(1..2) of NodePointer;
```

Figure 4-36 Definitions for sparse vectors in simulated heap implementation.

```
procedure StoragePoolInit is
begin
    Avail := 1;      -- Avail is global!

    for k in 1 .. MaxNonZero-1 loop
       Links(k) := k + 1;
    end loop;

    Links(MaxNonZero) := 0;

end StoragePoolInit;
```

Figure 4-37 Storage pool initialization (for array-based simulated heap).

In this way, a number of vectors can be stored in the same pool of space, and they can grow and shrink as required. The link structure maintains the logical order of each list; all the lists share the same physical "heap" space. The only time it is necessary to refuse to add a new item to a vector is in the event that all nodes in the list space are simultaneously occupied and allocated to vectors.

The name "cursor" is often given to a pointer which is simulated by a value in an array; the name is just used to distinguish this case from the "real" pointers available in Ada and other such languages.

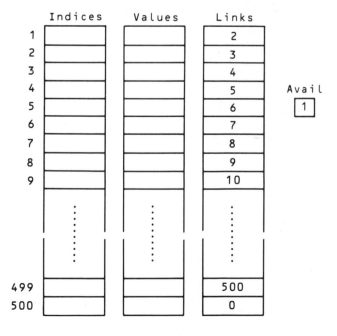

Figure 4-38 Initialized storage pool.

```
function MakeVectorElement(index: VectorRange;
                          value: ValueType) return NodePointer is
   p: NodePointer;
begin
   p := Avail;                -- point to next available node
   if p=0 then
      raise NoMoreSpace;
   end if;
   Avail := Links(Avail);     -- remove from available list
   Indices(p) := index;
   Values(p)  := value;
   Links(p)   := 0;
   return p;
end MakeVectorElement;

function IndexPart(p: NodePointer) return VectorRange is
begin
   return Indices(p);
end IndexPart;

procedure AddToFront(V1: in out SparseVector; p: NodePointer) is
   Next: constant integer := 1;
   Tail: constant integer := 2;
begin
   Links(p) := V1(Next);
   V1(Next) := p;
   if V1(Tail) = 0 then
      V1(Tail) := p;
   end if;
end AddToFront;

function Successor(V1: SparseVector: p: NodePointer)
             return NodePointer is
begin
   return Links(p);
end Successor;

function Retrieve(V1: SparseVector; i: VectorRange)
             return ValueType is
   p: NodePointer := Successor(V1(Next)); -- dummy in use!
begin
   while p /= 0 loop
      if    i = IndexPart(p) then
         return ValuePart(p);
      elsif i < IndexPart(p) then
         return 0;             -- it wasn't there!
      else
         p := Successor(p);
      end if;
   end loop;
   return 0;                   -- we got to the end
end Retrieve;
```

Figure 4-39 Some routines for sparse vectors (implemented with simulated heap).

Figure 4–39 gives the code for a few more routines equivalent to the ones given earlier for the case where built-in dynamic allocation is used. These routines are coded in Ada, our "design language," but they could be translated very straightforwardly into, say, Fortran, if the need ever arose.

In Figure 4–40 you will see a number of assignment statements assigning zero and nonzero values to vector elements as though they were stored in a "normal" array structure. Figure 4–41 shows a storage pool after the execution of the entire sequence of "assignments" has been done. Start with the initialized storage pool from Figure 4–38, then trace each statement's effect. Make sure you understand how this simulated dynamic memory scheme works!

From this example you can see the distinct advantages inherent in thinking of an application first in terms appropriate to that application: linked lists, pointers, type definitions, and so on, then recoding if necessary in whatever language is available. Having understood in the "right" way what linked lists and sparse vectors are about, you can convert to a cursor-oriented implementation with little difficulty, recoding only a small number of routines, then translate the whole into a less-well-equipped implementation language.

4.8 STYLE GUIDE TWO: ANOTHER VISIT TO PASCAL COMPLEX NUMBERS

It was mentioned previously that in Ada systems, space allocated from the heap which later becomes inaccessible can be recycled by a "garbage collector" module. This automatic recycling of inaccessible space usually relieves the programmer of having to think about storage reclamation.

```
V1 := MakeVector;
Store(V1, 5,-3);
V2 := MakeVector;
Store(V2,17, 2);
Store(V1, 2, 4);
Store(V1, 5,-3);
V3 := MakeVector;
Store(V3,18,-5);
Store(V1,10,-2);
Store(V1,20, 4);
Store(V1,10, 0);
Store(V2,10, 4);
Store(V3, 5, 2);
Store(V1,30,-3);
Store(V2 7, 0);
```

Figure 4-40 Sparse vector operations.

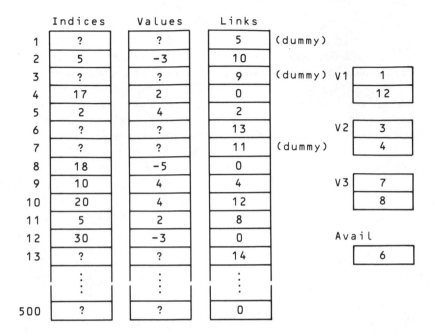

Figure 4-41   Storage pool and list variables after executing operations of Figure 4-40.

But other common programming languages—Pascal, Modula-2, C, PL/1—lack garbage collectors (there are interesting reasons for this, but they are beyond our scope). Inaccessible space remains inaccessible, thus unavailable for future use during that program execution. The programmer who is concerned about running out of heap space is responsible for doing something explicit about it.

As a vehicle for discussing this situation, let us return to the complex-number ADT package introduced in Chapter 1. Our objective there, as you will recall, was to build operations using *functions* so that these operations could be combined in expressions. For convenience, we repeat in Figure 4–42 the relevant type definitions and a few key functions from that package.

The function MakeComplex calls *new* each time it is called. This allocates a record to store the complex number. If C1 has been declared of type Complex, then

$$C1 := MakeComplex(1.5, -3.0)$$

will work exactly as intended. If C1, C2, and C3 are complex numbers, then

$$C3 := CSum(C1,C2)$$

will work correctly as well. But what about

```
type CompNum =
  record
     RealPart: real;
     ImagPart: real;
  end {CompNum};

Complex = @CompNum;


function MakeComplex (R,I: real): Complex;
  var P : Complex;
begin
  new(P);
  P@.RealPart := R;
  P@.ImagPart := I;
  MakeComplex := P
 end {MakeComplex};

function Re( C: Complex): real;
  begin
     Re := C@.RealPart
  end {Re};

function Im( C: Complex): real;
  begin
     Im := C@.ImagPart
  end {Im};

function Csum( X,Y: Complex): Complex;
  begin
     Csum := MakeComplex(Re(X) + Re(Y) , Im(X) + Im(Y) )
  end {CSum};
```

Figure 4-42 Types and functions for Complex numbers in Pascal (repeated from Chapter 1).

$$C3 := CProd(CSum(C1,C2), CDiff(C1,C2))$$

which is equivalent to $C3 := (C1 + C2) * (C1 - C2)$?

Since CSum and CDiff both call MakeComplex, two calls to *new* are made for the results of these operations. But these are only *temporary* or *intermediate* results. They are never assigned to program variables, so they should be reclaimed as soon as they are used as arguments to CProd. Unfortunately, Pascal's lack of a garbage collector leaves them allocated but inaccessible.

A solution is to be found in the fact that standard Pascal has a built-in procedure dispose(P) which, given a pointer P, returns to the heap whatever is pointed to by P. It's the inverse of *new*, in other words. The problem is for our complex-number package to be able to discern whether a given complex is temporary, as in the intermediate expressions above, or permanent, like A, B, C, D, and E.

```
type CompNum =
   record
       RealPart: real;
       ImagPart: real;
       IsTemp : boolean
   end {CompNum};



function MakeComplex (R,I: real): Complex;
   var P : Complex;
begin
   new(P);
   P@.RealPart := R;
   P@.ImagPart := I;
   P@.IsTemp:= True;
   MakeComplex := P
 end {MakeComplex};
```

Figure 4-43   Revised type definition and MakeComplex.

One way to do this is to add to each record a Boolean field IsTemp which is set to True by MakeComplex. This would change the type definitions and the MakeComplex function as shown in Figure 4–43.

Two questions remain: how to designate "permanent" complex numbers, and how to *dispose* of temporary ones. The first question can be answered by noticing that the only time we need a "permanent" complex is when we are assigning it to a declared variable. To do this, we need to write a procedure CAssign(C1, C2), which copies C2 into C1, *replacing the := operation*, and setting IsTemp to False.

To dispose of temporary structures, we can write a procedure CRelease(C) calls *dispose* just in case C is temporary. We shall have to call CRelease in each of our arithmetic functions, so that input arguments to these functions can be given back if temporary. CRelease is a sort of "conditional *dispose*." CAssign and CRelease are shown in Figure 4–44.

```
procedure CAssign (var C1, C2 : Complex);
   begin
      If  C1 <> nil then dispose(C1);
      { get rid of whatever C1 points to now }
      C1 := MakeComplex(Re(C2), Im(C2));
      C1@.IsTemp := False
   end {CAssign};



procedure CRelease (var C1 : Complex);
   begin
      If C1@.IsTemp then dispose(C1)
   end {CRelease};
```

Figure 4-44   Pascal procedures for CAssign and CRelease.

```
function CSum(X,Y : Complex) : Complex;
   begin
      CSum := MakeComplex (Re(X)+Re(Y), Im(X)+Im(Y));
      CRelease(X);
      CRelease(Y)
   end {CSum};
```

Figure 4-45   Modified Complex sum function in Pascal.

This may all seem a bit messy, but since Pascal will not collect garbage automatically, it's about the only way to reclaim the storage. As an example of where we'd use CRelease, consider the revised CSum given in Figure 4–45. In this scheme each arithmetic function has to be made responsible for calling CRelease for its arguments.

This scheme can also be used in applications such as the cursor-oriented sparse vector system shown in the previous section. There, of course, there are no built-in *new* and *dispose* operations as in Pascal, so the simulated ones are used instead.

4.9   SUMMARY

In this chapter we have worked with linked lists, with an emphasis on how they are handled in languages providing built-in support. The example of sparse vectors and matrices has served as an important vehicle for understanding list structures. You should be well aware that there is nothing in the linked-list abstraction that limits its use to numerical problems.

We have viewed several levels of abstraction here. There is first the abstraction of a "sparse vector" (or other appropriate application structure), which is implemented as a linked list. The list is in turn treated as an abstraction, with implementation either as a record-and-pointer structure in languages which permit it, or as an array-and-cursor structure in languages which don't.

Through a bit of performance analysis of vector addition, we have dealt with the oft-present tradeoff between *abstraction* and *run-time performance*. Further, the entire discussion of sparse vectors was built on the need to economize on *space;* thus another whole set of tradeoffs was considered.

The Style Guide sections in this Chapter showed how to deal with linked lists and storage reclamation in languages which don't provide these things as standard features.

In the coming chapters you will see many cases where linked structures are used in developing implementations of other abstractions.

4.10   EXERCISES

1. Implement the list operations Front, Delete, InsertBefore, and InsertAfter for the one-way list package specified in Figure 4–11.

2. Write a function to return the number of nodes in a one-way list.

3. Write a procedure which attaches one list to the end of another. Note that this procedure destroys the original lists.

4. Write a function which returns the concatenation of two lists L1 and L2, that is, a list containing copies of all the nodes of L1 followed by copies of all the nodes of L2. Note that this function does not destroy either L1 or L2.

5. Write a procedure Delete(L:list; K:KeyType), which deletes from an ordered list L the *first* node containing a given key K. Do this two ways: first for a list without a dummy node, then for a list with a dummy node.

6. Write a procedure DeleteLast(L:list; K:KeyType), which deletes from an ordered list L the *last* node containing a given key K. Do this two ways: first for a list without a dummy node, then for a list with a dummy node.

7. Write a procedure DeleteAll(L:list; K:KeyType), which deletes from an ordered list L *all* nodes containing a given key K. Do this two ways: first for a list without a dummy node, then for a list with a dummy node.

8. Write a function Search(L:list; K:Keytype) which searches a list L with a dummy node, returning a pointer to the first node containing a given key K.

9. Starting from the specification in Figure 4–11, develop a package for two-way lists.

10. Refer to the specification in Figure 3–23 for a vector-arithmetic package and implement the package for sparse vectors represented as one-way lists.

11. For the sparse-matrix implementation shown in Figure 4–29, calculate the space requirements for a matrix in this form which has K non-zero values. Assume that each pointer occupies P bytes, each index occupies I bytes, and each value occupies V bytes. Recalling that a "classical" square matrix with N rows and N columns occupies $V \times N^2$ bytes, find the crossover point, or the point where the classical and list methods require equal storage. Calculate the "sparseness ratio" K/N^2 for the realistic case in which $P = I = 2$ and $V = 4$.

12. Write a concatenation operation "&" for two text objects stored in the list form described in Section 4.6.

13. Complete the text-handler package discussed in Section 4.6.

14. In thinking about the text package discussed in Section 4.6, discuss the tradeoffs between the suggested method of concatenating Text objects—copying character-by-character and leaving no empty space at the ends of nodes—and an alternative strategy in which concatenation simply concatenates the *nodes* together. This uses extra space because both operands may have empty space at the ends, but saves time. How does this alternative design affect other routines in the package such as equality checking and substring searching?

15. Implement a sparse-vector package using the cursor-oriented memory scheme discussed in Section 4.7.

Chapter 5

QUEUES AND STACKS

5.1 GOAL STATEMENT

Two very common, important, and easy to understand structures in computing are the *queue* and the *stack*. These are distinguished from each other and from vectors and lists by the rules by which elements in them are accessed for storage and retrieval.

Recall that in a vector the access is *random* in the sense that we can store a value at an arbitrary location or retrieve a value from an arbitrary location, without having to search any other locations. In a list the access is *sequential* in that a sequential search must be done to locate the position of an arbitrary element. However, in stacks and queues we are allowed only a *controlled* method of access. In queues this is "First-In, First-Out" or FIFO; in stacks it is "Last-In, First-Out" or LIFO.

In this chapter you will see ADTs for these two structures, and various implementation schemes for them. Specifically, you will see how stacks and queues can be constructed using arrays as well as linked lists.

An important application of stacks, namely evaluating and translating arithmetic expressions, is shown in this chapter. The Design section develops an algorithm for translating an expression into *reverse Polish notation (RPN)* form.

5.2   QUEUES AND STACKS INTRODUCED

The queue is analogous to the waiting line at a supermarket checkout or bank teller: customers are served one at a time, in the exact order of their arrival. Because of this first-come, first-served serving strategy, the queue is often called a First-In, First-Out or FIFO structure. Notice that this means that customers must always get at the end of the line when they arrive, and the server (checkout clerk or whatever) waits on whoever is first in line. (We assume that all customers are polite and that "breaking in" never occurs.) That customer then leaves the line, and the line moves up. Obviously, it doesn't make sense for the server to try to serve an empty queue.

The stack, on the other hand, finds its intuitive analogy in the spring-loaded tray stackers often found in self-service restaurants. In such a stacker, only the top tray is visible. Only the top tray may be removed; when a new clean tray is placed on top of the stack all the others are pushed down, and when a tray is removed all the others move up. It doesn't make sense to remove the top tray on an empty stacker.

We shall see that there are a number of computing applications for the stack, which is often called a Last-In, First-Out or LIFO device because, carrying on with the restaurant analogy, the last tray put on the stacker is the first one removed.

With this intuitive introduction, let us formalize our consideration of queues and stacks.

5.3   QUEUES

Let us think of a queue as an abstract entity. It has a *head* and a *tail*, at any given time it has a certain *length* (the number of items awaiting service), and *items* arrive on the queue and are removed from it (the actual type of these items obviously depends on the application, so we shall leave it abstract and unspecified).

An item joins the queue only at the tail and leaves the queue only at the head, and only the head item can be examined. Thus the appropriate set of operations on queues are *MakeEmpty* (reset a queue to the empty condition), *IsEmpty* (test whether a queue is empty), *Enqueue* (put an item on the queue), and *Dequeue* (take an item off the queue). It is convenient to add another operation, *First*, which examines the item at the front of the queue without removing it. Accordingly, we will write the Dequeue operation so it just "throws away" the first item. This corresponds with the reality of most queues, in which the object at the front of the queue is first served, then leaves the queue. Figure 5–1 shows a sketch of a package specification for the queue ADT. The imple-

```
package Queues is

    type Item is ...

    type Queue is ...

    procedure MakeEmpty(Q: in out Queue);
    function  IsEmpty  (Q: Queue) return boolean;

    procedure Enqueue  (Q: in out Queue; E: Item);
    procedure Dequeue  (Q: in out Queue);
    function  First    (Q: Queue) return Item;

    QueueFull:  exception;
    QueueEmpty: exception;

end Queues;
```

Figure 5-1   Sketch of Queues package.

menting data types and the type of the element to be stored in the stack are omitted; we will fill them in later.

5.3.1 Array Implementation of Queues

A first attempt at implementing a queue uses an array with a cursor indicating the tail of the queue. The capacity of the queue is then determined by the length of the array. Initially the tail cursor is set to 1; a new arrival is inserted into the array at the location indicated by the cursor, then the cursor is incremented to indicate the next available location.

What happens when an item is removed from the head of the queue? In a supermarket, when a customer is finished at the checkout, the remaining customers move up one position in the queue. Our implementation works in an exactly analogous manner. The Enqueue and Dequeue operations in this implementation are demonstrated in Figure 5–2.

In Ada we can set up this implementation by declaring a type *queue*, which is a record containing the tail cursor and the queue array as its fields. This is shown in Figure 5–3; Figure 5–4 gives the procedure bodies for the various queue operations. Notice that we have used a general type Item to be stored in the queue, and that the queue has a maximum of MAX items. These two entities would have to be declared previously, for example by making the package generic. Notice that we have included exceptions for the QueueFull and QueueEmpty conditions. Unwittingly attempting to remove an item from an empty queue usually indicates a misuse of the queue abstraction; since in this implementation a queue can also become full, we need a way to signal that pragmatic condition as well.

You should always be keeping in mind the ways in which defensive programming or "antibugging" can be done, and the exception mechanism in Ada

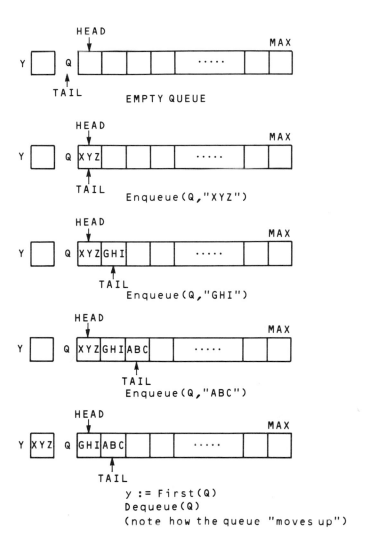

Figure 5-2   Operations on a queue Q: Enqueue, Dequeue, and First.

```
type ArrayList is array(1..MAX) of Item;

type Queue is
   record
      Store: ArrayList;
      tail: Integer range 0..MAX:=0;
   end record;
```

Figure 5-3   Record declaration for a Queue

```
package body Queues Is


   procedure MakeEmpty(Q: In out queue Is
   begin
      Q.tail := 0;
   end MakeEmpty;

   procedure Enqueue(Q: In out Queue; E: In Item) Is
   begin
      If Q.tail = MAX
         then raise QueueFull;
         else Q.tail := Q.tail + 1;
              Q.Store(Q.tail) := E;
      end If;
   end Enqueue;

   procedure Dequeue(Q: In out Queue) Is
   begin
      If Q.tail = 0 then
         raise QueueEmpty;
      else
         for I In 2..Q.tail loop
            Q.Store(I-1) := Q.Store(I);
         end loop;
         Q.tail := Q.tail-1;
      end If;
   end Dequeue;

   function First(Q: Queue) return Item Is
   begin
      If Q.tail = 0 then
         raise QueueEmpty;
      else
         return Q.Store(1);
      end If;
   end First;

   function IsEmpty(Q: In Queue) return boolean Is
   begin
      return Q.tail=0;
   end IsEmpty;

end Queues;
```

Figure 5-4   Queue implementation using array.

serves as a uniform way of thinking about error handling. Even if you are using Ada only as a design language, isolating exceptions and handlers for them is a good design discipline and the actual exceptions can usually be implemented easily enough in other languages.

5.3.2 Circular Array Implementation of Queues

The array implementation discussed previously has a major problem associated with it. It is true that an Enqueue operation requires a constant amount of time for its execution, namely a one-position move of the tail cursor. However, since the scheme requires moving the entire queue every time an element is removed from the head (as in real-life supermarket queues), a number of moves proportional to the queue length is required for this Dequeue operation.

Instead of requiring the queue to move whenever a Dequeue is done, let us "move the cash register" instead. We maintain a cursor to the current *head* of the queue, and move it ahead one position when an element is removed. Thus a constant amount of time will be needed to remove an element, since only the head cursor moves, and then only by one position.

This scheme works smoothly until the tail cursor reaches the upper limit of the array, at which time it breaks down since no new elements can be enqueued. Note that the queue is probably not full, since elements are presumably being dequeued as well, so there is space available if only we could discover how to use it.

One solution would be to reorganize the queue whenever the tail cursor reached the end of the array: simply move the element at the (current) head of the queue to the first array position, then move the others up behind it. This would require time proportional to the queue length as before, but would be done much less frequently.

A more elegant and "self-regulating" solution is to treat the array as though the last position were "glued" back to the first position, so that the tail cursor would "wrap around," using empty space at the beginning of the array for new arrivals—space that was vacated by previous departures. This "circular" arrangement is depicted in Figure 5–5; Figure 5–6 gives a type declaration. The queue is full whenever the tail cursor "catches up" to the head cursor, and so a "queue full" condition will only be evident if the queue is genuinely full.

A package body for this implementation is shown in Figure 5–7. We should point out that the head and tail pointers are initialized to MAX because of the "wrap-around"; that head and tail pointers are incremented modulo MAX; and that only MAX-1 positions of the array can be used, otherwise we cannot distinguish between the QueueFull and QueueEmpty conditions. Note in reading the code that all operations perform in O(1) time!

5.3.3 Linked Implementation of Queues

Yet another implementation for queues is through the use of linked lists. This is useful in cases where the programming language supports pointers and dynamic allocation. As in the sparse-vector case, we allocate a new list node

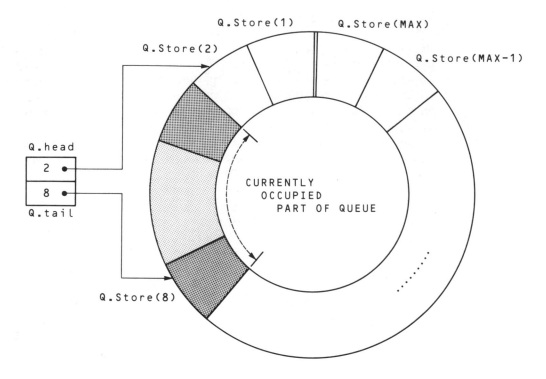

Figure 5-5 Array treated as a circular queue; locations 3 through 8 are occupied; note. Q head indicates the location of the most-recently-removed item!

whenever an item is to be enqueued; we use whatever de-allocation mechanism is available to free the node when an item is dequeued.

The header node for the queue contains pointers to the queue head and tail; as before, enqueueing and dequeueing are made easier by the presence of a "dummy" node at the actual head of the queue, and the MakeEmpty procedure sets this up.

```
type Index Is range 1..MAX;
type ArrayList Is array(Index) of Item;

type Queue Is
    record
        Store: ArrayList;
        head: Index := MAX;
        tail: Index := MAX;
    end record;
```

Figure 5-6 Type declaration for Circular Queue.

```
package body CircularQueues is

   procedure MakeEmpty(Q: in out queue) is
   begin
      Q.tail := MAX;
      Q.head := MAX;
   end MakeEmpty;

   procedure Enqueue(Q: in out Queue; E: in Item) is
   begin
      if (Q.tail mod MAX) + 1 = Q.head then
         raise QueueFull;
      else
         Q.tail := (Q.tail mod MAX) + 1;
         Q.Store(Q.tail) := E;
      end if;
   end Enqueue;

   procedure Dequeue(Q: in out Queue) is
   begin
      if Q.tail = Q.head then
         raise QueueEmpty;
      else
         Q.head := (Q.head mod MAX) + 1;
      end if;
   end Dequeue;

   function First(Q: Queue) return Item is
   begin
      if Q.tail = Q.head then
         raise QueueEmpty;
      else
         return Q.Store((Q.head mod MAX) + 1);
      end if;
   end First;

   function IsEmpty(Q: in Queue) return boolean is
   begin
      return Q.tail = Q.head;
   end IsEmpty;

end CircularQueues;
```

Figure 5-7 Package body for Queues using circular array implementation.

There are several advantages to using such an implementation. Enqueueing and dequeueing occur in a fixed amount of time, independent of the queue length, and—subject only to the compiler's heap-size limitations—a queue has no *a priori* fixed maximum length.

Figure 5–8 shows the necessary type declarations for the linked-list implementation; Figure 5–9 gives the package body.

```
type OneWayListNode;

type NodePointer is access OneWayListNode;

type OneWayListNode is
   record
      info: Item;
      next: NodePointer;
   end record;

type Queue is
   record
      head: NodePointer := null;
      tail: NodePointer := null;
   end record;
```

Figure 5-8   Type declaration for Queue implemented as linked list.

```
package body LinkedQueues is

   procedure MakeEmpty(Q: in out queue) is
   begin
      Q.tail := null;
      Q.head := null;
   end MakeEmpty;

   procedure Enqueue(Q: in out Queue; E: in Item) is
      P: NodePointer;
   begin
      P := new OneWayListNode;
      P.info := E;
      P.next := null;
      if Q.head = null then
         Q.head := P;
      else
         Q.tail.next := P;
      end if;
      Q.tail := P;
   end Enqueue;

   -- procedure Dequeue is left as an exercise

   -- procedure First is left as an exercise

   function IsEmpty(Q: in Queue) return boolean is
   begin
         return Q.head = null;
   end IsEmpty;

end LinkedQueues;
```

Figure 5-9   Package body for Queue implemented as linked list.

5.4   STACKS

Recall the intuitive explanation of a stack given at the beginning of the chapter. Here we make this intuition more concrete, defining a stack or LIFO device in ADT terms.

An item is inserted in the stack ("pushed") and deleted from it ("popped") only at the top, and only the top item can be examined. So the appropriate operations are *MakeEmpty*, *IsEmpty*, *Push*, and *Pop*. As in the queue case, we will add an operation *Top*, which examines the top item, and then write Pop so it just "throws away" the top item. Figure 5–10 gives a sketch of the package specification.

5.4.1 Array Implementation of Stacks

In the array implementation of a stack, we shall consider the stack to be a record consisting of a cursor pointing to the current stack top, and an array representing the stack itself. Notice that the "top" of the stack really keeps moving toward the "bottom" of the array, and this avoids the necessity of moving any other items when a new one arrives (alternatively we could fill the array from the bottom, which might be more intuitively clear). Thus Push and Pop operations are done in fixed time, independent of the current stack depth.

Figure 5–11 illustrates the array structure; in Figure 5–12 we show an appropriate type declaration. Note again that we require that Item be some type declared earlier, and that MAX be some natural number declared earlier. As in the case of queues, we have included StackFull and StackEmpty exceptions to isolate error detection and handling. Figure 5–13 gives the package body.

```
package Stacks is

    type Item is ...

    type Stack is ...

    procedure MakeEmpty(S: in out Stack);
    function  IsEmpty  (S: Stack) return boolean;

    procedure Push      (S: in out Stack; E: Item);
    procedure Pop       (S: in out Stack);
    function  Top       (S: Stack) return Item;

    StackFull:  exception;
    StackEmpty: exception;

end Stacks;
```

Figure 5-10 Sketch of Stacks package.

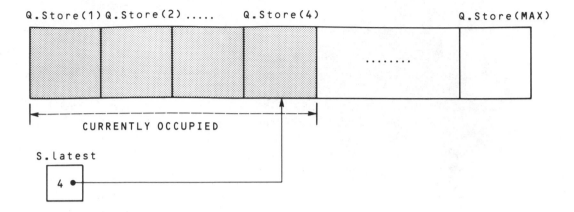

Figure 5-11   Stack implemented as an array; locations 1 through 4 are occupied; S.Store(4) is the most-recently occupied.

5.4.2 Linked Implementation of Stacks

A linked-list implementation of a stack is really quite staightforward. Items are both pushed and popped at the head of the list; both operations are thus done in fixed time. Given the full package body for queues in the previous section, you should have little difficulty in writing a package body for the linked-list implementation of stacks. This is left as an exercise.

```
type ArrayList is array(1..MAX) of Item;

type Stack is
    record
        Store: ArrayList;
        latest: Integer range 0..MAX:=0;
    end record;
```

Figure 5-12   Type declaration for Stack implemented as array.

```
package body Stacks is

    procedure MakeEmpty(S: in out Stack) is
    begin
        S.latest := 0;
    end MakeEmpty;

    procedure Push(S: in out Stack; E: in Item) is
    begin
        if S.latest = MAX then
            raise StackFull;
        else
            S.latest := S.latest + 1;
            S.Store(S.latest) := E;
        end if;
    end Push;

    procedure Pop(S: in out Stack; E: out Item) is
    begin
        if S.latest = 0 then
            raise StackEmpty;
        else
            E := S.Store(S.latest);
            S.latest := S.latest-1;
        end if;
    end Pop;

    function Top(S: in Stack) return Item is
    begin
        if S.latest = 0  then
            raise StackEmpty;
        else
            return S.Store(S.latest);
        end if;
    end Top;

    function IsEmpty(S: in Stack) return boolean is
    begin
        return S.latest=0;
    end IsEmpty;

end Stacks;
```

Figure 5-13 Package body for Stack implemented as array.

5.5   STACKS, EXPRESSION EVALUATION AND POLISH NOTATION

Consider the sort of lengthy computation often carried out on a hand-held calculator, for instance:

$$(5 * 2) - (((3 + 4 * 7) + 8/6) * 9)$$

A Brand X calculator allows the user to enter the above expression, parentheses and all; this form is called *parenthesized* or *infix* notation. On the other hand, a Brand Y calculator requires the user to convert the expression into something called *reverse Polish notation (RPN)*, often called *postfix* notation. The corresponding RPN form would be:

$$5\ 2 * 3\ 4\ 7 * + 8\ 6 / + 9 * -$$

which looks thoroughly unintelligible. Most people seem to prefer the parenthesized form.

Since the calculator is just a special-purpose computer, it follows some algorithm to *evaluate* (find the final result of) the expression, given in one form or the other. The purpose of this section is to introduce the relationship between a parenthesized or infix expression and RPN. You will see how a stack can be used to evaluate an RPN expression and also how to convert "by hand" from the parenthesized form to the RPN form (which is what the Brand X calculator does internally). Design Section 1 will give an algorithm for this conversion.

Polish notation got its name from the Polish mathematician Jan Lukasiewicz, who first published it in 1951. Lukasiewicz was more interested in mathematical logic than in computers *per se* (computers weren't very widespread in the early 1950s!), and his notation was developed as a convenient, *parenthesis-free* way to represent logic expressions. Today, Polish notation is very widely used in interpreters and compilers as an intermediate representational form for statements (a hand-held calculator is nothing but a kind of interpreter).

The term *reverse* or *postfix* is used to indicate that an operator *follows* its operands, instead of appearing in between them; there is also a *prefix* or *forward Polish notation* in which the operator precedes its operands. The latter form is considered in an exercise.

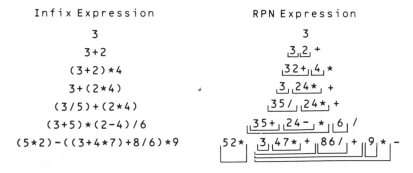

Figure 5-14   Infix and RPN expressions.

A bit later on, we shall consider how to convert an infix expression to its corresponding RPN form; for the moment, examine the examples in Figure 5–14. Brackets are used to indicate the two operands of each operator; they are not part of the RPN. Notice that the numerical quantities in each RPN expression occur *in the same order* as they do in the original infix form. This is always true.

5.5.1 Evaluating RPN Expressions

We will evaluate an RPN expression by a left-to-right scan. An operator is preceded by its two operands, so in evaluating the expression we need a way to remember what the operands are until we encounter the corresponding operator. This is easy if the expression has only one operator in it, like 3 5 +, for instance. We somehow store the first operand, 3, then store the second operand, 5, then, when the operator arrives, we determine that it is indeed + and so add the two operands together, obviously getting 8 as the result.

But suppose the RPN has more than one operator? Take the expression 3 5 + 10 * (the equivalent of (3 + 5) * 10 or 80). If we scan the expression left-to-right, we store 3, then store 5, then add them, getting 8 as before. But what do we do with the 8? We need to store *it*, then store the 10, then discover the * and multiply the 8 by the 10, getting 80.

Evidently we have to save intermediate results as well as input numbers, and then when we see an operator, apply it to the *last two* things we stored. The expression 3 5 2 * – (equivalent to 3 – (5 * 2) or –7) makes this even clearer. We need to store the 3, then the 5, then the 2. When the * is scanned, we multiply the last two numbers stored (2 and 5), then store this intermediate result. When the – arrives, we have two operands for it: 3 and the intermediate result from the multiplication, 10, so we get –7.

We have been saving values in such a way that the last two values saved become the first two retrieved. This is a perfect application for a stack. Let's represent the RPN expression in the form of a Text object using the text-handler package of Chapter 1, and assume it's well-formed, that is, follows the rules given above for forming an RPN expression. For simplicity, we just use single digits to represent numbers. We'll also use the array-stack package from this chapter, instantiated so a stack can hold integers. An Ada function is shown in Figure 5–15.

Here's how the algorithm works. We scan the text from left to right, removing the first character as we go, checking to see whether it's a number—we'll only use single numeric digits here for simplicity—or an operator—+, –, *, or /. If it's a numeric digit, we need to convert it to its integer form so we can do arithmetic with it, then push it on the stack. If it's an operator, we remove the top two items from the stack, do the operation, then push the result back onto the stack.

```
function EvalExp(X: Text) return Integer Is

    ZeroPos: Integer := character'pos('0');
    V: Integer;
    C: character;
    T: Text := X;
    S: Stack;
    Y, Z: Integer;
    WeirdChar: exception;

begin
    If Empty(T) then return 0; end If;

    loop
        C := Head(T);

        If    C In '0'..'9' then
            -- convert to Integer
            V := character'pos(C) - ZeroPos;
            Push(S,V);

        else
            Y := Top(S); Pop(S);
            Z := Top(S); Pop(S);

            case C Is
                when '+'    => Push(S, Z+Y);
                when '-'    => Push(S, Z-Y);
                when '*'    => Push(S, Z*Y);
                when '/'    => Push(S, Z/Y);
                when others => raise WeirdChar;
            end case;

        end If;

        T := Tail(T);
        exit when Empty(T);
    end loop;


    return Top(S);

end EvalExp;
```

Figure 5-15   Function for evaluation of RPN expression.

Assuming we started with a legal RPN expression, when all the characters in it have been exhausted, the final value will be the only value left on top of the stack.

Figure 5–16 shows the evaluation of an RPN expression by this algorithm; you should try the program "by hand" on a number of examples to be sure how it works. Be sure you understand that it works correctly even when the RPN expression is just a single digit.

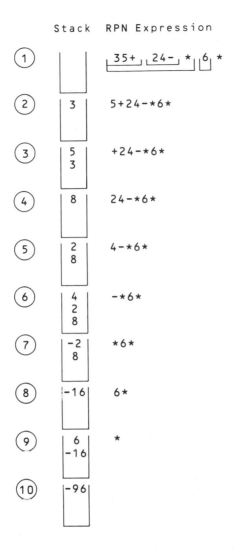

Figure 5-16   Evaluation of an RPN expression corresponding to $(3 + 5) * (2 - 4)$ * 6; each "snapshot" is taken just before the leftmost input character is examined.

5.5.2 Converting Manually from Infix to RPN Form

In this section we'll discuss the notions of *operator associativity* and *operator priority* or *precedence*, and develop an informal method for doing the translation "by hand." Our Design section, later on, will present a program for carrying out the translation.

The program in the preceding section, which emulates a hand-held calculator, works with RPN expressions containing only numeric values. Most other applications need to work with expressions containing variables as well. So we need a more general understanding of an expression. For our purposes, an arithmetic expression is a restricted version of the expressions you are familiar with from whatever programming languages you have used. An expression consists of identifiers or variable names (limited to single letters for simplicity), numerical constants (limited to one-digit integers for simplicity), the operators +, −, *, and /, which have their familiar meanings, and parentheses.

In the first instance, we consider only fully-parenthesized expressions, that is, expressions where parentheses are *always* used to indicate the order in which operations are to be performed, and show how these are transformed into RPN form.

An RPN expression is of one of two forms: it is either a single variable or constant, or it is two RPN expressions followed by an operator. The last (rightmost) operator in the RPN form is the "main" operator of the expression, that is, the operator which is performed *last* as the expression is evaluated, to produce the final result of the evaluation.

To give a few examples, Figure 5–17 shows the RPN expressions for A, A − B, (A − B) + C, A − (B + C), and (A + B)*(C − D). Notice carefully how these are constructed, and be sure that you understand well how (A − B) + C and A − (B + C) give rise to *different* expressions. In (A − B)+C the + is the main operation, since it is performed *last*; in A − (B + C) it is the – that is the main operation. If numerical values were assigned to A,B, and C, say 2,3, and 4, it is easy to see that the result of evaluating (A − B) + C is 3 while the result of evaluating A − (B + C) is –5. Try (A*B) − (C + (D/E)) and ((A − B) + (C/D))*E to make certain you understand how their RPN forms are produced.

Now we are ready to relax the condition that expressions be fully parenthesized. We do this by stating some assumptions about the order in which operations will be done. For example, in the expression A − B − C, how do we know whether to evaluate it as though it were (A − B) − C, or as though it were A − (B − C)? Most programming languages use the rule that a sequence of + and − operations, without parentheses, is evaluated *left to right*, so that A − B − C is treated as though it were (A − B) − C and A−B + C is done as

Infix Expression	RPN Expression
A	AB−
(A−B)+C	AB−C+
A−(B+C)	ABC+−
(A+B)*(C−D)	AB+CD−*

Figure 5-17   Infix and RPN expressions.

Unparenthesized	Assumed Parenthesized Form	RPN
A+B+C	(A+B)+C	AB+C+
A−B−C	(A−B)−C	AB−C−
W−X+Y	(W−X)+Y	WX−Y+
W+X−Y+Z	((W+X)−Y)+Z	WX+Y−Z+

Figure 5-18 Left-to-right associativity of + and −.

though it were (A − B) + C. That's the rule we'll use here. The mathematical term for a rule like this is an *association* or *associativity* rule; our addition and subtraction operators *associate* left-to-right.

Look at Figure 5–18 and compare the unparenthesized with the parenthesized forms and the RPN expressions.

The same associativity rule applies to sequences of * and / operators. These are also evaluated in left-to-right order. So A/B/C is always done as though it were (A/B)/C and A/B*C as though it were (A/B)*C. Figure 5–19 shows a number of expressions involving only * and /, their assumed parenthesized forms, and the corresponding RPN forms.

Left-to-right associativity is not the only possible way. Programming languages with a built-in exponentiation operator, often represented **, often apply a right-to-left rule for this operator, so that A**B**C is treated like A**(B**C). In an exercise, you are asked to explain why this rule is chosen. In this section we are ignoring exponentiation and using only left-to-right associativity.

What happens in the case of expressions where mixtures of all four operators can occur? This is usually handled by assigning *priorities* or *precedences* to the different operators. Usually + and − have the same priority and * and / have the same priority. For definiteness, let + and − be called "priority 2" operators, and let * and / be called "priority 1" operators. Given two adjacent operators, one of priority 1 and the other of priority 2, the priority 1 operator will be performed first. So the expression A + B*C will be evaluated *as though* it were parenthesized A + (B*C); A/B − C will be evaluated *as though* it were

Unparenthesized	Assumed Parenthesized Form	RPN
A*B*C	(A*B)*C	AB*C*
K/G/Z	(K/G)/Z	KG/Z/
Q/S*D	(Q/S)*D	QS/D*
P*D/E*K	((P*D)/E)*K	PD*E/K*

Figure 5-19 Left-to-right associativity of * and /.

Unparenthesized	Assumed Parenthesized Form	RPN
A+B*C	A+(B*C)	ABC*+
A*B+C	(A*B)+C	AB*C+
A+B*C+D	A+(B*C)+D	ABC*+D+

Figure 5-20 Operator priorities.

parenthesized (A/B) − C. So in the first expression + is the main operator, in the second it is −. These expressions and their RPN forms are shown in Figure 5–20.

You can now see how to convert, manually, an arbitrary expression, in which parentheses are *sometimes* used to group subexpressions. Following the two rules given just above, add the necessary parentheses (on paper until you have gained enough experience to do it by inspection) and then produce the RPN from the fully parenthesized version.

To give two examples, consider first A + B − C + D. Since adjacent operators of equal priority are handled left to right, we get ((A + B) − C) + D. Now look at A − (B + C)*D. Here the two adjacent operators of interest are − and * (the + doesn't count because it's inside a subexpression!), and the * is done first because it's priority 1. So this expression is handled as though it were A − ((B + C)*D). These RPN forms are shown in Figure 5–21.

Try A − B*C/(D − E) and A*B − (C + D) + E to be sure you've got it.

5.6 DESIGN: AN INFIX-TO-RPN TRANSLATOR PROGRAM

In the previous section you learned how to translate an expression manually from infix form to RPN. Here we shall develop a program to do it. Our program will be a function, taking as its input the infix expression, and returning the RPN expression as its result.

Consider first an *unparenthesized* expression with all operators of the same priority and left-to-right associativity. The operators and operands alternate in such an expression; the operands in the RPN appear in the same order as in the original.

Original	Assumed Parenthesized Form	RPN
A+B−C+D	((A+B)−C)+D	AB+ C − D +
A−(B+C)*D	A−((B+C)*D)	A BC+ D * −

Figure 5-21 Parenthesized expressions.

Assume that the input expression is implemented as a Text object T as defined in our text-handler package from previous chapters. Let us represent the resulting RPN expression R as a Text object as well. We scan the input expression from left to right. If the first character we see is an operand, we can immediately output it (concatenate it to the RPN string). If it is an operator, we need to remember it until after we've seen its other operand, which will be when the *next* operator is scanned. We then output the saved operator and save the new one.

An example of this operation is shown in Figure 5–22; an Ada function is given in Figure 5–23.

Now assume that operators of different priorities are allowed. Consider the infix expression A + B * C. Its RPN form is A B C * +. We cannot just output the + when the B is scanned, because the *, having higher priority, must be done first. So the + must be remembered longer, and we need to tackle the problem a bit more systematically. The priority of the incoming operator needs to be checked against the priority of the previous one; if the new operator has higher priority, we need to remember *it* as well, until we've scanned *its* second operand! When its second operand has been scanned and output, we can output the operator.

We have, in this case, remembered *two* operators, and the last one remembered is the first one output. This suggests that the best way to remember the operators is to put them in a stack, which, after all, is precisely a LIFO device. This is shown in Figure 5–24, where an example is worked through.

	RPN	OP	Input Expression
(1)			A + B − C + D
(2)	A		+ B − C + D
(3)	A	+	B − C + D
(4)	A B	+	− C + D
(5)	A B +	−	C + D
(6)	A B + C	−	+ D
(7)	A B + C −	+	D
(8)	A B + C − D	+	
(9)	A B + C − D +		

Figure 5-22 Simple Infix-to-RPN translation; each "snapshot" is taken just before the leftmost input character is examined.

```
function RPN(X: Text) return Text is
   C: character;
   T: Text := X;
   Op: character := ' '; -- to save 1 operator; start "empty"
   Result: Text := NullText;
   WeirdChar: exception;
begin
   if Empty(T) then return NullText; end if;
   loop
      C := Head(T);
      case C is
         when 'A'..'Z' =>
            Result := Result & C;
         when 'a'..'z' =>
            Result := Result & C;
         when '0'..'9' =>
            Result := Result & C;
         when '+' | '-' | '*' | '/' =>
            if Op = ' ' then      -- first operator seen
               Op := C;
            else
               Result := Result & Op;  -- get rid of old Op
               Op := C;                -- save new one
            end if;
         when others =>
            raise WeirdChar;
      end case;
      T := Tail(T);
      exit when Empty(T);
   end loop;

   Result := Result & Op;              -- get rid of last operator

   return Result;

end RPN;
```

Figure 5-23   Infix-to-RPN translator (simplest case, no priorities).

Figure 5–25 gives a simple function for determining the priority of an operator in the set ('+', '−', '*', '/'). A modified version of the Infix-to-RPN algorithm which uses priorities is shown in Figure 5–26; it is assumed that a package for stacks of characters is available.

In this new algorithm an operator is stacked until one of equal or lower priority comes along, then popped and added to the RPN. The new operator is then pushed onto the stack. The process continues until the input is empty, at which time the stack is emptied of all remaining operators. This function calls an auxiliary one to return the priority of an operator. Try the function on a few examples of your own, to be sure you understand its operation.

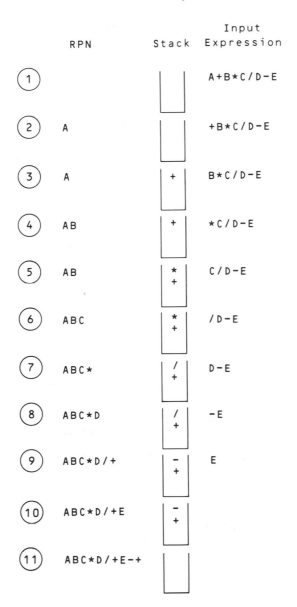

Figure 5-24 Infix-to-RPN translation with priorities; each "snapshot" is taken just before the leftmost input character is examined.

```
function Priority(Operator: character) return integer is
   begin
      if Operator = '+' or Operator = '-'
         then return 1;
         else return 2;
      end if;
   end Priority;
```

Figure 5-25   Function to calculate operator priority.

```
function RPN(X: Text) return Text is
   C: character;
   T: Text := X;
   S: Stack;
   Result: Text := NullText;
   WeirdChar: exception;
begin
   if Empty(T) then return NullText; end if;
   loop
     C := Head(T);

     case C is
       when 'A'..'Z' | 'a'..'z' | '0'..'9' =>
          Result := Result & C;

       when '+' | '-' | '*' | '/' =>
          if    IsEmpty(S) then
            Push(S,C);
            elsif Priority(Top(S)) < Priority(C) then
               Push(S,C);
            else
               loop -- clear higher priority operators
                  Result := Result & Top(S); Pop(S);
               exit when    IsEmpty(S)
                 or else Priority(Top(S)) < Priority(C);
               end loop;
               Push(S,C);
            end if;

       when others =>
          raise WeirdChar;
     end case;

     T := Tail(T);
     exit when Empty(T);
   end loop;

   while not IsEmpty(S) loop
      Result := Result & Top(S); Pop(S);
   end loop;

   return Result;

end RPN;
```

Figure 5-26   Infix-to-RPN translator, using operator priorities.

The final modification accommodates parentheses. How this is done becomes clear when it is realized that parentheses really *override* the priority scheme, essentially creating a whole new expression inside. We can change our algorithm to allow parentheses by pushing a *left* paren onto the stack, which creates a sort of "false bottom" in the stack. The algorithm progresses as in the previous case, but when a *right* paren is seen, the stack is emptied as far back as the "false bottom," then the "false bottom" is discarded.

In Figure 5–27 an example is worked; we leave it to you to modify the program as an exercise.

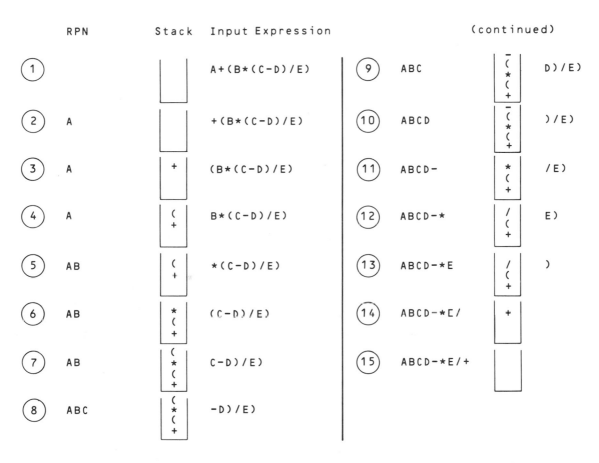

Figure 5-27 Infix-to-RPN translation with priorities and parentheses supported; each "snapshot" is taken just before the leftmost input character is examined.

5.7 SUMMARY

Stack and queues are two important data structures with restricted access. The stack is a Last-in-First-Out (LIFO) device; the queue is a First-In-First-Out (FIFO) device. The FIFO and LIFO access methods have many uses in computing applications: stacks are used in implementing general procedure calling and returning, and in language translation such as in the RPN example given here. Queues turn up in operating systems, and in any number of simulation problems where the physical system being simulated involves waiting lines.

A stack or queue can be implemented either using an array if its maximum size is known at compilation time, or else using a linear linked list. The chapter has presented full packages for some of these implementations; in other cases only a partial solution was given for you to complete.

The next two chapters present two more important structures: the graph and the tree, the latter being a special kind of graph. The stack and queue packages presented here will be re-used in the following chapters, as service packages for the applications to be discussed there.

5.8 EXERCISES

1. Write a package which implements stacks by one-way linked lists.

2. In some applications where two stacks are necessary, a bit of space can be saved by using an array representation but allowing the two stacks to share the same array. This is done by having one stack fill from the low-subscript end of the array forward, and the other stack fill from the high-subscript end backward. An exception must be raised if the two stacks "collide" in the middle somewhere. Design and implement a package to handle such a "double stack."

3. In most programming languages which have a built-in exponentiation (**) operator, this operator associates right to left. That is, A**B**C is treated as though it were written A**(B**C). Explain why this is a sensible convention.

4. A common parenthesis-free notation is *forward Polish* or *prefix Polish* notation. In this scheme an operator *precedes* its operands, so that for example A+B becomes +AB. For the infix expressions of sections 5.5 and 5.6, find the forward Polish forms.

5. Modify the Infix-to-RPN translator of Section 5.6 so that parenthesized expressions are handled correctly.

6. Modify the Infix-to-RPN translator of Section 5.6 so that the exponentiation operator is allowed and is handled correctly.

7. Write a translator that converts an infix expression to its forward Polish notation (FPN) form.

8. Write a translator that converts an RPN expression to its forward Polish notation (FPN) form.

Chapter 6

DIRECTED GRAPHS

6.1 GOAL STATEMENT

Graphs are an important mathematical structure, and one applied widely in computing problems. While this book is not the place for a really general treatment of graphs, we can introduce the mathematical structure of a graph, and go from there to a discussion of directed graphs.

A directed graph consists of a set of *points* or *nodes*, and a set of *edges* or *arcs*, which represent connections between the points. We shall consider a number of important mathematical properties of directed graphs, and then look at some implementation methods. These implementations are the *adjacency matrix, adjacency list, weighted adjacency matrix,* and *state table*.

You will learn two important *traversal* algorithms for directed graphs. A traversal is a "walk" around a graph in a systematic fashion, in such a way that each node is officially "touched" or *visited* exactly once. The algorithms to be introduced are called *Depth-First Search* and *Breadth-First Search*. These algorithms use the packages for sets and queues developed in earlier chapters.

The Design section in this chapter shows how to build a very simple *lexical scanner*, representing it as a state table. This is an application area which will be revisited in a Design section in Chapter 7.

One of the most important characteristics of the directed graph is that the *tree* is just a special case. Armed with an understanding of directed graphs, you will be able more readily to see in Chapter 7 just what makes a tree a tree.

6.2   INTRODUCTION

A *graph* G is an ordered pair of sets <N,E> where N is a set of *nodes* (which may be thought of as points) and E is a set of *edges* (which may be thought of as lines connecting the points). Other authors refer to nodes as *points* or, frequently, *vertices*; they often refer to edges as *arcs*. An edge is given as a pair {m,n} where m and n are in the node set N. Notice that no direction is given to the edge, and so {m,n} and {n,m} really represent the same edge.

Figure 6–1 shows some undirected graphs. This is all we shall do with undirected graphs, since in this book we are interested mainly in *directed graphs*, or graphs in which the edges have direction.

A *directed graph* G (sometimes abbreviated *digraph*) is a graph G = <N,E>. Unlike the previous case, in a digraph an edge is given as an *ordered pair* <s,d> where s and d are in the node set N. The node *s* is called the *source* node and the node *d* is called the *destination* node. This imposes a certain "directionality" to the edge, and this is why G is called a *directed* graph.

Figure 6–2 shows some directed graphs. Note that in graph G1 the edge <1,3>, for example, is *not* the same as the edge <3,1>, because even though they connect the same pair of nodes the direction is different.

For convenience in the sequel, we shall write "sGd" to mean "the edge <s,d> is in the edge set of G." If sGd, we say that *d is adjacent to s*. The set of all nodes adjacent to s is called the *adjacency set of s*.

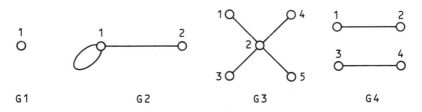

G1   G2   G3   G4

Figure 6-1   Some undirected graphs.

G1   G2   G3   G4

Figure 6-2   Some directed graphs.

6.3   PROPERTIES OF DIGRAPHS

There are a number of properties of digraphs which have important applications and which it is thus interesting to study. In defining these properties we shall always use G to refer to an arbitrary digraph, and lower-case letters to refer to nodes in G's node set. Further, the abbreviation *iff* will be used—as is common in mathematics—to mean "if and only if."

Reflexivity

G is *reflexive* iff xGx for all nodes x in N. Intuitively, if we refer to <x,x> as a *self-loop*, then G is reflexive iff *every* node in G's node set has a self-loop.

Irreflexivity

G is *irreflexive* if *no* node has a self-loop. Note that it is quite possible for G to be neither reflexive nor irreflexive. This will be so if *some* but not *all* nodes have self-loops. Be careful not to confuse the assertion "G is *not* reflexive" with the assertion "G is *ir*reflexive."

Figure 6–3 shows some digraphs which are reflexive, some which are irreflexive, and some which are neither.

Symmetry

G is *symmetric* iff for every case where xGy it is true that yGx. Note carefully that this does *not* say that every pair of nodes must be connected by an edge! It says only that *if* there is an edge <x,y> then there must be an edge <y,x> for G to be symmetric. For example, a digraph consisting of a single node with *no* edges (this is possible because nothing in the definition requires E to be non-empty!) is symmetric. You might consider this to be a "pathological" situation, but it does make the point.

Antisymmetry

G is *antisymmetric* iff xGy and yGx imply x = y. This is a way of saying that no two *distinct* nodes have edges in both directions, but that self-loops are permitted. As in the case of reflexivity, be careful with your language: saying "G is *not* symmetric" is *not* the same as saying "G is *anti*symmetric," since G may have *some* pairs of nodes with edges both ways and some pairs with edges only one way. Thus G is neither symmetric nor antisymmetric. To get pathological again, it is interesting that the digraph with one node and no edges is *both* symmetric *and* antisymmetric!

Some authors do not permit antisymmetric graphs to have any nodes with self-loops. This would make the definition simpler: we could just say that if we have xGy then we cannot have yGx. On the other hand, then a reflexive graph could never be antisymmetric—indeed an antisymmetric graph would be *irreflexive*—and this would mix up two properties that we prefer to keep independent.

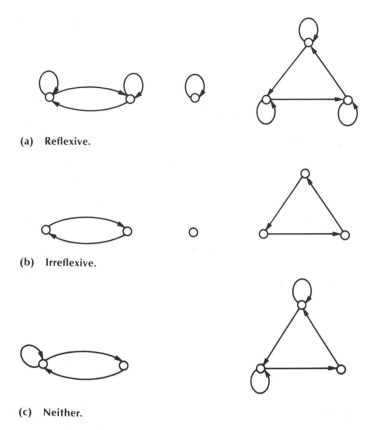

(a)   **Reflexive.**

(b)   **Irreflexive.**

(c)   **Neither.**

Figure 6-3   Reflexivity and irreflexivity.

In Figure 6–4 you can see some symmetric digraphs, some antisymmetric ones, and some which are neither.

Transitivity

G is *transitive* iff for each triple of nodes such that xGy and yGz it is true that xGz. In other words, if we can get from x to z by way of y, then we can get there directly if G is transitive. Note again that this does *not* mean that there must ever be edges <x,y> and <y,z>. It says only that *if* there are, then if G is to be transitive there must be an edge <x,z>. There is also no requirement that x, y, and z be distinct, so that self-loops must be considered in determining transitivity. Is it possible for a digraph to be symmetric and transitive without being reflexive?

Figure 6–5 shows some transitive digraphs, and some others where it is explained why they are not transitive.

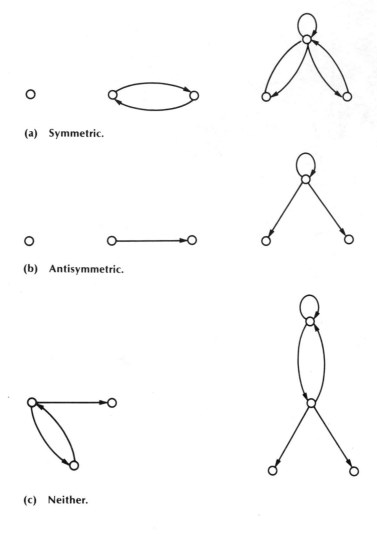

(a) **Symmetric.**

(b) **Antisymmetric.**

(c) **Neither.**

Figure 6-4   Symmetry and antisymmetry.

Paths

A *path* is a sequence of edges <n1,n2>, <n2,n3>, ... ,<n k-1, n k>, i.e. a sequence of edges such that the destination of one is the source of the next. The path is *simple* iff all nodes in the path, except possibly for the first and the last, are distinct. The *length* of the path is the number of *edges* (not nodes) in it. Thus a single edge <x,y> is a path of length 1. Note that a self-loop <x,x> is a path of length 1. If there is a path *from* x *to* y, we say that *y is reachable from x.*

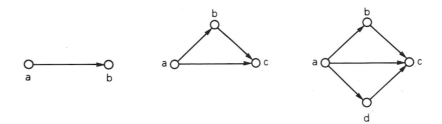

(a) Transitive.

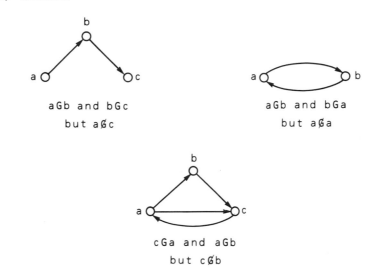

aGb and bGc
but aᴓc

aGb and bGa
but aᴓa

cGa and aGb
but cᴓb

(b) Not transitive.

Figure 6-5 Transitivity.

Cycles

A *cycle* is a path such that the destination of the last edge is the source of the first edge (it gets back to where it started). Note then that a self-loop is a cycle of length 1. A digraph is *acyclic* if it has no cycles in it. A *simple cycle* is a simple path which is a cycle.

Connectivity

Intuitively, a graph (directed or otherwise) is *connected* iff it is "all one piece." In other words, a digraph is connected iff, treating *all* edges as though they were two-way—or, equivalently, adding edges to make the graph symmetric— we can find a path from any node to any other. The "pieces" of a graph which is in several pieces are called *connected components*.

(a)   Not connected.

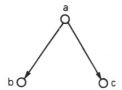

(b)   Connected but not strongly connected (*a* cannot be reached from *b* or *c*).

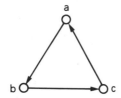

(c)   Strongly connected.

Figure 6-6   Connectivity and strong connectivity.

Strong Connectivity

A digraph G is *strongly connected* iff from each node there is at least one path (not necessarily of length 1!) to all the other nodes, *even if we take directionality into account*. Can a strongly connected digraph ever be acyclic?

Figure 6–6 illustrates connectivity and strong connectivity.

In-degree and Out-degree

The *in-degree* of a node z in a digraph G is the number of edges which have z as their destination (visually, the number of arrowheads arriving at z). The *out-degree* of a node z is the number of edges with z as their source (or the number of arrowtails leaving z).

6.4   IMPLEMENTATIONS FOR DIRECTED GRAPHS

In this section we shall look at several of the common ways of implementing directed graphs in programs. These are the *adjacency matrix*, *adjacency list*, *weighted adjacency matrix*, and *state graph*.

6.4.1 Adjacency Matrix

The most straightforward way to represent a digraph G with K nodes is by a K × K boolean matrix G', called the *adjacency matrix*, where G'(x,y) = true iff xGy, false otherwise. So row x of the matrix indicates the adjacency set of node x.

In this matrix it is easy to determine whether y is adjacent to x, and this is done in O(1) time, since only a subscript calculation is involved. But a disadvantage of using this scheme is that even if the graph has few edges, K^2 cells are needed to store it and any algorithm to examine the whole graph, or even read or print it, must be $O(N^2)$. A digraph and its adjacency matrix are given in Figure 6–7.

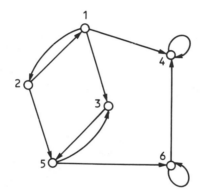

(a)   A digraph.

	1	2	3	4	5	6
1	F	T	T	T	F	F
2	T	F	F	F	T	F
3	F	F	F	F	T	F
4	F	F	F	T	F	F
5	F	F	T	F	F	T
6	F	F	F	T	F	T

(b)   Adjacency matrix for this digraph.

Figure 6-7   Adjacency matrix for a digraph.

6.4.2 Adjacency List

In most graphs, the nodes have relatively small adjacency sets, so the adjacency matrix is sparse, with most of its elements false. For this reason a variant of the sparse-matrix technique is often used to implement a digraph. This representation is the *adjacency list*. Each node x is a header for a linear list, each cell of which represents a destination node for edges leaving x. The headers can be stored in an array. This structure is shown in Figure 6–8.

Assuming that Booleans, pointers, and integers identifying nodes all occupy the same number of bytes of storage, when is this scheme more economical than an adjacency matrix? Let L be the average number of cells in a single node list. The pointer array requires K cells, each of one storage unit; each list cell requires two storage units and there are KxL such cells. So the structure requires $K + 2*K*L$ or $K*(1 + 2*L)$ storage units. To find the crossover point, we set $K^2 = K*(1 + 2*L)$, or $L = (K - 1)/2$.

The assumption we just made—that Booleans, pointers, and node identifiers are all the same size—is often wrong. Many programming languages, including Ada, give the programmer a way of implementing an array of Booleans in such a way that each array entry is represented by a *single bit*. In such a situation, the "dense" matrix (two-dimensional array) can be considerably more economical of space than the "sparse" matrix (list).

We cannot neglect differences in time performance, though. To print the entire adjacency list takes $O(K*L)$ operations, which is usually much less than $K*K$. On the other hand, just determining whether xGy takes $O(L)$ operations (on the average) whereas it was $O(1)$ in the adjacency matrix representation. We have here another clear example of the tradeoffs inherent in selecting implementations for abstract objects.

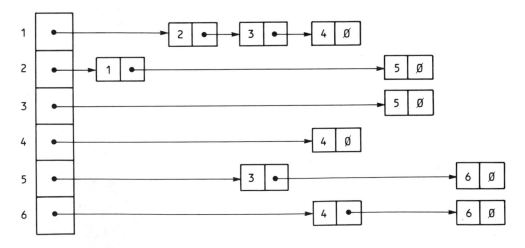

Figure 6-8   Adjacency list structure for the digraph of Figure 6-7.

6.4.3 Weighted Adjacency Matrix

The implementations just described give the *structure* of a digraph, but provide no information about its *content*. In many graph applications, nodes or edges are associated with data values of one kind or another. These are often called *weights*. For example, in Figure 6–9 is a digraph with numbers attached to the edges. One interpretation of such a number might be the distance between points on a graph representing a road map. Another interpretation might be the time required to perform a certain task in a complex project. Implementing such a weighted graph is a straightforward extension of the adjacency matrix: each entry of the matrix contains the weight, instead of just a Boolean; entries which correspond to missing edges contain some indication to that effect, for example zero or null.

Weights can also be used in the list implementation: weights for edges emanating from a given node are just stored in the nodes of the corresponding adjacency list.

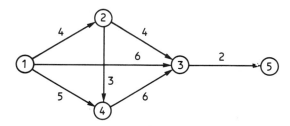

(a)   A weighted digraph.

	1	2	3	4	5
1	0	4	6	5	0
2	0	0	4	3	0
3	0	0	0	0	2
4	0	0	6	0	0
5	0	0	0	0	0

(b)   Weighted adjacency matrix for this digraph.

Figure 6-9   Weighted digraph and adjacency matrix.

6.4.4 **State Table**

A certain kind of weighted digraph, the *state graph*, comes from the field of abstract machine theory, and is useful in hardware design and also in building language translators. A Design section will discuss an application of state graphs, but here we limit ourselves to a description of the structure.

Until now we have said nothing about the nature of the weights in a weighted digraph. Indeed, in most cases the weights can be arbitrary values. In a state graph, however, it is required that the weights be a (usually small) discrete set of values, for example the letters of the alphabet or the numeric digits.

The graph is implemented as a two-dimensional array, with a row for each node and a column for each *weight*. Each row represents a source node; entries in the matrix represent *destination nodes*, not weights as before. For an example, look at the graph in Figure 6–10. The nodes of this state graph are called A,B,C, and D; the weights are just the digits 0 and 1. The corresponding state table is shown in Figure 6–11.

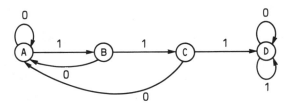

Figure 6-10   A state graph.

	0	1
A	A	B
B	A	C
C	A	D
D	D	D

Figure 6-11   A state table.

6.5   GRAPH TRAVERSALS

Some applications of graphs require the graph to be *traversed*. This means that, starting from some designated node, the graph is "walked around" in a systematic way such that every node reachable from that starting node is officially "touched" or *visited* exactly once. Two often-used traversal algorithms are called *Depth First Search* and *Breadth First Search*.

The Depth-First Search algorithm finds all graph nodes reachable from a particular starting node, in a way that explores a given path from the starting node before starting another path. The search strategy, then, is to probe deeper and deeper along a path, hence the designation "depth-first."

The Breadth-First Search algorithm visits all nodes adjacent to the starting node, then visits all nodes adjacent to *those* nodes, and so on. Since all adjacent nodes are visited before probing further away, the search is broad rather than deep, hence the name "breadth-first."

These algorithms are introduced in this section, and programs are given for them.

6.5.1 Depth-First Search

A traversal algorithm requires that each node be "officially" visited exactly once. Since a node can be adjacent to many other nodes, and since graphs can have cycles, we need a way of keeping track of the nodes that have already been visited. Accordingly the Depth-First Search algorithm uses an auxiliary set, called Visited, initially empty. A node of G is added to the set when it is visited. The algorithm is recursive, and operates as follows:

Depth-First Search:

1. Place the designated starting node x in the set Visited.

2. Do whatever application-dependent things need to be done upon visiting a node.

3. For each node y adjacent to x, if y has not been visited, call Depth-First Search recursively with y as the starting node.

This algorithm pursues a given path until a previously-visited node is reached, then returns to the original node and pursues another path. If it terminates with the entire node set in Visited, then all nodes were reachable from the given starting node.

Figure 6–12 shows an example of the Depth-First Search in action.

For a program to carry out this algorithm, we number the nodes of our graph, then use the adjacency matrix to implement it. The line of the algorithm "for each node y adjacent to x" becomes a loop which walks across x's row of the matrix. For the set Visited, we call upon the NaturalSet package introduced

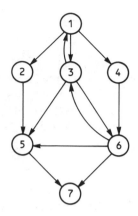

(a) A directed graph.

```
      starting at 1 : 1-2-5-7-3-6-4
      starting at 2 : 2-5-7
(graph isn't strongly connected, so only
        three nodes are visited!)
      starting at 3 : 3-1-2-5-7-4-6
```

(b) Some depth-first searches of the digraph.

Figure 6-12 Depth-first search on a graph.

in Chapter 1. We let the set Visited be an **in out** parameter, so we can keep adding members to it.

Depth-First Search is really just a framework for a program whose real work is application-dependent. Therefore we implement step two of the algorithm as a simple call to a procedure Visit(x), which has the job of carrying out this application-dependent task, whatever it be. An Ada procedure for Depth-First Search appears in Figure 6–13.

6.5.2 Breadth-First Search

In Breadth-First Search, we start from a node x and first visit all nodes adjacent to x. Then all nodes adjacent to *those* nodes are visited, and so on. We use a queue to keep track of nodes we have visited but whose adjacent nodes we haven't yet visited. The same set Visited is used to keep a record of visited nodes. We now give an algorithm for Breadth-First Search.

```
procedure DepthFirstSearch(G: Graph; start: natural;
                           Visited: In out NaturalSet) Is

  begin

    Visit(start);
    Insert(Visited,start);

    for dest In 1..MaxNodes loop

      If IsAdjacent(G,start,dest)
         and not IsIn(Visited,dest) then
            DepthFirstSearch(G, dest, Visited);
      end If;

    end loop;

  end DepthFirstSearch;
```

Figure 6-13   Procedure to carry out depth-first search.

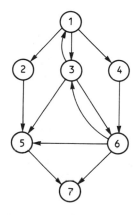

(a) A directed graph.

```
starting at 1 : 1-2-3-4-5-6-7
starting at 3 : 3-1-5-6-2-4-7
```

(b)   Some breadth-first searches of the digraph.

Figure 6-14   Breadth-first search on a graph.

Breadth-First Search:

1. Clear the queue Q.
2. Place the designated starting node x in the set Visited.
3. Enqueue x on Q.
4. Do whatever application-dependent things need to be done upon visiting a node.
5. Repeat the remaining steps as long as Q is not empty:
6. Dequeue a value y from Q.
7. For each node z adjacent to y, if z has not been visited, place z in Visited; do the application-dependent task for z; enqueue z on Q.

An example of Breadth-First Search in action appears in Figure 6–14; an Ada procedure, which uses both the NaturalSets package and a Queues package, is given in Figure 6–15.

```
procedure BreadthFirstSearch(G: Graph; start: natural;
                             Visited: in out NaturalSet) is

    source, dest: natural;
    Q: Queue;

begin

    Visit(start);
    Insert(Visited,start);
    Enqueue(Q,start);

    while not IsEmpty(Q) loop

        source := First(Q);
        Dequeue(Q);

        for dest in 1..MaxNodes loop

            if IsAdjacent(G,source,dest)
               and not IsIn(Visited,dest) then
                Visit(dest);
                Insert(Visited,dest);
                Enqueue(Q,dest);
            end if;

        end loop;

    end loop;

end BreadthFirstSearch;
```

Figure 6-15   Procedure to carry out breadth-first search.

6.6   DESIGN: A SIMPLE LEXICAL SCANNER

An Ada identifier consists of a letter followed by zero or more letters, digits, and underscore characters. In this section we describe a program or algorithm capable of deciding whether an arbitrary string of characters is a valid Ada identifier. This is a simple *lexical scanner*; lexical scanners are used for the initial phase of a language translation, for checking the validity of commands in an interactive system, and other similar applications.

We represent the scanner by a state graph. In this graph, one node is designated as the *start state*; two other nodes are designated as the *accepting* and *rejecting states*. A node which is a source is called a *current state*; a node which is a destination is called a *next state*; a weight is used to represent each possible character in the string.

The state graph operates as a little machine: it is started in its start state, "reads" the first character of the string, then moves to the next state corresponding to the character just seen. The next state thus becomes a current state. The machine reads another character, moves to a new state, and so on. If the machine is in its accepting state when the input string is empty, the string was a valid identifier; if it is in its rejecting state, the string had an invalid character in it.

To keep this example simple, we use a very small alphabet for our identifiers. The only *letter* allowed is 'L'; the only digit is '5.' Underscore characters are permitted; all illegal characters are represented by @. These are the only characters that ever appear in a string. Figure 6–16 gives a number of legal and illegal identifiers in this limited alphabet.

Figure 6–17 shows the state graph for this machine; Figure 6–18 gives a diagram of the state table. In Figure 6–19 are shown some Ada type definitions for the state table implementation. Note the use of *enumeration types* to list the states (the node set N of the graph) and the input alphabet (discrete set of weights).

```
_        invalid   (starts with _)
L        valid
L5       valid
5        invalid   (starts with 5)
L_       valid
_L       invalid   (starts with _)
LL5L     valid
L___5    valid
L@5L     invalid   (contains @)
5LLL     invalid   (starts with 5)
```

Figure 6-16   Valid and invalid words in a language over a limited alphabet.

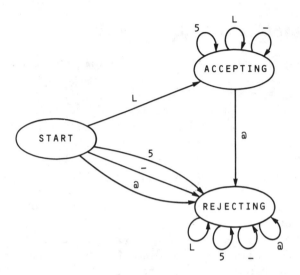

Figure 6-17   State graph for simple scanner.

	L	5	—	a
START	ACCEPTING	REJECTING	REJECTING	REJECTING
ACCEPTING	ACCEPTING	ACCEPTING	ACCEPTING	REJECTING
REJECTING	REJECTING	REJECTING	REJECTING	REJECTING

Figure 6-18   State table for simple scanner.

```
type State      is (Start, Accepting, Rejecting);
type InputClass is (Letter, Digit, Underscore, Illegal);

StateTable: array(State,InputClass) of State :=
   ((Accepting, Rejecting, Rejecting, Rejecting),
    (Accepting, Accepting, Accepting, Rejecting),
    (Rejecting, Rejecting, Rejecting, Rejecting));
```

Figure 6-19   Definitions for state table.

To make this data structure work as a machine, we need a program to "run" it. We'll write this as an Ada function ValidIdentifier, which accepts a Text object, starts the state graph in its start state, then reads characters, returning a Boolean which indicates whether the input string was a valid identifier. Formally, a machine like this is called a *finite state machine*; in this case the finite-state machine keeps running until its input string is empty; if it ever gets

```ada
function ValidIdent(T: Text) return boolean is

    type State       is (Start, Accepting, Rejecting);
    type InputClass  is (Letter, Digit, Underscore, Illegal);

    StateTable: array(State,InputClass) of State :=
       ((Accepting, Rejecting, Rejecting, Rejecting),
        (Accepting, Accepting, Accepting, Rejecting),
        (Rejecting, Rejecting, Rejecting, Rejecting));

    S: Text := T;
    C: character;
    Class: InputClass;
    CurrentState: State := Start;

begin

    if Empty(S) then return false; end if;

    loop
       C := Head(S);

       if    C = 'L' then
          Class := Letter;
       elsif C = '5' then
          Class := Digit;
       elsif C = '_' then
          Class := Underscore;
       else
          Class := Illegal;
       end if;

       CurrentState := StateTable(CurrentState,Class);

       S := Tail(S);
       exit when Empty(S);

    end loop;

    if CurrentState = Accepting then
       return true;
    else
       return false;
    end if;

end ValidIdent;
```

Figure 6-20 Function simulating a Finite-State Machine.

to the rejecting state, it keeps reading characters and cycling in that state until the input is empty. This program, which really implements a lexical scanner, is shown in Figure 6–20.

We shall return to the lexical scanner idea in Chapter 7, where one of the Design sections introduces a finite-state machine for scanning English text, in order to build a cross-reference generator.

6.7 SUMMARY

Graphs have many uses: they are used to show relationships between elements in a set, for example orderings or precedences; sequencing of activities in a project; sequences of characters in a string; and others. This book cannot treat graphs in a completely general way; graph theory and application is an entire mathematical discipline in itself. But we have presented a number of important concepts of directed graphs: mathematical properties like reflexivity, symmetry, transitivity, connectedness; traversals like depth-first and breadth-first search; and a bit of application.

We are now ready to proceed to the study of *trees*, which are directed graphs with certain special properties. Chapter 7 will consider trees at length.

6.8 EXERCISES

1. One interpretation of a digraph is a relation on a set. The nodes in the graph represent elements of the set; an edge from node x to node y means "x is related to y." A relation is called an *equivalence relation* if it is reflexive, transitive, and symmetric. Clearly a relation has these properties iff its digraph representation does. Write a function to determine if a graph G, implemented as an adjacency matrix, represents an equivalence relation.

2. A relation is called a *partial ordering* if it is reflexive, transitive, and antisymmetric. Using the graph interpretation from the preceding problem, write a function to determine whether a graph G represents a partial ordering.

3. Given a digraph with node set (A,B,C,D,) and edge set ((A,A), (A,B), (A,D), (B,B), (C,B), (C,D), (D,C)), draw the graph and its adjacency matrix and adjacency list forms.

4. For the digraph specified in the preceding problem, indicate whether or not the graph has each of the following properties: reflexive, irreflexive, symmetric, antisymmetric, transitive, connected, strongly connected, acyclic. For each property the graph *doesn't* have, make a list of the *minimum* number of changes necessary to give the graph property.

5. For the digraph specified above, find the depth-first and breadth-first searches starting with each of the four nodes.

6. Repeat the preceding three problems for the digraph with the node set (A,B,C,D) and edge set ((A,B), (A,C), (B,B), (B,C),(C,C), (C,A), (C,C), (C,D)).

7. Show that it is possible to renumber the nodes of a digraph G so that its adjacency matrix is lower-triangular iff G is acyclic.

8. Given a graph G represented by its unweighted adjacency matrix M. Consider the matrix product of M with itself (the square of M) gotten by using "or" and "and" as the addition and multiplication operators in the matrix product. Calling this matrix MM, show that MM(r, c) = true iff there is a path of length two or less from node r to node c.

9. Starting from the previous problem, show that in the matrix representing the $p - th$ power of M, a true entry in the $r - th$ row and $c - th$ column indicates that there is a path of length p or less from node r to node c, of the matrix M.

Chapter 7

TREE STRUCTURES

7.1   GOAL STATEMENT

A tree is a special case of a directed graph, with many applications in computing. Specifically, a tree is just a connected digraph such that exactly one node (the *root*) has an in-degree of zero and all other nodes have an in-degree of one. The consequence of this definition is that, starting from the root, there is exactly one path to each of the other nodes. This makes a tree useful for representing hierarchical relationships.

This chapter focuses mainly on the important special case of the *binary tree*, in which no node has more than two outgoing edges. Here we shall see two important applications. One is the *expression tree*, which is used in translating or interpreting programming language statements; the other is the *binary search tree* or BST, which is yet another implementation of a mapping or dynamic table.

An important concept in the study of trees is the *traversal*. A traversal is an algorithm for "walking around" the tree so that all its nodes are visited exactly once in some systematic sequence. There are many possible traversals; we shall study three of them. All are written as recursive algorithms.

Even though we concentrate on binary trees, section 7.6 briefly introduces two important applications of more general trees: *digital search trees*, used in applications like spelling checkers, and *B-trees*, often used as a basis for organizing large structured files on secondary storage devices.

There are two Design sections in this chapter. Design One shows how to construct a parser for simple arithmetic expressions; Design Two shows how an indexing or cross-reference program can be constructed using a binary search tree. The Style Guide in this chapter focuses on some alternative implementations of binary trees to reduce algorithm run times and avoid recursive traversal programs.

7.2   INTRODUCTION

A tree is a certain kind of directed graph. It is a mathematical structure whose main application is in expressing purely hierarchical relationships of some kind. For example, Figure 7–1 shows the basic structure of an hypothetical company, with a single president, a few vice-presidents, some managers, and some workers; Figure 7–2 shows a family tree representing three generations of descendants of a person; and Figure 7–3 illustrates the operator-operand relationship in a programming language assignment statement.

The common characteristic of all these examples is the fact that there is a single node that can be identified as the "top" of the tree—we call this the *root*—and that from the root to any other node in the tree there is *exactly one path*.

Now let us formalize the definition of a tree as a special case of a directed graph:

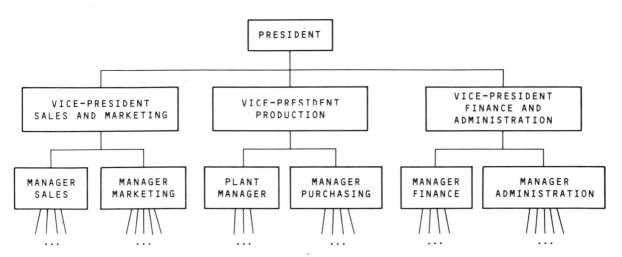

Figure 7-1   Hypothetical corporate structure.

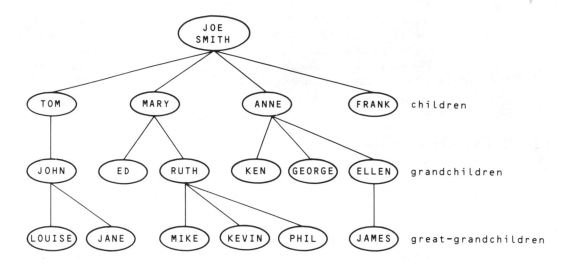

Figure 7-2   Descendants of Joe Smith.

$$X := Y+Z-(A*B/W)+G$$

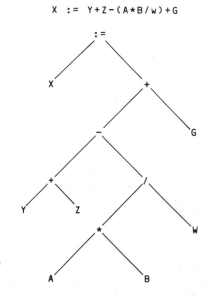

Figure 7-3   Operator-operand relationships
in an arithmetic assignment statement.

A *tree* is a connected digraph with these properties:

1. There is exactly one node (the *root*) with in-degree = 0.
2. All other nodes have in-degree = 1.

Notice that we have said nothing about out-degree. In a general tree there is no restriction on the out-degree of a node, nor indeed on whether the node set must even be finite. In most of the important applications, however, the tree has a finite number of nodes and so there is necessarily a subset of the node set with out-degree = 0. These nodes are at the "bottom" of the tree; we call them *leaves* or sometimes *terminal nodes*. The remaining nodes are called *interior* or sometimes *nonterminal nodes*. In this book you may assume that all trees are finite.

Look at Figure 7–4 and be sure you understand why the structures in Figure 7–4a are trees and those in Figure 7–4b are not.

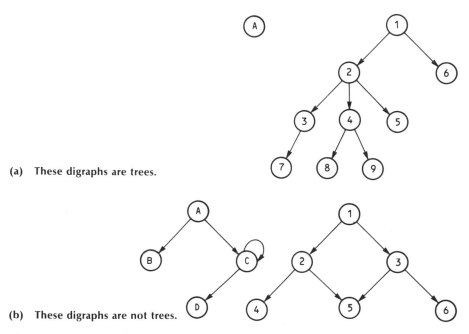

(a) These digraphs are trees.

(b) These digraphs are not trees.

Figure 7-4 Some trees and some digraphs that are not trees.

A tree is a digraph, so it makes sense to consider which graph properties pertain to trees. This can be done by looking directly at the definition of a tree. Since a node in a tree has at most one edge leading to it, there are certain graph properties that all trees must have, others that no tree can have. For instance, there is *at most* one path from any node to any other node, and there is *exactly* one path from the root to any leaf. Therefore a tree is necessarily antisymmetric and irreflexive; we leave consideration of the other graph properties to an exercise.

By the way we have defined trees, the node at the destination end of an edge for which the root is the source, is itself the root of a tree. We shall sometimes call this structure a *subtree*. Note that a single node, by itself, is a tree.

Let us define the *depth* of a tree as the length of the longest path from the root to a leaf. We will also refer to the *level* of a node as the length of the path (remember, there is only one path!) from the root to that node. The level of the root itself is then 0. Figure 7–5 shows some trees and indicates their depths.

Drawing some terminology from genealogical (family) trees, we shall refer to the destination nodes of a node as its *children*, and a node from which one or more children grow as the *parent* of those children. Children of the same parent are referred to as *siblings*. All nodes reachable from a given node are called that node's *descendants*. Also, note that a child of any node is itself the root of a tree. That tree is called a *subtree* of the parent.

The analogy with family trees is imperfect, though, because while humans and most animals have precisely *two* parents, a node in our type of trees has precisely *one* parent!

Since we are interested in applications of trees in computing, there will often be certain information associated with each of the nodes of a tree. Obviously the nature and interpretation of this information depends on the appli-

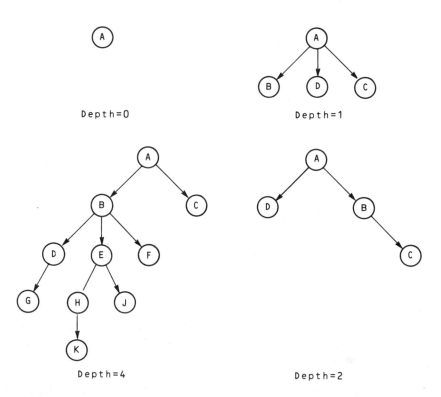

Figure 7-5 Some trees and their depths.

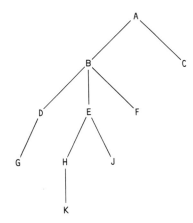

Figure 7-6   Simplified tree notation.

cation; we shall refer to it generically by a number of names, for example *label*, *data*, *value*, or *key*.

In general we do not bother to draw the arrowheads on the edges of a tree, but write the root at the top and "grow" the tree in a downward direction on the page. Thus it is obvious which direction is meant. Also, it is sometimes convenient to omit the circle indicating a node, simply writing the data instead, as in Figure 7–6.

We shall return to the subject of general trees later in the chapter; for now, let us limit our attention to the special and useful case of *binary trees*.

7.3   BINARY TREES

A *binary tree* is a tree all of whose nodes have out-degree <= 2. Furthermore, the subtrees of a binary tree are *ordered* in the sense that there is a *left* child and a *right* child. If a node has only one child, it must be clearly identified as left or right. The two trees given in Figure 7–7a are different binary trees; so are the two trees in Figure 7–7b.

7.3.1 Properties of Binary Trees

Strictly binary

T is a *strictly binary tree* iff each of its node has out-degree = 0 or out-degree = 2. Nodes with out-degree = 1 are not allowed in strictly binary trees.

Complete

T is a *complete binary tree of depth K* iff each node of level K is a leaf and each node of level less than K has nonempty left and right children. So a complete

(a) These are *different* binary trees.

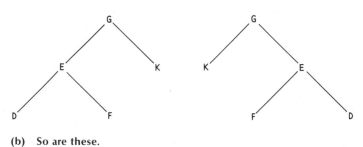

(b) So are these.

Figure 7-7   Binary trees have ordered children.

binary tree has all its leaves at the same level and every non-leaf node has both children present. Notice that a complete binary tree of depth K always has *exactly* 2^{K+1} nodes: a tree consisting of a single node has depth = 0; a complete binary tree of depth = 1 has three nodes; one of depth = 2 has seven nodes, and so on.

Viewed another way, a complete binary tree of N nodes has depth equal to $\log(N+1) - 1$, where the log is to the base 2.

Almost complete

T is an *almost complete binary tree (ACBT) of depth K* iff it is either complete, or fails to be complete only because some of its leaves are at the right-hand end of level K-1. This has the effect of concentrating all the level K leaves at the left end of the level, and all the level K-1 leaves at the right end. The three parts of Figure 7–8 show complete and almost-complete binary trees, and some trees with neither property.

Almost-complete binary trees are very useful in certain sorting applications, for example *heap sort*, which we will examine in detail in Chapter 9. An almost complete binary tree is useful because an ordinary array may be viewed as an implementation of an ACBT. The first element of the array is considered to be the root of the tree; the second and third elements are the children of the root, and so on. If we number the nodes of an ACBT, starting at the root and proceeding level by level and left to right within a level, these numbers correspond to the subscripts of the array, as indicated in Figure 7–9.

A note on terminology: some authors use the term "full binary tree" for a tree we call "complete"; those authors use the term "complete" to mean a tree we call "almost complete."

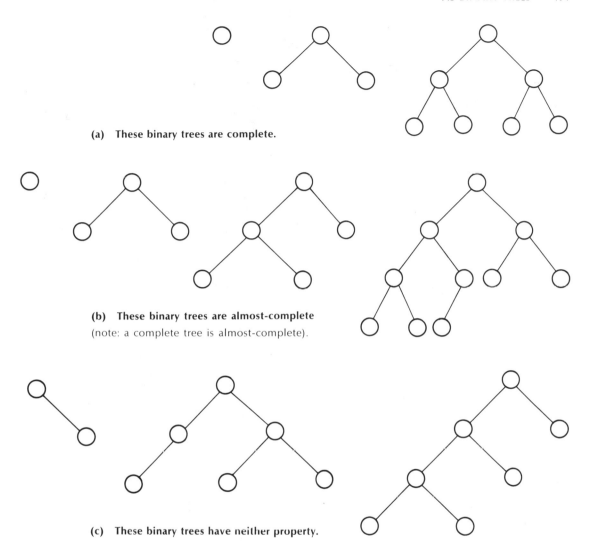

(a)   **These binary trees are complete.**

(b)   **These binary trees are almost-complete**
(note: a complete tree is almost-complete).

(c)   **These binary trees have neither property.**

Figure 7-8   Complete and almost-complete binary trees.

Balanced

T is a *balanced* (sometimes called *height-balanced*) binary tree iff *for each node t in T*, the depths of t's right and left subtrees differ by at most one. If one subtree is null, the other subtree must either be null or a leaf.

It is important to understand that for a tree to be balanced, the property must hold for every node in the tree, not just its root. For all the trees in Figure 7–10, be sure you know why each is either balanced or not balanced. The notion of balance in a binary tree is important in the study of binary search trees.

The definition of balance can also be stated recursively:

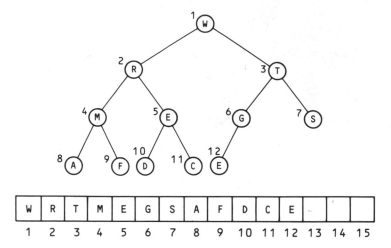

Figure 7-9 An array, viewed as an almost-complete binary tree (it would be complete if elements 13, 14, and 15 were present).

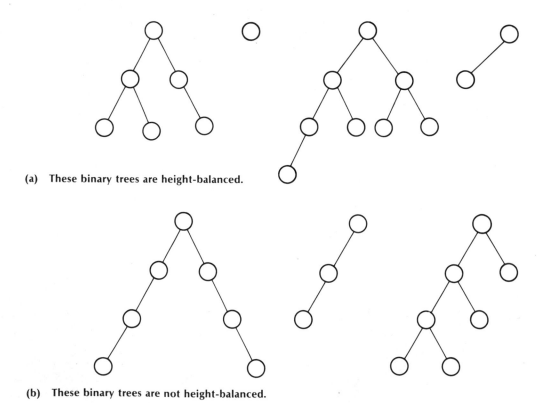

(a)   **These binary trees are height-balanced.**

(b)   **These binary trees are not height-balanced.**

Figure 7-10   Balanced (or height-balanced) binary trees.

A binary tree consisting of a single node is balanced.

A node with a single subtree is balanced iff that subtree is a leaf.

A binary tree is balanced iff its left and right subtrees are balanced and their depths differ by at most one.

7.3.2 Implementing Binary Trees

Since a binary tree is really just a digraph, we could implement it using one of the graph representations. However, it is usually better to make use of our knowledge that a binary tree has right and left subtrees and create a more specialized structure.

A node is defined as a record, with an information field, a pointer to the left subtree, and a pointer to the right subtree. Thus a tree can be built as a linked structure using dynamic storage allocation if that is available in the coding language, cursor allocation otherwise.

In Figure 7-11 we show some Ada type definitions for these nodes and pointers (of course using the built-in pointer and allocation facilities of the language). This simple definition assumes that the information field in each node is just a key; for many applications this field will, of course, be a composite record of some kind. A sequence of statements declaring and manipulating nodes is given in Figure 7-12, along with diagrams showing the results of each operation.

Generally we will avoid drawing "boxes" to represent the nodes and just use the more abstract diagrams as in all the other previous examples.

7.3.3 Traversals of Binary Trees

Many applications require *traversing* or "walking around" a tree in a particular way so that all the nodes are *visited* or "touched" in a certain order. Three tra-

```
type KeyType is ...;

type BinaryTreeNode;

type tree is access BinaryTreeNode;

type BinaryTreeNode is
  record
    Key:   KeyType;
    left:  tree := null;
    right: tree := null;
  end record;
```

Figure 7-11 Type definitions for binary tree node.

Statement   Resulting Structure

T1: tree; t: tree;

T1   := new BinaryTreeNode;
T1.key := 'D';

T1.left   := new BinaryTreeNode;
T1.left.key   := 'B';
T1.left.right   := new BinaryTreeNode;
T1.left.right.key := 'C';

t   := new BinaryTreeNode;
t.key := 'F';

T1.right := t;

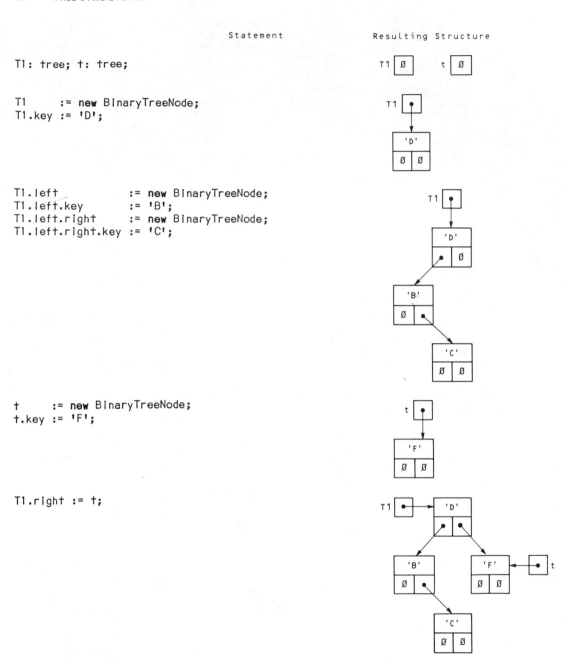

Figure 7-12   Operations on binary tree nodes.

versal algorithms are particularly useful in dealing with binary trees. These are often called *Preorder, Inorder,* and *Postorder,* but different authors occasionally disagree on what these three terms should mean.

To avoid any confusion, we shall call these three by names which are more descriptive once they are understood, namely TraverseNLR, TraverseLNR, and TraverseLRN, respectively. In these names, L stands for "left subtree," R stands for "right subtree," and N stands for "node." The order of the letters indicates the traversal order: for example, in TraverseNLR a node is visited, then its left subtree is traversed, then its right subtree is traversed. In TraverseLNR, the left subtree is traversed before the node is visited, and the right subtree thereafter.

How do these algorithms work? They are recursive. Since a binary tree is recursively defined (every subtree of a binary tree is a binary tree), a traversal defined for a tree is also defined for any subtree. We can thus write the three traversal algorithms recursively as shown in Figure 7–13.

The three parts of Figure 7–14 show the steps in performing these three traversals for the given tree. In each one, the details of the "Visit" operation are deferred, since precisely what "visit" should accomplish is application dependent. For completeness, the figure includes a "visit" operation which simply prints the key. The applicability of each of these traversals will become apparent below.

7.4   EXPRESSION TREES

One common application of binary trees is in interpreters or compilers for programming languages, where the statements of a source program are converted into trees so that the structure of the statements is apparent. As a simple case of this, we shall consider *expression trees*, which are transformations of arithmetic expressions into binary trees.

We will use, for simplicity, the same restricted expressions that we used in Chapter 5, in the discussion of stacks and RPN. As a reminder, an expression consists of single-letter identifiers or variable names, one-digit integer constants, the four arithmetic operators +, −, *, and /, and parentheses.

7.4.1 Constructing Expression Trees

Design One shows how to construct a scanner or parser program that can construct an expression tree for these simple expressions. For now, let us just see how to construct an expression tree manually. The general idea is very similar to the way we constructed an RPN expression from an infix one.

We consider first only fully-parenthesized expressions. An expression tree

```
procedure TraverseNLR(T: tree) is
   begin
      if T = null then
         return;
      else
         VisitTree(T);
         TraverseNLR(T.left);
         TraverseNLR(T.right);
      end if;
   end TraverseNLR;


procedure TraverseLNR(T: tree) is
   begin
      if T = null then
         return;
      else
         TraverseLNR(T.left);
         VisitTree(T);
         TraverseLNR(T.right);
      end if;
   end TraverseLNR;


procedure TraverseLRN(T: tree) is
   begin
      if T = null then
         return;
      else
         TraverseLRN(T.left);
         TraverseLRN(T.right);
         VisitTree(T);
      end if;
   end TraverseLRN;


procedure VisitTree(T: tree) is
   begin
      put(T.key);
   end VisitTree;
```

Figure 7-13   Recursive tree traversals.

always has an operator at its root and identifiers or constants at its leaves. (The exception is for an expression consisting only of a single identifier or constant; there is just one node, both root and leaf.) The root operator is the "main" operator of the expression, that is, the operator which is performed *last* as the expression is evaluated. Interior nodes are the operators of subexpressions.

To give a few examples, Figure 7–15 shows the expression trees for A, A−B, (A − B) + C, A − (B + C), and (A + B)*(C − D). Notice carefully how these trees are constructed, and be sure that you understand well how (A − B) + C and A − (B + C) give rise to *different* trees. In (A − B) + C the + is the main operation, since it is performed *last*; in A − (B + C) it is the – that is the main operation.

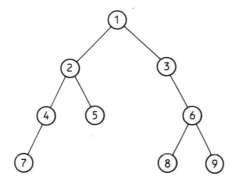

(a)   A binary tree.

1   2   4   7   5   3   6   8   9
_____

(b)   NLR (node-left-right or Preorder) traversal.

7   4   2   5   1   3   8   6   9
_____

(c)   LNR (left-node-right or Inorder) traversal.

7   4   5   2   8   9   6   3   1
_____

(d)   LRN (left-right-node or Postorder) traversal.

Figure 7-14   Three traversals of binary trees.

Try building expression trees from $(A*B) - (C + (D/E))$ and $((A - B) + (C/D))*E$ to make certain you understand how these trees are produced.

As we did in Chapter 5, let us now relax the condition that expressions be fully parenthesized. We use the same association and priority rules developed in the earlier discussion: + and – are priority 2 operators; * and / are priority 1 operators, and adjacent operators of equal priority associate left to right. The expression $A + B * C$ will be treated *as though* it were parenthesized $A + (B*C)$; $A/B - C$ will be evaluated *as though* it were parenthesized $(A/B) - C$. So in the first expression + is the main operator, in the second it is –. Their expression trees are as shown in Figure 7–16.

Expression   Expression Tree

A   A

A–B

(A–B)+C

A–(B+C)

(A+B)*(C–D)

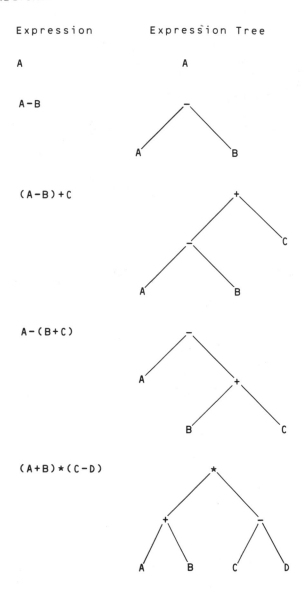

Figure 7-15   Some expression trees.

Using the left-to-right rule in the case of equal-priority operators, $A - B - C$ is treated as though it were written $(A - B) - C$, and A/B*C is treated as though it were written (A/B)*C.

As we did in Chapter 5, let's look at expressions containing a mixture of parentheses and operators of both priorities. Consider first $A + B - C + D$. Since adjacent operators of equal priority are handled left-to-right, we treat it as though it were $((A + B) - C) + D$. Now look at $A - (B + C)*D$. As before,

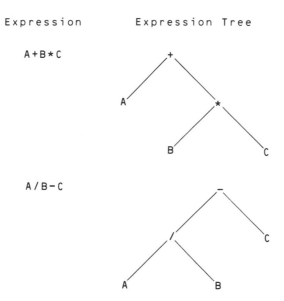

Expression   Expression Tree

A+B*C

A/B-C

Figure 7-16   More expression trees.

the two operators of interest are – and * (the + doesn't count because it's inside a subexpression!), and the * is done first because its priority is one. So this expression is handled as though it were A − ((B + C)*D). These trees are shown in Figure 7–17. Try A − B*C/(D − E) and A*B − (C + D) + E.

7.4.2 Traversing Expression Trees

The three parts of Figure 7–18 show the three traversals TraverseNLR, TraverseLNR, TraverseLRN performed on the given expression trees. It is interesting that TraverseNLR produces the "forward Polish" or "prefix" form of the original expression, and TraverseLRN produces the RPN form!

What about TraverseLNR? This traversal turns out not to be terribly useful for expression trees, since it produces an infix form of the expression *with the parentheses removed*. This leads to possible ambiguities, since, for example, the expressions (A − (B − C)) and ((A − B) − C), which clearly have different expression trees, have the same TraverseLNR infix form. Indeed, if numerical values were substituted for A, B, and C, the two original expressions would evaluate to different results, only one of which would result from evaluating the infix form!

Convince yourself, please, that similar ambiguities do not arise in the prefix and postfix cases. Even though TraverseLNR is not very useful for expression trees, we shall see in the next section that it does have a very useful application.

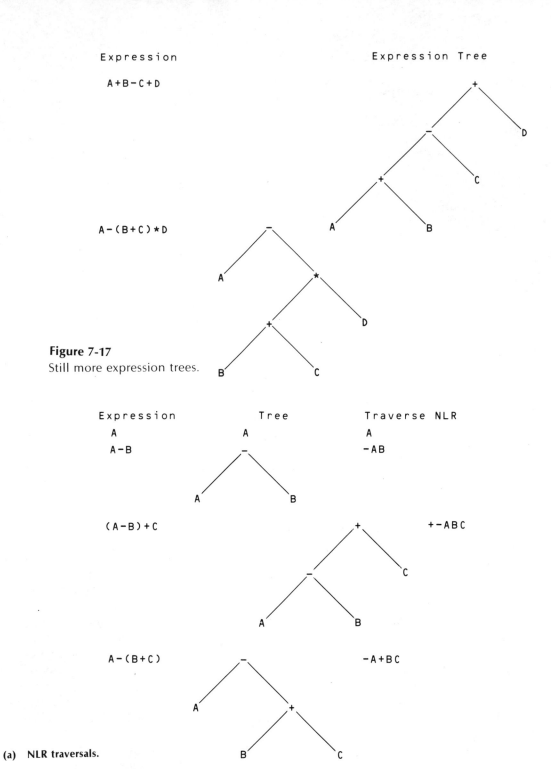

Expression

A + B − C + D

Expression Tree

A − (B + C) ∗ D

Figure 7-17
Still more expression trees.

Expression	Tree	Traverse NLR
A	A	A
A − B		− A B
(A − B) + C		+ − A B C
A − (B + C)		− A + B C

(a)   NLR traversals.

Figure 7-18   Traversals of expression trees.

You have seen that there is an intimate relationship between an infix expression, its tree, and its forward and reverse Polish forms. In compiler applications, some form of the expression tree is often used as a convenient intermediate internal representation of a program. An expression tree is a structure that can easily be manipulated by a program, and even restructured to optimize the object-program instructions that are generated.

7.5   BINARY SEARCH TREES (BSTs)

Another useful application of binary trees is in the implementation of efficient insertions and deletions in tables with dynamically varying entries. To get

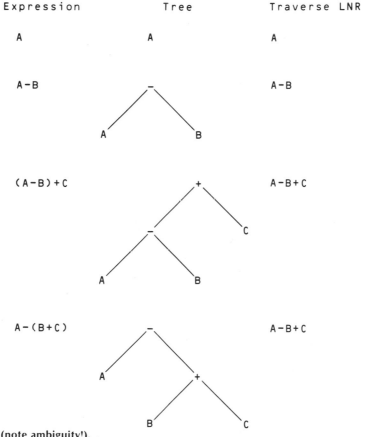

(b)   LNR traversals (note ambiguity!).

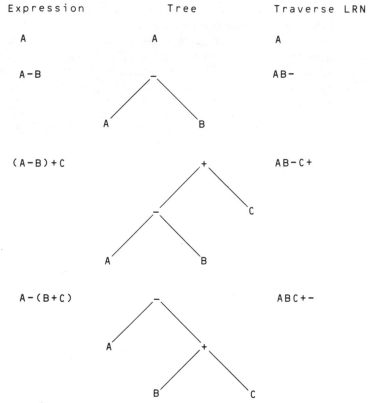

Expression	Tree	Traverse LRN
A	A	A
A−B		AB−
(A−B)+C		AB−C+
A−(B+C)		ABC+−

(c)   NLR traversals.

started, let us define a *binary search tree (BST)* as a binary tree with the property that the value of the key at any node is greater than all values in that node's left subtree, and less than or equal to all values in that node's right subtree. We can state this property recursively as follows:

A leaf node is a BST.

A node is the root of a BST if its key value is greater than that of its left child and less than or equal to that of its right child, and if both of its children are either null or the roots of BSTs.

Figure 7–19 gives some trees which are BSTs and some which are not. As usual, be sure you can distinguish them.

In Figure 7–20 the specification for a dynamic table handler is repeated for convenience. It turns out that the BST is often an effective implementation of such as a dynamic table; the next several sections explain how each of the table operations can be implemented as operations on a BST. We have kept the examples uncluttered by using records consisting only of a single-letter key; the generalization to records with value fields should be obvious.

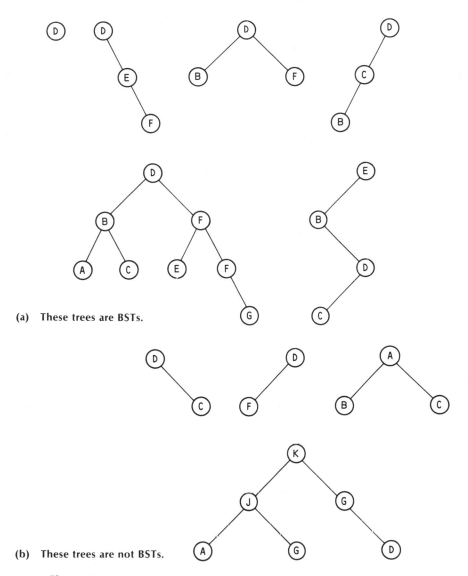

(a) These trees are BSTs.

(b) These trees are not BSTs.

Figure 7-19 Binary Search Trees.

7.5.1 The Report Operation: Traversing a BST

It was mentioned above that the LNR or inorder traversal of a binary tree has an interesting use. Specifically, it can be used to implement the "report" or "print in order" operation for a dynamic table.

A BST has the property that an LNR traversal will visit the nodes in the order of their key values. This can be readily understood by realizing that every key in the root's left subtree is necessarily less than the root key (otherwise it wouldn't be a BST!), and so visiting all the nodes in the left subtree prior to visiting the root will visit smaller keys. Similarly, visiting nodes in the right subtree after visiting the root will visit the root before visiting any keys greater than or equal to the root.

Now since LNR traversal is recursive, and the left and right subtrees of the root are themselves BSTs, the nodes must be visited in "sorted" order. This is illustrated in Figure 7–21.

```
package TableHandler Is

    type KeyType Is ...
    type TableType Is ...

    procedure Create(T: In out TableType);
    procedure Update(T: In out TableType; K: KeyType);
    function  Search(T: TableType; K: KeyType) return tree;
    procedure Delete(T: In out TableType; K: KeyType);
    procedure Report(T: TableType);


    end TableHandler;
```

Figure 7-20   Sketch of table handler package (repeated from Chapter 2).

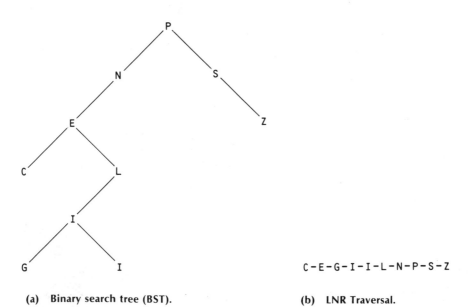

(a)   Binary search tree (BST).

C – E – G – I – I – L – N – P – S – Z

(b)   LNR Traversal.

Figure 7-21   LNR Traversal of a binary search tree.

7.5.2 The Update Operation: Inserting a Record in a BST

Since BSTs are recursively defined we can discover a very natural recursive algorithm for inserting a new key in the tree. Assuming first that the tree is not empty, we just test the key against the root key. If it is less, we insert it in the left subtree; if it is equal or greater, we insert it in the right subtree. Eventually, after several recursive calls, we will reach a point where the subtree into which the new key is to be inserted is empty. At this point, we just create a new node for it and link it to the appropriate pointer in the parent node. Figure 7–22 gives a procedure for inserting in a BST.

In Figure 7–23 we show four "auxiliary routines" called by the insert procedure. Two of these procedures, ConnectLeft and ConnectRight, are responsible for connecting a leaf node, created by the function MakeNode, as the left or right child of its parent respectively. The fourth procedure is called Process-Duplicate, and handles the case where a "duplicate key" is encountered, that is where a given key is seen for the second time. The action to be taken for a duplicate key is application-dependent: sometimes duplicate keys are not allowed, therefore ProcessDuplicate should raise an exception. In the present application, we treat the second occurrence of a key as though it were *greater*

```
procedure UpdateBST(T: in out tree; K: KeyType) is
   begin

      if T = null then
         T := MakeNode(K);

      elsif K < T.Key then
         if T.left = null then
            ConnectLeft(T,K);
         else
            UpdateBST(T.left,K);
         end if;

      elsif K > T.Key then
         if T.right = null then
            ConnectRight(T,K);
         else
            UpdateBST(T.right,K);
         end if;

      else
         ProcessDuplicate(T,K);
      end if;

   end UpdateBST;
```

Figure 7-22   Binary search tree Update.

than the original; this forces the second occurrence into the right subtree. This strategy gives what is known as a *stable sort*, in which equal keys appear in the LNR traversal in precisely the order in which they arrived.

What is the time performance of this algorithm? Suppose the BST is balanced. Then if there are K nodes in the tree, the number of levels will be (approximately) log K, and finding the right place for a new arrival will take (approximately) log K comparisons.

The problem is that since the BST was built by the above algorithm, there is no guarantee whatever that it is balanced, since this property depends on the order of arrival of the new keys.

How bad can it get? Suppose that the keys arrive *in sequential order*, for example sorted ascending. Then each new arrival will necessarily be greater than the previous one, and will thus go into the right subtree. No arrival ever goes into a *left* subtree! Thus the tree will be badly deformed: it will look like a linear list! So adding a new arrival will be a *linear* function of the number of keys already there, instead of a *logarithmic* one. Figure 7–24 shows this worst-case situation.

The best case performance of Update, then, is logarithmic; the worst case is linear; the average case will be somewhere in between. In practice, BSTs are not useful for applications in which there is a high probability that the incom-

```
function MakeNode(K: KeyType) return tree is
      Result: tree;
   begin
      Result := new BinaryTreeNode;
      Result.Key := K;
      return Result;
   end MakeNode;


procedure ConnectLeft(T: in out tree; K: KeyType) is
   begin
      T.left := MakeNode(K);
   end ConnectLeft;


procedure ConnectRight(T: in out tree; K: KeyType) is
   begin
      T.right := MakeNode(K);
   end ConnectRight;


procedure ProcessDuplicate(T: in out tree; K: KeyType) is
   begin
      UpdateBST(T.right,K);
   end ProcessDuplicate;
```

Figure 7-23   Auxiliary functions for BST Update.

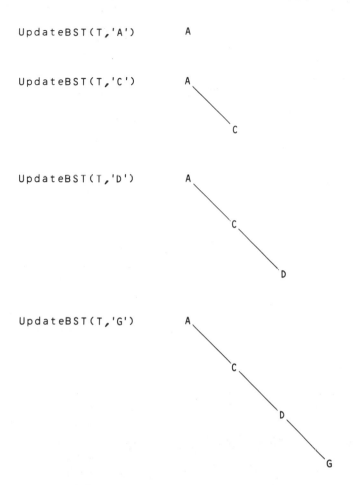

Figure 7-24   A worst-case situation for BST Update.

ing data items are already sorted. In situations where the data is reasonably "mixed up," the average performance is acceptable.

As it happens, algorithms exist for balancing BSTs. A balanced BST is sometimes called an AVL tree, after Adel'son-Vel'skii and Landis; the algorithm they discovered is rather complicated and unintuitive, and beyond the scope of this book.

7.5.3 The Search Operation: Finding a Record in a BST

The algorithm for Search is really very similar to the first part of the Update operation. Given a key to search for, we simply start at the root of the tree, comparing our key with the one we find at that node. If our key is equal, we

```
function SearchBST(T: tree; K: KeyType) return tree is
    begin

        if    T = null then
            return null;
        elsif K = T.Key then
            return T;
        elsif K < T.Key then
            return SearchBST(T.left,K);
        elsif K > T.Key then
            return SearchBST(T.right,K);
        end if;

end SearchBST;
```

Figure 7-25   BST Search function.

have found the record we are looking for and return its location; if our key is less, we search in the left subtree; if it is greater, we search in the right subtree. If we reach a null subtree, we know the key we are looking for is not in the tree.

This algorithm is shown as an Ada function in Figure 7–25; clearly its performance depends upon the structure of the particular tree, varying from logarithmic in the best case to linear in the worst case.

The Update and Search operations show clearly where a Binary Search Tree got its name. The operations are the tree equivalents of their counterparts for ordered arrays, and are very similar to binary search. The Binary Search Tree can be seen as a binary tree used for searching (*binary* search tree) or as a tree which implements binary search (*binary search* tree).

7.5.4 The Delete Operation: Deleting a Record from a BST

We are studying BSTs in part because they are useful for storing dynamically varying sets of records. Thus records are deleted as well as added. Deletions need to be done, of course, in such a way that the BST property of the remaining tree is preserved.

Assuming that deletion of a node from a BST always takes the form "delete the record containing a given key," what is the algorithm? If the desired node is a leaf, we have an easy problem: just cut it off the tree. Otherwise, it has subtrees and we need to rearrange the subtrees so that the BST property is not disturbed. If only one subtree is present, we can just delete the node by making its parent point to whichever child is there. If both subtrees are present, we replace the node by its *LNR* or *Inorder Successor*. Formally, we have:

To delete a node from a BST:

1. Locate the desired node by a search; call it t.

2. If t is a leaf, disconnect it from its parent (set the pointer in the parent's node equal to null).

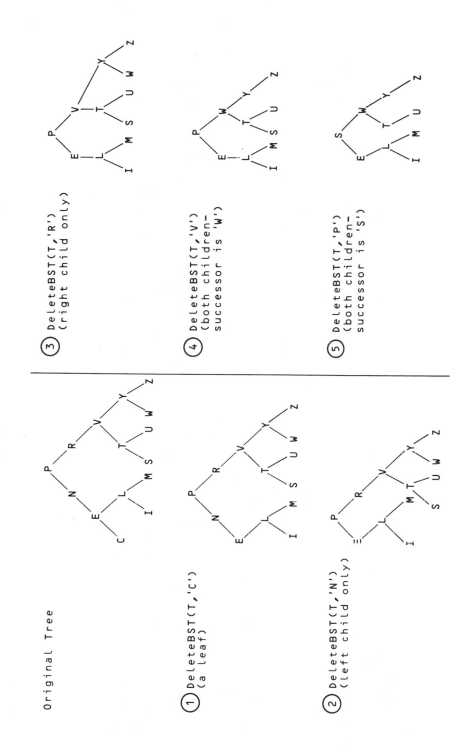

Figure 7-26 Deletions from a BST.

209

3. If t has a left child but no right child, remove t from the tree by making t's *parent* point to t's *left child*.

4. If t has a right child but no left child, remove t from the tree by making t's *parent* point to t's *right child*.

5. Otherwise, find t's LNR successor, which is the node in t's *right subtree* with the *smallest* key. Copy this node's information into t; delete the node.

In Figure 7–26 you will see some deletions from a BST which illustrate each case above.

To arrive at a procedure for Delete, consider the last case in the algorithm above. To handle that case, we write an auxiliary procedure DeleteSmallest(T,K), which finds the node in a tree T with the smallest key, deletes that node, and returns the key in K. This procedure is shown in Figure 7–27; the full DeleteBST procedure is given in Figure 7–28.

There are really two possible Delete algorithms; we could just as well have used t's "in-order predecessor," the node in its *left* subtree with the *largest* key. Finding an algorithm for this is left as an exercise.

Notice that a deletion clearly affects the tree's balance. Experimental results have shown that in a "real-world" BST, with many insertions and deletions, all coming in random order, the tree's balance is best maintained by *alternating* successor and predecessor deletions.

```
procedure DeleteSmallest(T: in out tree;
                         K: out KeyType) is

  begin
    if T.left = null then

        -- T ALREADY POINTS TO THE SMALLEST KEY
        K := T.Key;
        T := T.right;

    else

        -- T HAS A LEFT CHILD, SO LOOK THERE
        DeleteSmallest(T.left,K);

    end if;

  end DeleteSmallest;
```

Figure 7-27   DeleteSmallest procedure.

```
procedure DeleteBST(T: in out tree; K: KeyType) is
    TempK: KeyType;
begin

    if   K < T.Key then
        DeleteBST(T.left,K);
    elsif K > T.Key then
        DeleteBST(T.right,K);
    else  -- FOUND THE NODE TO BE DELETED

        if   T.left = null and
             T.right = null      then
        -- T IS A LEAF; DELETE IT
            T := null;

        elsif T.right = null then
        -- REPLACE T BY ITS PREDECESSOR
            T := T.left;

        elsif T.left = null then
        -- SUCCESSOR IS T'S RIGHT CHILD
            T := T.right;

        else
        -- BOTH CHILDREN THERE
            DeleteSmallest(T.right,TempK);
            T.Key := TempK;

        end if;

    end if;

end DeleteBST;
```

Figure 7-28   BST Delete procedure.

7.6   GENERAL TREES

We have concentrated in this chapter on binary trees. In this section, we will present two examples of the use of more general tree structures. The first example is the *digital search tree*, which is an application of a tree in which a node has a number of children which is potentially large and highly variable. The second example is the *B-tree*, a structure used frequently in structuring large files on secondary storage devices. In a B-tree each node has a number of children which is variable but has a fixed, usually relatively small, maximum. The balanced BST turns out to be a special case of the B-tree.

7.6.1 Digital Search Trees

Consider the problem of designing a program to check whether the words in a report are spelled correctly. This is usually solved by creating a dictionary of all those words likely to be used in the report. Then the report is scanned, word-by-word, and all words not appearing in the dictionary are reported to the user as possible spelling errors. A word will be reported if it is misspelled, but also if it is a valid word that just isn't in the dictionary.

Theoretically, any kind of table can be used to represent the dictionary: an ordered array or a balanced BST, for example. The difficulty is that for real-world dictionaries, the amount of space required would be enormous, since in the usual tables each word would have to be stored in full.

The digital search tree provides a solution: only a single character is stored in each node. There are as many separate trees as there are possible first letters (such a collection of trees is usually called a *forest*); each tree has a different first letter at its root. The children of the root contain the second letters of all the words with the given first letter; the children of a given second-letter node contain the third letters of words with the given second letter, and so on.

A search for a word in such a forest then involves starting with its first letter and trying, letter by letter, to find a path through the appropriate tree. If one is found, the word is valid; otherwise it is reported.

Figure 7–29 shows a diagram of a pair of digital search trees for some words beginning with C and D. Notice that we have added a special character '#' to indicate "end of word," so that, for example, the word "DEE" (not a valid English word) would not be erroneously reported as correct by going part-way down the path for "DEER."

If we can find an appropriate implementation of this tree, great storage savings can be achieved; indeed, this savings can make it feasible to build a dictionary which can be loaded into primary memory in its entirety, thus avoiding time-consuming disk accesses.

A possible implementation is to represent a node by an array of twenty-seven pointers, one for each letter and the "end of word" character, so a parent can have up to twenty-seven children. This has the advantage of letting us determine in constant time whether, say, the letter "s" in a given node has a child for letter "q": we just check to see whether the pointer for "q" is the "s" node is null or not. On the other hand, this implementation uses space very inefficiently, since such arrays will normally be sparse—whatever the language of the dictionary—many letter combinations do not appear. A given letter, at a given "level" of the words being indexed, will have only a few successors.

A better approach is to treat the node as a "sparse vector," by analogy with the approach we used in Chapter 4. Represent the children of a given parent as an ordered linear list, as shown in Figure 7–30. Now each node has only *two* pointers: one to its leftmost child, the other to its immediate right sibling. The trees in the forest are all connected at the top level to an artificial "super-root,"

CAN,CANE,CON,CONE,COP,COPE,CURE,CURT,CUT,CUTE,CUTS

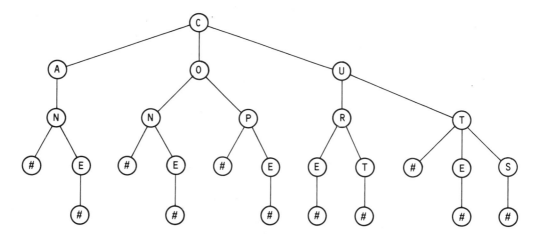

DEBT,DEBTOR,DEEP,DEEPLY,DO,DON,DONATE,DONE

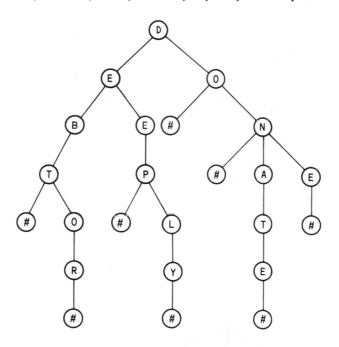

Figure 7-29 Two digital search trees.

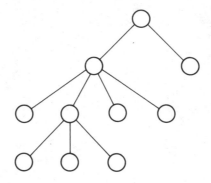

(a) Abstraction.

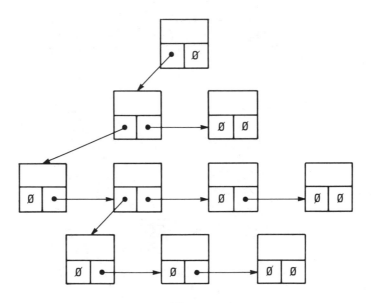

(b) Implementation.

Figure 7-30 Left child/right sibling implementation of a general tree.

representing "beginning of word" (we can use the same artificial "end-of-word" '#' here). A part of the dictionary used in the previous figure is shown in this form in Figure 7-31.

As in other sparse-vector techniques, we have traded space for time. Determining whether a certain letter has another given letter as a child requires a linear search through the child list. On the other hand, the child lists are likely to be short for this type of application. You can write an appropriate package

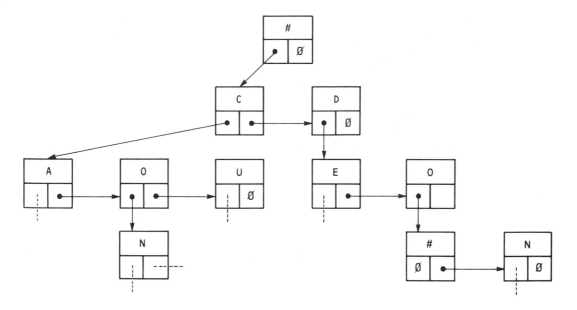

Figure 7-31   Digital search tree implementation.

for the digital search tree as an exercise; another exercise examines the space and time requirements.

The use of a linked list to represent the siblings is not limited to the spelling-checker application; it is a common implementation structure for general trees. Sometimes each node carries a pointer back up to its parent as well.

7.6.2 B-Trees

The B-tree is a generalization of the balanced BST (or AVL tree), frequently used as a basis for structuring large files on external devices like disks.

The BST developed in section 7.5 can obviously be generalized to allow the nodes of the tree to be stored on disk instead of memory: all that's involved is to use a disk input/output package that permits addressing individual records on disk, then letting node pointers represent disk-record addresses rather than main-memory locations.

For a BST large enough to provoke consideration of storing it externally, this scheme could use too many disk accesses, and disk accesses are slow because of the time required to search for a given record on the device. A balanced BST with N nodes, however stored, requires O(log(N)) record accesses in the worst case. For really large files, ten, twenty or thirty disk operations to carry out a search is just too many.

On the other hand, if the entire tree is large enough to justify disk storage, we do not usually need more than a few records at a time in main memory. So these records can be rather large. Moreover, disk storage is relatively inexpensive as well, and the time for retrieving a large record from disk is about the same as the time for retrieving a small one, since most of the time is used to *find* the record, not to transfer it to main memory.

This all gives rise to the idea of a *B-tree of order K*, in which each node is of *fixed size*, capable of holding K keys and K+1 child pointers, as shown in Figure 7–32. A balanced BST is a special case: a B-tree of order one. Another special case, the B-tree of order two, often goes by the name "2–3 tree."

The keys in a given node are *ordered*. Looking at the diagram in the figure, we construct the tree so that the two pointers surrounding a given key point to subtrees in such a way that the BST property is preserved! All the values in a given key's left subtree are less than that key; the values in its right subtree are greater than it *but less than the adjacent key*. A 2–3 tree, or B-tree of order two, is shown in Figure 7–33b; its corresponding balanced BST is shown in Figure 7–33a for comparison.

Note the difference in the depths of the two trees. In this particular case, the depths differ by only one, but notice that there is still a good bit of "extra capacity" for keys in the 2–3 tree, which can be filled before more levels are added. Generally speaking, we maintain the balance in a B-tree by requiring that a node must always be at least half full. Combining a number of keys into each node leads to a "flatter" tree, thus to fewer disk accesses.

For completeness, we should add that B-tree nodes don't usually carry the entire record around, since that would require more space per node, much of it

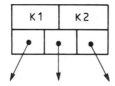

(a)   B-tree node, order 2.

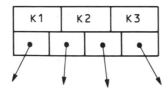

(b)   B-tree node, order 3.

Figure 7-32   B-tree nodes.

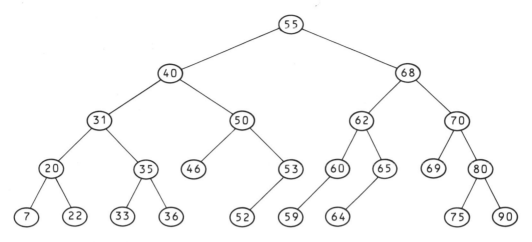

(a)   A balanced BST (or AVL tree).

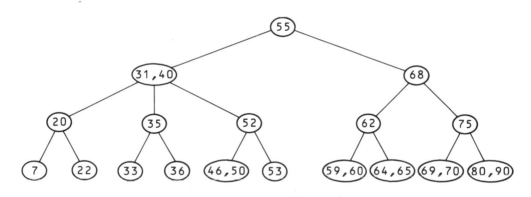

(b)   A 2-3 tree (or B-tree of order 2) for the same data.

Figure 7-33   Balanced BST compared with 2-3 tree.

unused. The tree is used as a directory structure: along with the K keys, the actual disk addresses of the corresponding records are often stored; addresses take a lot less space than full records!

Detailed implementation of the B-tree stucture is left to the exercises.

7.7   DESIGN ONE: BUILDING AN EXPRESSION TREE

In the Design section of Chapter 5 a function was developed to translate an arithmetic expression to its RPN form. It turns out that the algorithm to produce the expression tree is very similar, and the decision process for pushing and popping operators on and off the stack is exactly the same.

There is a difference, though. In the previous case, when an operand (letter or number) was scanned, it was immediately output (concatenated to the RPN string). Similarly, an operator popped from the stack was immediately output.

In this situation, we need to retain those operands and operators, connecting them together in a tree. We do this by maintaining a separate stack for intermediate *tree* results, letting items in the stack be pointers to subtrees instead of just characters. Our operator stack is also converted to hold pointers to nodes; an operator is placed in such a node before being pushed.

At the end of the algorithm, a pointer to the root of the resultant tree is left on top of the node stack. Figure 7–34 shows the conversion of an expression to a tree. All the details of the nodes are illustrated.

The main loop of an Ada function for the translator is shown in Figure 7–35; Figure 7–36 gives the detailed code. The translator uses a local procedure, PopConnectPush, which pops an operator node from the operator stack, pops the two top nodes from the node stack, connects the operator node as the root of the new tree, then pushes this node back onto the node stack. This procedure is really the difference between the expression-to-RPN translator and this expression-to-tree translator.

The similarity of these two algorithms illustrates once again the intimacy of the relationship between infix expressions, trees, and Polish notation.

7.8   DESIGN TWO: A CROSS-REFERENCE GENERATOR

A cross-reference generator is an example of an indexing program. Two applications come from the fields of programming and text analysis.

A programmer uses a cross-reference listing of a program to help debug that program. The cross-reference listing indicates, for each identifier in the program, in which statements that identifier appears. A person analyzing text in a natural language uses a cross-reference listing of that text (this kind of cross-reference listing is sometimes called a *concordance*) to indicate how frequently and in which lines each important word occurs. For example, a hundred or two years ago—long before computers, in any case—a number of monks in England produced a concordance of the entire Bible, all by hand, of course!

A cross-reference generator, whatever its application, consists of two parts. One part is some kind of *dynamic table handler* to hold the words read from the text, and all their references, in some efficient way. The other part is some kind of *scanner* or *parser*, which knows the specifics of the language being analyzed and therefore how to distinguish a meaningful word from other things.

The main loop of the cross-reference generator is shown in Figure 7–37. The scanner procedure GetWord is called to read text from the input file and return the next word it finds; GetWord also keeps the line counter up to date and reports end-of-file at the right time. A word and its line number are put in

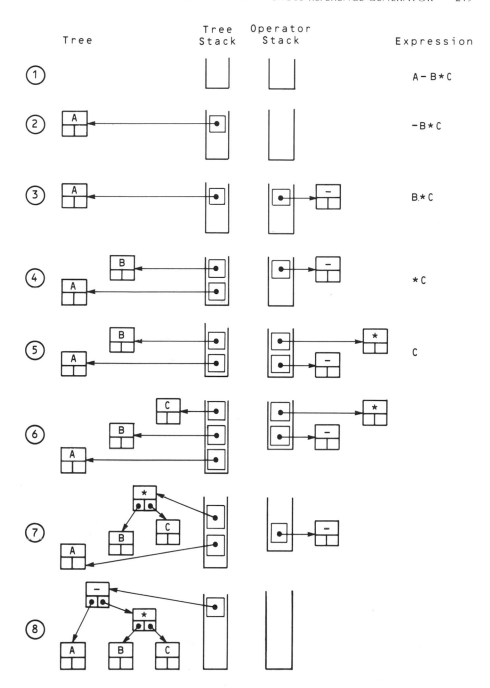

Figure 7-34   Translation of infix expression to tree.

```
function ExpTree(X: Text) return Tree is
   C: character;
   T: Text := X;
   Ops, Nodes: Stack;
   Temp:   Tree;
   WeirdChar: exception;

      procedure PopConnectPush is
         begin
            Temp := Top(Ops); Pop(Ops);
            Temp.right := Top(Nodes); Pop(Nodes);
            Temp.left  := Top(Nodes); Pop(Nodes);
            Push(Nodes,Temp);
         end PopConnectPush;

begin

   if Empty(T) then
      return null;
   end if;

   loop

      C := Head(T);
      case C is

         -- BODY OF case STATEMENT GOES HERE

      end case;

      T := Tail(T);
      exit when Empty(T);

   end loop;

   while not IsEmpty(Ops) loop
      PopConnectPush;
   end loop;

   return Top(Nodes);

end ExpTree;
```

Figure 7-35 Expression-to-tree translator.

the table by a call to Update. When the input file is exhausted, Report is called to print out the cross-reference listing. Notice how all the details of the scanning and table handling are hidden.

7.8.1 The Table Handler

Let us look first at the requirements for the table handler. We assume that the distinct words in the text or program are few enough in number that the table

```
case C is

   when 'A'..'Z' | 'a'..'z' | '0'..'9' =>
      Push(Nodes, MakeNode(C));

   when '+' | '-' | '*' | '/' =>
      if    IsEmpty(Ops) then
         Push(Ops,MakeNode(C));

      elsif Top(Ops).key = '(' then
         Push(Ops,MakeNode(C));

      elsif Priority(Top(Ops).key) < Priority(C) then
         Push(Ops,MakeNode(C));

      else
         loop -- clear stack of higher priority operators
            PopConnectPush;
         exit when    IsEmpty(Ops)
            or else Top(Ops).key = '('
            or else Priority(Top(Ops).key) < Priority(C);
         end loop;
         Push(Ops,MakeNode(C));

      end if;
   when '(' =>
      Push(Ops,MakeNode(C));

   when ')' =>
      while Top(Ops).key /= '(' loop
         PopConnectPush;
      end loop;
      Pop(Ops); -- throw away the '('

   when others =>
      raise WeirdChar;

end case;
```

Figure 7-36   Body of translator case statement.

can be constructed in main memory. The input text will be scanned, the cross reference built, then the results reported *once*. Also, we do not know either precisely how many different words will arrive nor how many references each will have. Furthermore, words and references are only added, never deleted. These facts argue for a table structure whose Update and Search operations are efficient. The Report operation is not worrisome, since it's done only once per run, and Delete is never done at all.

Unless the total number of words is very large, the BST structure is a useful solution. Since people don't often write either programs or essays with the words in alphabetical order, the chances of getting a badly unbalanced tree are slim and both Update and Report then perform in roughly O(log(N)) time.

```
with Text_IO,TableHandler,DataTypes,Scanner,Text_Handler;
use  Text_IO,TableHandler,DataTypes,Scanner,Text_Handler;
procedure EnglishXref is

    FileName: string(1..12);
    F: File_Type;

    T:          XrefTable;
    LineNumber: integer := 1;
    ThisWord:   Word;

    EOF: boolean := false;
    EOL: boolean := false;

begin
    Put_line("Please enter name of data file");
    get(FileName);
    open(F,in_file,FileName);

    loop

        GetWord(F,ThisWord,EOL,EOF);

        if not Empty(ThisWord) then
            Update(T,ThisWord,LineNumber);
        end if;

        if EOL then
            LineNumber := LineNumber + 1;
        end if;

        exit when EOF;

    end loop;

    new_page;
    put("Cross Reference Listing for ");
    put_line(FileName);
    new_line;
    Report(T);


end EnglishXref;
```

Figure 7-37   Main program for cross reference.

A first attempt to build a BST package would carry a node for each word and reference (line number): the word would be the key, the reference would be the value. A moment's thought reveals that this is wasteful of space, since we really only need one copy of each word. Let's put all the references to a given word in a one-way list, then use the value part of the tree node as the list header. A diagram for this is shown in Figure 7–38, using a small number of words of English text.

```
1 We wish to point out the difference
2 between the terms "data type," "abstract
3 data type," and "data structure."
```

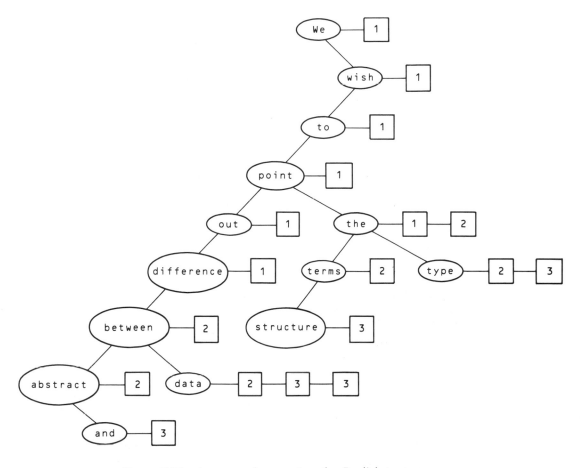

Figure 7-38   A cross-reference tree for English text.

How should Update work? Recall that the update procedure for BSTs, given in section 7.5.2, calls two lower-level procedures, ProcessFirst and ProcessDuplicate. In this application, ProcessFirst should create a node for the newly arrived word—which is being seen for the first time—and then set up the reference list with the current line number in the first node of the list. ProcessDuplicate should just create a list node for a new reference, adding it to the tail of the list. Since additions are made only to the tail of the list, it helps if the list header keeps a pointer to the tail.

Given type definitions for Word and Reference, some type definitions for the tree and list nodes are shown in Figure 7–39. Figure 7–40 gives the modified Ada code for Update, and Figure 7–41 shows the necessary auxiliary routines.

The other important operation is Report, which, for a BST, is just a TraverseLNR operation. The Visit procedure in TraverseLNR prints the word in the tree node and then traverses the reference list, printing out line numbers as it goes. The modification of TraverseLNR is left to an exercise.

7.8.2 The Scanner

Developing scanners for languages is a science in itself, and a general treatment is well beyond the scope of this book. For this example, we'll simplify the scanner by relying on some key assumptions about the text to be scanned. We assume that the text is English, that upper-case and lower-case letters are treated separately, and that numeric digits are treated just like letters, so dates, phone numbers, etc., will be indexed along with normal words. Punctuation is not to be indexed; there is no embedded punctuation like an apostrophe or a hyphen. A word is never broken across two lines. In the exercises you have the chance to relax some of these assumptions.

```
type OneWayListNode;
type list is access OneWayListNode;
type OneWayListNode is
  record
    val:   Reference;
    next:  list := null;
  end record;

type ListHeader is
  record
    head:  list := null;
    tail:  list := null;
  end record;

type XrefTreeNode;
type XrefTable is access XrefTreeNode;
type XrefTreeNode is
  record
    key:   Word;
    val:   ListHeader;
    left:  XrefTable := null;
    right: XrefTable := null;
  end record;
```

Figure 7-39 Type definitions for cross reference.

```
procedure Update(T: in out XrefTable;
                   K: Word; V: Reference) is
  begin

    if T = null then
      T := MakeNode(K,V);

    elsif K < T.key then
      if T.left = null then
        ConnectLeft(T,K,V);
      else
        Update(T.left,K,V);
      end if;

    elsif K > T.key then
      if T.right = null then
        ConnectRight(T,K,V);
      else
        Update(T.right,K,V);
      end if;

    else
      ProcessDuplicate(T,K,V);
    end if;
  end Update;
```

Figure 7-40   Modified Update for cross reference.

```
function MakeNode(K: Word; V: Reference)
                     return XrrefTable is
      Result: XrefTable;
      L: list;
  begin
    L := new OneWayListNode;
    L.val := V;
    Result := new XrefTreeNode;
    Result.key := K;
    Result.val.head := L;
    Result.val.tail := L;
    return Result;
  end MakeNode;

procedure ProcessDuplicate(T: in out XrefTable;
                             K: Word; V: Reference) is
      L: list;
  begin
    L := new OneWayListNode;
    L.val := V;
    T.val.tail.next := L;
    T.val.tail      := L;
  end ProcessDuplicate;
```

Figure 7-41   Auxiliary operations for cross reference.

Our scanner can be implemented using a structure which generalizes nicely to many other scanning applications, namely the *finite-state machine*. In Figure 7–42 is shown a simple diagram for this structure, which was introduced in Chapter 6 as a *state graph*, or *transition graph*. The circles represent *states* of the machine. The arrows represent *transitions* from one state to another. An arrow is labeled with two things: the left part is the *class* of input character just scanned, and the right part is an *action* to be taken just before the machine moves to its new state.

Figure 7–43 gives the state graph for our scanner. It begins in its *Start* state, and continues to cycle in that state until it sees a letter. If a "carriage return" is seen, it updates the line counter and returns to the *Start* state (we need to account for the possibility of a line containing all blanks or all punctuation).

Once a letter is seen (remember, digits count as letters!), the machine executes an action called *StartWord*, which initializes a string in which to store the word, stores the letter in this string, and transfers to a state called *Build*.

While in the *Build* state, the machine reads characters, adding the letters it finds on to the word string using an action called *AddLetter*. When a non-letter character is seen, the word is complete and the machine transfers to its *Finish* state. If the non-letter was a "carriage return," the line counter is incremented.

How is the finite-state machine implemented? We hide it in a package which exports only the procedure GetWord. The state names, input classes, and actions are written as *enumeration types*, as shown in Figure 7–44. The transition graph is implemented as a two-dimensional array, which uses the

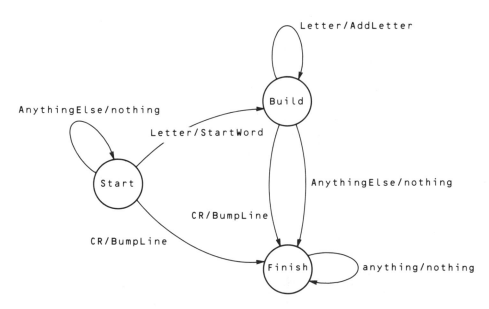

Figure 7-42   Graph and table notations for finite-state machine.

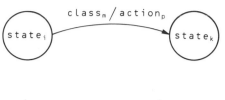

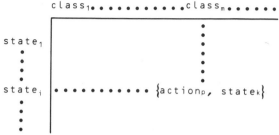

Figure 7-43   State graph for scanner for simple English.

states as its row subscripts and classes of inputs as its column subscripts. Each entry in the array is itself a record, containing an action field and a new-state field. The filled-in array for our scanner is shown in Figure 7–45.

The procedure GetWord is the "machine" that actually moves around the state graph. It reads a character, classifies it (by calling a function shown in Figure 7–46), determines the action to be taken by looking in the array using its current state and input class as subscripts, executes the action, then goes to its new state. If the new state is *Finish*, the procedure returns to the caller. The main loop for GetWord is given in Figure 7–47; details appear in Figure 7–48.

This design example has shown the advantages of separating the independent functions of scanning and table handling into manageable pieces; it has

```
type State      is (Start,Build,Finish);

type InputClass is (Letter,CR,AnythingElse);

type Action     is (Nothing,StartWord,BumpLine,AddLetter);

type LexicalEntry is
  record
    NewState: State;
    ThisAction: Action;
  end record;

type FSM_Table      is array(State,InputClass)
                       of LexicalEntry;
```

Figure 7-44   Types of lexical scanner.

```
EnglishText: FSM_Table :=

--    entries for current state = Start,    current input =

      (((Build,        StartWord),    --  Letter
        (Finish,       BumpLine),     --  CR
        (Start,        Nothing)),     --  AnythingElse

--    entries for current state = Build,    current input =

       ((Build,        AddLetter),    --  Letter
        (Finish,       BumpLine),     --  CR
        (Finish,       Nothing)),     --  AnythingElse

--    entries for current state = Finish,   current input =

       ((Finish,       Nothing),      --  Letter
        (Finish,       Nothing),      --  CR
        (Finish,       Nothing)));    --  AnythingElse
```

Figure 7-45   FSM state table for English cross-reference.

also illustrated the clarity with which structures like tables can be written using enumeration types. A number of the exercises invite the reader to develop various modifications to this design.

7.9   STYLE GUIDE: THREADING TREES FOR EFFICIENCY

Sometimes it is useful to have a nonrecursive algorithm available for tree traversal. Not every language supports recursion directly, and even in those that do, recursion requires extra storage and time for all those subprogram calls.

```
function Classify(Char: in character)
                  return InputClass is
  begin
    if    (Char in 'A'..'Z')
      or  (Char in 'a'..'z')
      or  (Char in '0'..'9')
    then    return Letter;
    else    return AnythingElse;
  end if;
end Classify;
```

Figure 7-46   Character classification function.

```
procedure GetWord(F:      in  File_Type;
                  ThisWord: out Word;
                  EOL:  out boolean;
                  EOF:  out boolean) is

    Char: character;
    ThisClass: InputClass;
    PresentState: State;
    ThisEntry: LexicalEntry;
    NewAction: Action;


begin
    EOL := false;
    EOF := false;
    Clear(ThisWord);
    PresentState := Start;

    loop

        -- MAIN LOOP OF GetWord GOES HERE

    end loop


end GetWord;
```

Figure 7-47   Framework for GetWord.

For that reason, we show in this Style Guide a technique called "thread-ing." We illustrate for the case of a BST; it is equally applicable to expression trees and the details are left to an exercise.

Threading is a very simple idea: as we build a BST, we utilize empty pointer fields to contain pointers helping us move *up* the tree as well as down. This helps us to find the successor of a node during a Report or TraverseLNR operation. Figure 7–49 shows several threaded BSTs with the threads shown as dashed lines. Such a tree is often called "right in-threaded," because it contains threads to facilitate its right inorder traversal.

Where are the threads stored? If a node has a right child, then its LNR successor is *below* it, somewhere in the right subtree. Otherwise, its LNR suc-cessor is *above* it in the tree. A node needs a thread only if it has no right child. Therefore, common practice is to store the thread in the right-child field of a node with a null right child, using some kind of flag to indicate that it is a thread and not an ordinary pointer. In a cursor implementation of a tree-node storage pool, the pointers are always positive integers and so a thread can be distinguished by making it negative. We are using the dynamic implementation

```
loop

   If PresentState = Finish then
      return;
   end if;

   If    End_of_File(F) then
      EOF := true;
      return;
   end if;

   If    End_of_Line(F) then
      Skip_Line(F);
      ThisClass := CR;
   else
      get(F,Char);
      ThisClass := Classify(Char);
   end if;

   ThisEntry := EnglishText(PresentState, ThisClass);
   NewAction := ThisEntry.ThisAction;
   case NewAction is
      when Nothing =>
         null;
      when StartWord =>
         ThisWord := MakeText(Char);
      when AddLetter =>
         ThisWord := ThisWord & Char;
      when BumpLine =>
         EOL := true;
   end case;

   PresentState := ThisEntry.NewState;

end loop;
```

Figure 7-48   Main loop of GetWord.

here, so we shall add to each node a Boolean field called Thread, which is true if a thread is stored in the right child field, and false otherwise. Figure 7–50 gives the modified type definition.

Now let us give a modified TraverseLNR procedure. Essentially, the procedure just moves all the way down the left side of the tree to find the first node to be visited, follows the threads back up until a node with a right child is encountered, then starts back down the left side of the child subtree. This program is shown in Figure 7–51; note that it is nonrecursive.

Finally we develop a nonrecursive Update procedure which threads the tree as it goes along. When a node is inserted as the *left* child of another node, its parent is its LNR successor. When a node is inserted as the *right* child of another node, *it* becomes its parent's LNR successor; the LNR successor of the

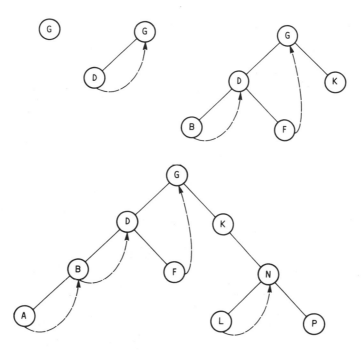

Figure 7-49 Some threaded binary search trees.

new node is the *parent's* former LNR successor. Figure 7–52 gives several examples of how new nodes are added. The new procedure and its auxiliary routines appear in Figure 7–53 and Figure 7–54 respectively.

Nonrecursive Search and Delete routines for right in-threaded BSTs are left as exercises.

```
type ThreadedBinaryTreeNode;
type tree is access ThreadedBinaryTreeNode;
type ThreadedBinaryTreeNode is
  record
    Key:   KeyType;
    Val: ValueType;
    left:  tree := null;
    right: tree := null;
    thread: boolean := false;
  end record;
```

Figure 7-50 Threaded binary search tree node.

```
procedure TraverseLNR(T: tree) is
    p: tree := T;
    q: tree;
begin

    loop

        q := null;

        -- DOWN LEFT BRANCH TO BOTTOM
        while p /= null loop
            q := p;
            p := p.left;
        end loop;

        if q /= null then
            VisitTree(q);
            p := q.right;

            -- NOW BACK UP FOLLOWING THREADS
            while q.thread loop
                VisitTree(p);
                q := p;
                p := q.right;
            end loop;

        end if;

        exit when q = null;

    end loop;

end TraverseLNR;
```

Figure 7-51   Nonrecursive LNR traversal.

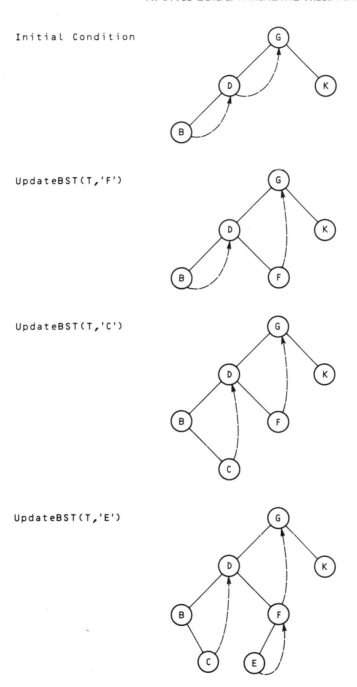

Figure 7-52 Updating a threaded BST.

```
function MakeNode(K: KeyType; V: ValueType) return tree is
    Result: tree;
begin
    Result := new ThreadedBinaryTreeNode;
    Result.Key := K;
    Result.Val := V;
    return Result;
end MakeNode;


procedure ConnectLeft(T: in out tree;
                      K: KeyType; V: ValueType) is
begin
    T.left := MakeNode(K,V);
    T.left.thread := true;
    T.left.right := T;
end ConnectLeft;


procedure ConnectRight(T: in out tree;
                       K: KeyType; V: ValueType) is
    Temp: tree := MakeNode(K,V);
begin
    if T.right /= null then
        Temp.thread := true;
        Temp.right := T.right;
    end if;
    T.right := Temp;
end ConnectRight;
```

Figure 7-53   Nonrecursive BST Update.

```
procedure UpdateBST(T: in out tree; K: KeyType) is
     p: tree;
   begin

     if T = null then
        T := MakeNode(K);
        return;
     end if;

     p := T;        -- SET UP SEARCH POINTER
     loop

        if K < p.Key then
           if p.left = null then
              ConnectLeft(p,K);
              exit;
           else
              p := p.left;
           end if;

        else  -- DUPLICATES TREATED AS GREATER
           if p.right = null or p.thread then
              p.thread := false;
              ConnectRight(p,K);
              exit;
           else
              p := p.right;
           end if;

        end if;

     end loop;

   end UpdateBST;
```

Figure 7-54   Modified auxiliary procedures.

7.10   SUMMARY

This chapter has presented a number of definitions pertaining to trees. Binary trees were emphasized, and the two applications covered in detail were expression trees and binary search trees or BSTs.

An important part of this chapter has been the traversal of a binary tree, that is, visiting each node of the tree in some specified order. The usefulness of three of these traversal schemes, the NLR, LNR, and LRN algorithms, has been considered in detail, and you have seen the close connection between trees and expressions in infix or Polish form.

To illustrate some of the uses of general trees, the digital search tree and B-tree were introduced. In the Design sections, an expression parser and a cross-reference generator were discussed. Finally, some nonrecursive tree-handling programs were shown, and their associated data structures were developed.

This chapter is the last one in which data structures *per se* are presented. The remaining chapters take up two important applications, namely sorting files and searching tables. In these chapters much use is made of all the structures we have used until now; there is also important emphasis on performance issues.

7.11   EXERCISES

1. Given a connected digraph represented by its *adjacency matrix* G, write a Boolean function IsTree(G) which returns true iff G represents a *tree*. Hint: review the definition of a tree!

2. Given a connected digraph represented by its *adjacency matrix* G, write a Boolean function IsBinaryTree(G) which returns true iff G represents a *binary tree*.

3. Given a connected digraph represented by its *adjacency matrix* G, write a Boolean function IsStrictlyBinaryTree(G) which returns true iff G represents a *strictly binary tree*.

4. Which properties of digraphs must *all* trees have? Which properties does *no* tree have?

5. Given a binary tree T, write a Boolean function Balanced(T) which returns true iff T is height-balanced, false otherwise. Hint: Think recursively.

6. Given a binary tree T, write a function Depth(T) which returns the depth of the tree. Hint: Think recursively.

7. In a binary tree T, each leaf node can be reached by only one path from the root. Write a function MinPathLength(T) which returns the length of the *shortest* of all such paths. Hint: Think recursively.

8. Write a procedure implementing a Delete operation for a binary search tree in which, if the element to be deleted possesses both children, it is replaced by its LNR *predecessor* instead of its successor.

9. Write a Delete operation for a BST in which successive deletions are done alternately by the successor and predecessor methods.

10. Develop a procedure implementing the Report operation for a digital search tree.

11. Develop a procedure implementing the Update operation for a digital search tree.

12. Develop a procedure implementing the Delete operation for a digital search tree.

13. An interesting application of the digital search tree is the implementation of a *multi-dimensional array*. One of the difficulties with row- and column-major implementations is that the storage mapping functions contain multiplications, which may be rather slow to execute. Instead, use a digital search tree which has as many levels as the array has dimensions. For example, an array dimensioned (1..10,1..5,1..8) has three levels. The root has ten children; each child points to a node with five children; each of these points to a 1-dimensional, 8-element array. Storing and retrieving values becomes a matter of following pointers instead of doing a subscript calculation. Design a package implementing such a scheme.

14. Develop a procedure implementing the Report operation for a cross-reference tree.

15. Develop a procedure implementing the Delete operation for a cross-reference tree. Be careful: this depends upon whether all references associated with a key are to be deleted, or only one.

16. Develop a nonrecursive Search operation for a threaded BST.

17. Develop a nonrecursive Delete operation for a threaded BST.

18. Develop a threading scheme suitable for NLR traversal of an expression tree and a corresponding nonrecursive traversal procedure.

19. Develop a threading scheme suitable for LRN traversal of an expression tree and a corresponding nonrecursive traversal procedure.

20. Write a package implementing the abstract table operations for a 2–3 tree.

Chapter 8

HASH TABLE METHODS

8.1 GOAL STATEMENT

We now take up again the problem of updating and searching for items in a table, implemented as an array, whose contents vary dynamically, with a mixture of insertions or updates, searches or "locate" operations, and deletions. After a reconsideration of the issues and time performance associated with our old friends linear search and binary search, we shall develop the idea of a "hash table" or "scatter storage" method. This is a table scheme in which updates, searches and deletions are done, ideally, in *constant time*. As we shall see, in actuality the performance of these operations can be made to approximate constant time, but rarely to achieve it exactly.

In a hash table scheme, we identify a record by its key field, and assume that there are many more possible key values than there are storage positions in the table. We then seek a mathematical function called a "hash function" or "key-to-address transformation," which produces a table address when supplied with a key.

Since there are many more possible key values than addresses, this is a many-to-one function, in which many different key values can lead to the same table address. Since we do not know which keys will actually arrive for placement in the table, it is possible that two keys with the same address actually *will* arrive. Two or more keys with the same hash address are called *synonyms* of each other; an arrival of a second key after its synonym has already been placed in the table is called a *collision* or sometimes a *hash clash*.

There are many different hash functions; in fact there are a number of *classes* of hash functions, with the details depending upon the structure and distribution of the keys. Designing a hash table involves two essential parts: finding a hash function that minimizes the likelihood of collisions, and finding an appropriate scheme for resolving those collisions which do occur.

8.2 SEQUENTIAL AND BINARY SEARCH REVISITED

Let us go back to the table searching strategies we considered in Chapter 2. Remember that these are grouped into two main strategies: sequential (or linear) and binary (or logarithmic).

In the sequential case, the items in the array, which we always assume have a key part and a value part, are maintained in unordered form. The *Update* operation depends upon simply keeping track of the location of the next "empty" position in the array, then inserting a new arrival just by placing it in that position. On the other hand, the *Search* and *Delete* operations require looking sequentially through the array, item by item, until either the desired item is found or the end of the array is reached.

In the binary case, we store the table elements in order, sorted by their key. *Update* then requires a logarithmic operation (finding the correct position) followed by a linear one (moving the elements to make room for the new one). For tables large enough for us to care about performance, the linear component dominates. *Search* is purely logarithmic; *Delete* is similar to *Update*.

Figure 8–1 gives a summary, just repeated from Chapter 2, of the "big O"'s of these operations for the two implementations. In the next section we introduce the notion of a hash table, where update, search, and delete operations are carried out in approximately *constant* time.

	UNORDERED	ORDERED
Create	O(1)	O(1)
Update	O(1)	O(N)
Search	O(N)	O(Log(N))
Delete	O(N)	O(N)
Report	O(N x Log(N))	O(N)

Figure 8-1 Comparative performance of table operations for linear and binary strategies.

8.3 THE HASH TABLE

Let's assume—as is the case in most applications—that the set of possible keys K is much larger than the table we wish to maintain. Suppose you have around 100 friends whose phone numbers you wish to keep in your list, and you want to retrieve a friend's number according to, say, the first four letters of his or her name. Since you keep making new friends, and you don't know in advance what their names will be, you have to assume a large number of possible four-letter combinations. There are 26**4 or 456,976 four-letter combinations in the English alphabet. Of course not every combination shows up in people's names—QQQQ would be very unlikely, for instance—but the realistic number is still quite large.

Another example is a university with 10,000 students in which each student is assigned, say, a six-digit number when first arriving at the school. There are one million possible numbers but only 10,000 students. A teacher keeping a list of students in a given course may be dealing with only a hundred or so of those. Of course, since the numbers are assigned purely sequentially, the group of numbers "in use" will tend to drift over time so that at a given moment all *currently registered* students have numbers with a leftmost digit of, say, 3 or 4. But this still leaves 200,000 possible keys.

Yet a third example is the symbol table used by a compiler or assembler to keep track of the machine addresses it allocates to program variables or identifiers. The keys are the identifiers; the values are the assigned addresses. The number of possible identifiers is huge: Fortran, for example, allows a letter followed by up to five letters or digits and Pascal and Ada permit even longer names. In practice, of course, a given program will have only a few dozen variables or so, but obviously the compiler writer cannot predict which ones a programmer will choose.

In the hash table or "scatter storage" technique the entries are scattered around the table in an approximately uniform fashion. This involves designing a mathematical transformation, called the *hash function* or *key-to-address transformation*, which accepts a key as its input and returns a table address (array subscript) as its result. Such a function is usually designated h(k), where k represents a key. A pictorial representation of this is shown in Figure 8-2.

In the next section you will be introduced to a number of these transformations; for the moment, realize that a typical transformation might be simply

Figure 8-2 A key-to-address transformer.

to take the first few digits or the last few digits of the key, or to multiply the key by some number and select the middle few digits of the result. The point is that these computations generally have constant performance, since arithmetic operations generally don't depend on the value of their arguments and therefore are independent of the number of items in the table and usually of the table size as well. Given a well-chosen transformation, a table address can be delivered in O(1) time.

If, for a given key structure and desired table size, we can invent a good h(k), then the *Update* operation consists simply of passing the key of an arriving item through this "transformer" to get a table address, usually called the *hash address* or *hash code*, then storing the item there (in constant time, of course!).

Search works in similar fashion, passing the key whose value is sought through h(k), then looking in that table location. Similarly, *Delete* just removes the item to be deleted by finding its location and marking that location as "available."

All this would work wonderfully—and with guaranteed O(1) performance—were it not for the fact that there are many more possible keys than there are locations in the table, and we don't know just which keys will arive. Therefore the h(k) function *cannot* be one-to-one, and so will deliver the same table address for many different keys. So, potentially, many items will compete for the same table location.

We denote by *synonyms* the set of keys for which a given h(k) will deliver the same hash address. An entire set of synonyms is, mathematically, an equivalence class. A situation in which a given table location is occupied by one item, and then one of its synonyms arrives, is called a *collision* or *hash clash*. Designing a good hash table depends upon finding good solutions to the following two problems:

1. Find an h(k) which will minimize the number of collisions by spreading arriving records around the table as evenly and uniformly as possible.

2. Since *any* h(k) must be many-to-one, and therefore collisions are inevitable, find a good way of resolving them.

The term "hash function" derives from our desire to "chop up" or "hash together" the characters or digits of the key to get a high degree of randomness in the hash code. The next two sections of this chapter introduce, respectively, a number of different kinds of h(k) functions, and some methods of resolving collisions.

A word about one operation we haven't mentioned: *Report*. The items in a hash table are, by definiton, scattered around the table in no particular order. Moreover, in any good hashing scheme they're not even stored in contiguous locations. So Report is a rather expensive operation involving a sort. This is, of course, not much worse than Report for an unordered array, but it's worth pointing out.

8.4   CHOOSING A HASH FUNCTION

In this section we shall introduce the four main classes of h(k) functions: *truncation*, *division*, *mid-square*, and *partitioning* or *folding*. There is no one "best" hash function in general. Choice of an h(k) depends heavily on the structure of the keys, the degree of unpredictability, and the amount of extra table space the designer is willing to tolerate in the interest of achieving a fast search.

The only generalizations to be made are that certain hash functions can turn out to be disastrous, and that in the end the best way to know whether a hash function is effective is to try it in practice on real data.

8.4.1 Truncation

By *truncation* we mean just taking the first few or the last few characters or digits of the key as the hash code. We cannot do this naively: in some cases the method will work acceptably; in other cases it can be disastrous.

Consider a student ID consisting of six decimal digits, as described above. The school assigns these numbers first-come first-served, so of the million possible numbers only a fairly dense subset will be in active use at a given time. For example, at the author's college at this writing, almost all active student ID's have a high-order digit of 4 or 5.

Now take the three high-order digits of the ID as a hash code into a 1,000-item table. Almost all codes will begin with 4 or 5, and thus only about 200 of the 1,000 possible codes from 000 to 999 will actually be generated by this code. Frequent collisions are guaranteed by the fact that arriving items are really competing for only 20 percent of the available positions! On the other hand, taking the low-order three digits is much better, since at least any of the 1,000 combinations has an equal likelihood of occurrence.

This example shows one of the criteria of a good h(k): it must at least be capable of generating the full range of table addresses! Taking the first three digits of the student ID is an approach that is *obviously* wrong because it is so extreme; other key sets can have biases that are less obvious but just as damaging. It is important, then, in designing an h(k), to study the set of keys thoroughly to determine what bias there might be and then design a function which will minimize the effect of the bias.

The truncation method has an important advantage: it can be coded to run very fast, since—at least in assembly language—selecting digits or characters from a memory word is just a shifting or masking operation. This kind of operation is usually faster than an arithmetic operation like multiplication or division.

8.4.2 Division

An alternative to truncation, which works reasonably well given a hardware implementation of fixed-point division, is division of the key by the size of the table, which we will call MaxItems, then taking the remainder as the hash code. It can be shown that the best policy here is to choose a *prime number* as MaxItems—that is, make the table size a prime number. You can consider why this is so in an exercise.

8.4.3 Mid-Square

In the mid-square method the key is multiplied by itself (*squared*) and then the *middle* few digits of the result are selected as the hash code. This is shown in Figure 8–3; note that because of the "long multiplication," *all* digits of the key participate in the calculation, not just a few.

The mid-square approach is advantageous because it guarantees equal participation of all digits, so unbiased digits tend to diminish the effect of biased ones. In this way we hope to be able at least to generate all table addresses. An obvious disadvantage of the method is that squaring a long quantity like a key involves a long-multiplication operation, which can be fairly slow on most computers.

8.4.4 Folding or Partitioning

The folding or partitioning method is another way of ensuring a good randomizing of the digits of the key. The key is partitioned or divided into several

```
      K=510324

        510324
    ×
        510324
    _____
      2041296
      1020648
      1530972
      000000
      510324
    2551620
    _____
    26043|058|4976

for a 1000-element table, h(k)=058
```

Figure 8-3 Mid-square hashing function.

pieces, then the pieces are operated upon together in some way, typically by adding them together, then taking the necessary number of digits of the result as the hash code. Two different ways of doing this are shown in Figure 8–4.

This method is somewhat similar to the mid-square method in its advantages and disadvantages. All digits of the key are "hashed" together, but with possibly slow performance because of the amount of arithmetic necessary.

Having discussed a number of methods for arriving at a hash code for each arriving item, let's move on to look at some things we can do to resolve collisions when they occur.

8.5   RESOLVING COLLISIONS IN HASH TABLES

If a collision arises in attempting to place an item in the table, we need to search in a systematic and repeatable fashion for an alternative position. This is called "probing," and several different methods exist for doing it. They all depend upon selecting an "increment" function, which we shall denote inc(i), which takes a hash address (not a key) i, and produces another hash address. If *that* position is occupied, we take *that* hash address and pass it again through

```
                    K=510324
```

(a)   A key.

```
Folding Method 1: "slide" left and right sections
                51
                03
              + 24
              ————
                88
```

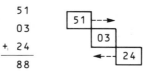

```
        for a 1000-element table,h(k)=088
```

(b)   Folding method 1: "slide" left and right sections.

```
Folding Method 2: "fold" left and right sections
                15
                03
                42
              ————
                60
```

```
        for a 1000-element table,h(k)=060
```

(c)   Folding method 2: "fold" left and right sections.

Figure 8-4   Folding method.

the increment function, and so on until we find an open position. With luck and good choices of h(k) and inc(i), we should be able to do this, in most cases, with only a few additional probes, so we still have approximately O(1) performance.

Finding an unoccupied position in the table depends upon our being able to tell that the position is empty; the two most common ways of doing this are to have the Create operation initialize all the positions of the table with some value we can use to indicate "unoccupied," and to associate with each table position a flag or code indicating "unoccupied." You will see shortly that we need to make a distinction between "currently unoccupied" and "never occupied," so whatever indicator we use will need three states, not two.

The framework for a hash-table package incorporating hash and increment functions (whose details are not supplied) is given in Figure 8–5. Update, Search, and Delete operations are shown; also, we assume that two functions CurrentlyUnoccupied and NeverOccupied are available, which hide the details of the occupancy indicator.

This kind of hash table scheme is often called *closed hashing*, because all items are stored in the same table, which is of fixed size. In the next section you will see other schemes called *open hashing* and *bucket hashing*.

8.5.1 Linear Probing

In linear probing, we let the increment function be

$$inc(i) := (i + 1) \bmod MaxItems,$$

that is, we just add one to the hash address and "wrap around" if we reach the end of the table. If that position is occupied, we add one again, continuing to search linearly for an open position. As long as there is "enough" extra space in the table, and it doesn't become too densely filled, we should be able to find a position in a reasonable number of tries.

Now let's see how Search and Delete work in such a scheme. Intuitively, we should just apply the same sequence of h(k) followed by as many calls to inc(i) as we need, checking the key of every item we find along the way until we arrive at the right one. A problem arises when we ask how we know that we've searched long enough. The simple answer—stop when we reach an "open" position—just isn't enough.

Consider the example in Figure 8–6. Suppose keys K1 and K2 are successfully placed in their "own" positions, i.e. just after being transformed by h(k). Now suppose K3, a synonym of K1, arrives. By linear probing, it will be placed adjacent to K1. K4, another synonym of K1, arrives and of course is placed just beyond K2. At this point a Search for any of the items will succeed.

Now suppose we need to Delete(K3). No problem yet: K1 is in the "official" position for K3, so we try the next position, find K3, then mark the posi-

```
package body TableHandler is

    -- THESE SIX OPERATIONS ARE NOT EXPORTED TO THE USER

    function Hash(k: KeyType) return IndexType is ...
    function Increment(i: IndexType) return IndexType is ...
    function CurrentlyUnoccupied(T: Table; i: IndexType)
            return boolean is ...
    function NeverOccupied(T: Table; i: IndexType)
            return boolean is ...

    procedure Store(T: in out Table; i: IndexType; K: KeyType) is ...
        -- store item in array; turn occupancy indicator on
    procedure Remove(T: in out Table; i: IndexType) is ...
        -- turn occupancy indicator off

    -- REMAINING OPERATIONS ARE EXPORTED TO USER

    procedure Update(T: in out Table; K: KeyType) is
        ProperHome: IndexType := Hash(K);
        Probe:      IndexType := ProperHome;
    begin
        loop
            exit when CurrentlyUnoccupied(T, Probe);
            Probe := Increment(Probe);
            if Probe = ProperHome then
                raise TableFull;
            end if;
        end loop;
        Store(T,i,K);
    end Update;

    function Search(T: Table; K: KeyType) return IndexType is
        ProperHome: IndexType := Hash(K);
        Probe:      IndexType := ProperHome;
    begin
        loop
            if    K = KeyPart(T, Probe) then
                    return Probe;
            elsif NeverOccupied(T, Probe) then
                    return Zero;
            else
                    Probe := Increment(Probe);
                    if Probe = ProperHome then
                        return Zero;
                    end if;
            end if;
        end loop;
    end Search;

    -- details omitted for Create, Report, Delete

end TableHandler;
```

Figure 8-5 Framework for a hash-table package.

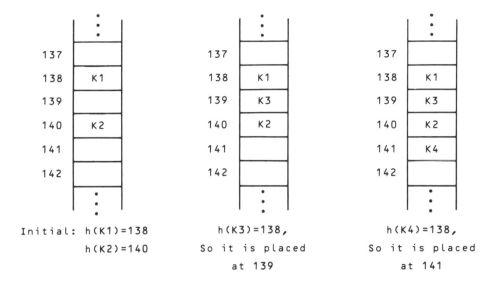

Figure 8-6   Linear probing and the clustering problem.

tion as "open." Now comes trouble: let's try to Search for K4! We'll stop at the position formerly occupied by K3 and think K4 isn't there!

The problem arises because we haven't distinguished between two meanings of "open": "never occupied" and "formerly occupied." We really need *three*, not two, states for the status indicator. One state indicates "never occupied," one indicates "formerly occupied," and the third indicates "currently occupied." We use "never occupied" as an indicator that we can stop looking in a Search or Delete operation: finding a "never occupied" position indicates that the target item isn't in the table. In an Update operation, either the "never occupied" or "formerly occupied" states can be used to place the arriving item.

Clearly linear probing will result in a situation called "clustering" where a group of synonyms will all be placed adjacently and mixed together with some "official" occupants. As the table system runs, these clusters will inevitably grow larger and larger, making the Update, Search, and Delete operations run progressively more slowly.

8.5.2 Non-Linear Probing

Other probing methods have been proposed and analyzed, to reduce clustering and thus speed up the average search performance. One way is to keep track of the number of probes, then give the increment function *two* arguments: the value of the previous hash address, and the number of probes carried out thus far to place the current item. So instead of

$$\text{inc(i)} := i + 1 \bmod \text{MaxItems},$$

we get

$$\text{inc(i,p)} := (i + p) \bmod \text{MaxItems},$$

where p is the number of probes. The first increment will be one position away; the next probe will move two positions from the last, the next probe three positions, and so on. This scheme tends to put more space between successive synonyms and thus reduces clustering.

Another method is the so-called *quadratic* hashing method, where

$$\text{inc(i,p)} := (i + ap + bp^2) \bmod \text{MaxItems}$$

where a and b are constants, usually +1 or –1. You can show in an exercise that this method spreads items out over the table and will cover exactly half the table before repeating. There is little clustering, because—as you can show in the exercise—if one search starts at location i1 and continues over i2,i3,i4,...,iN, then another search which *starts* at, say, i2 will *not* touch any of the locations i3,i4,...,iN.

Still another method is to use a pseudo-random number generator as an increment function. This will eliminate clustering, but may be a slower computation than those previously described.

All of these methods assume that successive synonyms are placed in the same closed or fixed-size table. In the next section we discuss another strategy called *bucket hashing* or *chained hashing*.

8.5.3 Bucket Hashing

The bucket hashing method establishes a "bucket" or separate storage area for all members of a given synonym (equivalence) class. Then h(k) is used just to determine in which bucket the new arrival belongs.

The most common way to do this is to use a linear-list structure for the buckets. In this case, the original table contains not records but list headers; each arriving entry goes into its appropriate list. An illustration of this appears in Figure 8–7.

This method has the obvious disadvantage of requiring extra space for the lists, but this is offset by the fact that the list nodes can be allocated dynamically (given a programming language with that feature), and thus the space not used is shared with other program structures. Furthermore, the amount of space allocated to the original table can be reduced.

There is a time/space tradeoff operating here: if the number of buckets is B, then the average list length is ActualItems/B (assuming a decently random h(k)). The linear search to find an item in the list is obviously O(Actual Items/B), so a larger B results in a shorter search.

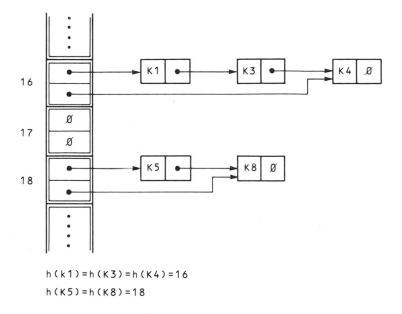

h(k1)=h(K3)=h(K4)=16
h(K5)=h(K8)=18

Figure 8-7   Bucket hashing.

A minute's thought reveals that the bucket method is really a miniaturization of the other sequential table-handling strategies. The bucket idea just cuts down the length of the sequential searches by reducing the list length from ActualItems to (an average of) ActualItems/B.

8.5.4 Ordered Hashing

In an application where it frequently happens that a Search operation frequently reports "the item is not in the table"—we call this an unsuccessful search—and the unsuccessful search is not immediately followed by an Update of that item, we can cut down the time for an unsuccessful search by inserting synonyms into a bucket in an ordered sequence, say in ascending order. Thus an *unsuccessful* search takes the same time as a successful one, because the search can stop when an item with a key greater than the target is found. Of course this strategy also *increases* the time for an Update, since a new arrival cannot just be placed at the end of a bucket.

Note that this ordering can also be used in a closed-hashing scheme (the details are left to an exercise). Remember that it is only worth the trouble where there are frequent unsuccessful searches that are *not* followed by Updates, thus for example useless in compiler symbol-table applications in which an unsuccessful search is almost *always* followed by an Update!

8.6   DESIGN: HYBRID SEARCH STRATEGIES

There is no law requiring an application to use only a single search strategy. Often several methods can be combined, perhaps in earlier and later stages of the application's task.

A good example of this is a translator—compiler or assembler—symbol table. When the translator makes an early pass over the source program, the main goal is to discover the *first* appearance of an identifier or program variable, so that an object-program address can be assigned to it. A fast Update operation is then of interest: unsuccessful searches are always followed by insertions; successful searches (the identifier is already in the table!) are not interesting at all.

In the code-generation pass of the translation, each time an identifier is discovered in the source program its address must be looked up in the symbol table. Therefore a fast Search is most desirable; Updates don't occur after the table has been built, and Deletes never occur at all in this application!

Some translator designers use *different* table structures for these two passes. For example, a binary search tree or bucket hash table is used for the scanning pass, because neither the number of identifiers nor their spelling is known before the source program is scanned, and in most languages a tremendous number of possible identifiers exists. The BST Update will probably perform reasonably close to O(log(N)) because programmers rarely if ever declare or use their identifiers in alphabetical order. Both the BST and bucket hash methods handle dynamic space allocation with ease.

On the other hand, once that pass is completed, the table contents are *fixed*, and *only* Search operations are ever done. Therefore compiler designers sometimes re-organize the symbol table between passes, sorting it and storing it in an ordered array, so that the Search operation is guaranteed to perform in O(log(N)) time.

Working out the details of this hybrid structure is left to an exercise.

8.7   SUMMARY

Our goal has been to establish a method for maintaining a dynamic table such that the performance of the Update, Search, and Delete operations approximates O(1) or constant time. We have seen that by constructing an appropriate hash function h(k), just a mathematical transformation of the key, the "official" position of an item can certainly be calculated in O(1) time.

Unfortunately, hash functions are inherently many-to-one, with many different keys—synonyms—all yielding the same hash address. Therefore the problem is really twofold: find an h(k) which minimizes the likelihood of these coincidences or collisions, then find a good way of resolving those collisions that do occur.

The truncation, division, mid-square, and partitioning methods are all commonly used as hash functions. There is no mechanical way to decide on a best h(k), but two important considerations are the uniformity with which h(k) spreads the items around the table, and speed of calculation.

The two most common ways of resolving collisions are the closed method and the open or bucket method. In the closed method, when the "official" position of an arriving item is already occupied, a search ensues which probes for the first open position by using an increment function inc(i), then places an arriving item there. Several different increment functions are possible, for example linear, quadratic, or random. Each of these methods has its strengths and weaknesses regarding uniform spread and speed; what they have in common is a sequential search, whose linear performance damages the ability to place or search for an item in constant time. So in practice, our goal of O(1) performance is achieved only approximately.

In the open or bucket collision-resolution method, items in the same synonym class are all placed in a bucket, typically a linear list. While detailed implementations vary and small optimizations are possible, there is usually a linear search involved in at least one of the operations.

8.8 EXERCISES

1. In designing a hash table where h(k) is a division-method function, show why it is best that the divisor and therefore the table size be a prime number.

2. A certain computer does all its arithmetic and array subscripting in *binary-coded decimal,* not the usual binary integer. A word in this machine consists of *eight* decimal digits; characters are coded as two decimal digits, according to the following code:

0 − 9	00 thru 09
A − I	11 thru 19
J − R	21 thru 29
S − Z	32 thru 39

    Now consider this hash-coding problem. There is a table of 100 items, indexed by 2-digit decimal subscripts. The key part of each item is a four-letter sequence. A hashing method is proposed in which h(k) is computed by dividing the key by 10 (integer division!) then taking the rightmost two digits of the result. Find h(k) for each of the keys MARY, JACK, WILL, and MACK. Is this a good hashing method? Why or why not?

3. Suggest strategies for implementing the Report operation for a hash table. Don't forget that Report must print out the table in sorted order by key.

4. Clearly the midsquare method is easier to implement if the table size is a power of 2 and h(k) is written in a language (assembler, for example) which allow easy extraction of bits. Design a high-level language implementation of this method, using some programming language that doesn't allow direct bit manipulation.

5. Show that the quadratic method of collision resolution eliminates clustering and covers exactly one half the table before repeating.

6. Starting with the table handler framework given in Section 8.3, fill in the details for specific hash and re-hash functions and implement the handler package.

7. Design a symbol-table scheme for a high-level or assembler language with which you are familiar, using a bucket hash method for the scanning pass of the translator and an ordered array for the code-generation pass. Show how you will reorganize the table between passes.

Chapter 9

INTERNAL
SORTING
METHODS

9.1 GOAL STATEMENT

Sorting, or putting a list of records in sequence, is an important part of all aspects of computing. To take a somewhat extreme example, one data-processing installation with which the author is familiar conducted a survey of its applications which were being run on a multi-million-dollar large-mainframe computer. It turned out that somewhere near *fifty percent* of the central-processor machine cycles were absorbed just in sorting!

In smaller-scale situations, putting a list in order is often a part of a larger program, and so it is important to understand how to develop sort procedures that will work correctly and speedily to carry out this function.

Also, the technology of sorting is well understood and many different and varied algorithms exist. Therefore comparative study of sorting algorithms gives useful experience in predicting run-time performance.

The goal of this chapter is to study various algorithms for sorting a list, where the number of records involved is small enough for all of them to fit simultaneously into main memory. We call this *internal* sorting. For each of the algorithms we consider, we will study briefly how each one performs, in "big O" terms. Most algorithms are $O(N^2)$ or $O(N \times \log(N))$, but there are some exceptions.

9.2   INTRODUCTION

Before we introduce methods for sorting arrays, we need to establish some terminology. We are given an array A(1..N) of some kind of records, each with a key of some kind (in the simplest case the record consists only of the key). Then that array is said to be *upward sorted* or *sorted in ascending order* if for every index I from 1 to N it is true that A(I)<=A(I+1). If for each I it is true that A(I) > = A(I + 1), the array is said to be *downward sorted* or *sorted in descending order*.

A *sort algorithm* or *sort procedure* is one which, given A originally unsorted, will produce a sorted array. For simplicity, we will use only *ascending* sorts, and so "sorted" will mean "upward sorted."

An *internal sort* is one which assumes that the array is of sufficiently small size that all records can fit into main memory at one time. An *external sort* is one which assumes that the number of records is so large that some of them must reside on external storage (tape or disk) at any given instant.

Given an array A, we say that a record R1 *precedes* a record R2 if R1 is located at A(I) and R2 is located at A(J) and I < J. A sort is said to be *stable* if for any pair of records R1 and R2 such that R1 precedes R2 and key(R1) = key(R2) in the unsorted array, then R1 precedes R2 in the sorted array. In other words, a stable sort preserves the relative positions of records with equal keys.

An *in situ* sort is one in which the unsorted and sorted arrays occupy the same space, possibly with the use of a small amount of auxiliary working storage to carry out the sort. In other words, no copy of the array is needed for an in situ sort.

Chapter 10 is devoted to the study of external sorting; in this chapter we shall concentrate on the presentation and performance prediction of various internal sorting methods. It must be borne in mind that each of these algorithms is designed to operate on an array of arbitrary size, whose contents are initially in arbitrary order. In predicting performance, then, we can make no assumptions about the structure of the records. We will, though, try to find the *best case*, *average case*, and *worst case* performance of a sort algorithm. Years of work on sorting theory and practice have established that most internal sorts are of growth rate $O(N^2)$ or $O(N \times \log(N))$.

9.3   SORT ALGORITHMS WITH GROWTH RATE $O(N^2)$

The simplest and most straightforward sort methods are those with growth rate $O(N^2)$. These methods are easy to understand and require little additional memory; they also have relatively small time-per-operation characteristics. For occasional sorting of reasonably small arrays, the payoff in simplicity and ease of debugging of these methods is often worth the price of quadratic performance.

The five sorts to be presented here are *Simple Selection, Delayed Selection, Bubble Sort, Linear Insertion,* and *Binary Insertion.*

9.3.1 Simple Selection Sort

Our first sort is intuitively very easy to understand. Given the array A(1..N) we are asked to sort ascending, we *select* the smallest item in the array and place it in the first position, then the second smallest and place it in the second position, and so on. This is done, say, for the first position by comparing key(A(1)) with key(A(2)), and *exchanging* if key(A(2)) is smaller. We then compare (the possibly new) key(A(1)) with key(A(3)), exchanging if necessary, and so on until key(A(1)) and key(A(N)) are compared. It should be clear to you that this procedure will guarantee that the smallest item ends up in the first position.

This being the case, we can forget about A(1), and do the same thing with A(2) through A(N), which will bring the second smallest item to the second position. If we call each scan of the partial array a *pass*, then we will finally execute a pass such that A(N − 1) and A(N) find their proper places, and the array will be sorted. The sort process is illustrated in Figure 9–1; a procedure appears in Figure 9–2. This procedure uses an auxiliary procedure Swap(x,y:**in out** valuetype) which interchanges two values. An invocation like Swap(A(i),A(j)) interchanges the i-th and j-th values in the array A. The procedure Swap will be used by many of the algorithms in this chapter.

What is the time performance of this algorithm? The structure of this program is a double loop with a decision inside. We accommodate the decision, as outlined in Chapter 2, by assuming that the slower leg is always executed. So we assume that an exchange is done every time a comparison is done. The first pass requires N − 1 operations, the second N − 2 operations, and so on. The N-1st pass requires one operation. Thus the total number of operations is (N − 1) + (N − 2) + ... + 1 or N*(N − 1)/2 as you might remember from Chapter 2. Multiplying out, we get (N*N/2) − N/2, and so the algorithm is

```
25 12        12            12              12
57           57 48 37 25   25              25
48           48 57         57 48 37 33     33
37           37 48         48 57           57 48 37
12 25        25 37         37 48           48 57
92           92            92              92
86           86            86              86
33           33            33 37           37 48

First  Pass  Second  Pass  Third  Pass     Fourth  Pass
```

Figure 9-1 Simple selection sort (the reader can fill in the additional passes).

```
procedure Swap(x,y: in out KeyType) is
  Temp: KeyType;
begin
  Temp := x;
  x := y;
  y := Temp;
end Swap;


procedure SelectSort(V: in out vector) is

    Top:     integer:= V'first;
    Bottom: integer:= V'last;

begin

    for SlotToFill in Top..Bottom-1 loop
      for Candidate in SlotToFill+1..Bottom loop

        if V(Candidate) < V(SlotToFill) then
           Swap(V(SlotToFill),V(Candidate));
        end if;

      end loop;
    end loop;

end SelectSort;
```

Figure 9-2 Procedure for simple selection sort (and auxiliary Swap routine).

$O(N^2)$, since the squared term will dominate the linear term for nontrivial N (even for N = 10 we are only off by 10 percent).

Our assumption that an exchange is done for each comparison corresponds to worst-case conditions, where the original array is sorted downwards. If the original array is sorted upwards, there will be no exchanges at all done. The actual execution time, then, will be faster, but the growth rate is still proportional to the square of the array size.

9.3.2 Delayed Selection Sort

We can speed up the selection sort a bit if we try to reduce the number of exchanges that are made, under less-than-best-case conditions. We do that by delaying any exchange until the end of the pass. Instead of, for example, exchanging A(1) and A(2) if A(2) is smaller, we note in an auxiliary variable that A(2) is the smallest key we've seen in this pass, by setting this variable to 2. This is the location whose key we test against A(3), keeping track of which is smaller. At the end of the first pass, this variable will clearly have the location of the smallest key. We then exchange that record with the one at A(1).

Since in this improved algorithm we do at most one exchange per pass, the overall running time will generally be faster even though it is still a $O(N^2)$ algo-

```
function MinIndex(V: vector) return indextype is

    Min:    KeyType    := V(V'first);
    Index: indextype := V'first;

begin

    for current in V'first..V'last loop
        if V(current) < Min then
            Min := V(current);
            Index := current;
        end if;
    end loop;

    return Index;

end MinIndex;




procedure DelayedSelectSort(V: in out vector) is

    Top:    integer:= V'first;
    Bottom: integer:= V'last;
    Index: integer;

begin

    for SlotToFill in Top .. Bottom-1 loop
        Index := MinIndex(V(SlotToFill..Bottom));
        Swap(V(SlotToFill),V(Index));
    end loop;

end DelayedSelectSort;
```

Figure 9-3 Delayed selection sort (and auxiliary routine to find location of minimum value).

rithm. Figure 9–3 shows the procedure for this algorithm. The procedure uses an auxiliary function MinIndex, which finds the index (or location) in an array of the smallest value in the given array. This function is called by the main procedure using the Ada notation for an "array slice" or section of an array. For example, an invocation like MinIndex(A(i..N)) will return the index of the smallest value in the *section* of the array A from the i-th to the N-th locations, inclusive.

9.3.3 Bubble Sort

Bubble sort is another simple sort with O(N^2) worst-case performance. In this algorithm we compare the keys of *adjacent* items, exchanging if necessary. We begin with key(A(1)) and key(A(2)), then key(A(2)) and key(A(3)), and so on.

At the end of the first pass, as shown in Figure 9–4, the "heaviest" item will have "sunk" to the bottom, one location at a time.

Continuing as in the first two sorts above, we then start a second pass which runs through A(1) to A(N − 1), sinking the second-heaviest item down to the next-to-last position. As before, we will, after N − 1 passes, have the array sorted.

At first glance, this looks no better than the exchange sort. But there is a way to improve it which can make a difference. Since only adjacent items are ever compared, if we ever make a complete pass in which no exchanges are necessary, we know that the array is sorted. Indeed, if the array is *received* in sorted order, then only one pass is necessary to make that determination, and so the best-case performance is O(N)!

What we need to do, then, is maintain a Boolean, AnotherPassNeeded, which is initialized to false at the start of each pass, then set to true whenever an exchange is made. If AnotherPassNeeded is false at the end of a pass, we can stop the sort. A procedure for this is given in Figure 9–5.

Bubble Sort, then, has a running time of O(N) in the best case, O(N²) in the worst case (where the array is originally in *reverse* order). In general, of course, it will lie somewhere between.

You may be wondering why this algorithm is called "bubble" sort. Taking a close look at the process, you can see that a pass can just as easily be run "upside down," comparing first, say, key(A(N)) and key(A(N − 1)), so that "light" items "bubble up," instead of "heavy" ones "sinking down." We chose

```
 25             25             25
 57 48          48 37          37 12
 48 57 37       37 48 12       12 37
 37 57 12       12 48          48
 12 57          57             57 33
 92 86          86 33          33 57
 86 92 33       33 86          86
 33 92          92             92

First Pass     Second Pass    Third Pass


 25 12          12             12
 12 25          25             25
 37             37 33          33
 48 33          33 37          37
 33 48          48             48
 57             57             57
 86             86             86
 92             92             92

Fourth Pass    Fifth Pass     Sixth Pass (Sorted!)
```

Figure 9-4 Bubble sort.

```
procedure BubbleSort(V: in out vector) is

    CurrentBottom:     integer:= V'last;
    AnotherPassNeeded: boolean := true;
    Top:               integer := V'first;

begin

    while AnotherPassNeeded loop

        AnotherPassNeeded := false;

        for Current in Top..CurrentBottom-1 loop

            If V(Current+1) < V(Current) then
                Swap(V(Current+1),V(Current));
                AnotherPassNeeded := true;
            end if;

        end loop;
        CurrentBottom := CurrentBottom - 1;

    end loop;

end BubbleSort;
```

Figure 9-5   Procedure for bubble sort.

the algorithm the way we did to make it more intuitively comparable with the selection sort.

What factors determine how many passes will be required? It turns out that the most important factor is the fact that even though a "heavy" item can move all the way from top to bottom in one pass, a "light" one only moves up one position at a time! So the number of passes is determined by the number of positions in the longest upward trip. Because of this, the overall performance of bubble sort can often be improved by running alternate passes in opposite directions, so that a "light" item which only moved one position in a given pass will get to move much further in the next pass. You are asked in an exercise to write a program for this algorithm, which is sometimes called "shaker sort."

9.3.4 Linear Insertion Sort

Linear insertion is yet another simple sort with O(N^2) running time. This method is very similar to what one does in preparing to play a game of cards, where one receives cards one at a time and orders them in the hand. As each new card arrives, the player scans his hand, conceptually left-to-right, searching for the correct place for the new arrival, then inserts the arrival in that place.

In a programming context, let us assume that an N-element array A exists, with K < N elements in ascending order already in the first K locations. Here is an algorithm to put a new arrival in its place.

To place a new arrival:

1. Search sequentially through the array until a key is found which is greater than that of the new arrival. Call its location J.

2. Make space for the new arrival by moving the contents of A(J) through A(K) to locations A(J + 1) through A(K + 1).

3. Insert the newly-arrived element at A(J).

To sort N new arrivals, then, we begin by inserting the first arrival in A(1), then looping N − 1 times through the above algorithm.

The preceding has assumed that there are "arrivals." Where do they arrive from? We can make this an *in situ* sort by having the new arrivals simply come from the array itself. Since the first K arrivals are sorted into the first K locations of the array, the K + 1st will fit in somewhere in the first K+1 locations, and so the K + 1st location can be used to hold A(K) as it is moved. In other

25	25	25	25
⑤⑦ ← "new arrival"	57	48	37
48	④⑧	57	48
37	37	③⑦	57
12	12	12	①②
92	92	92	92
86	86	86	86
33	33	33	37
Original array	57 inserted	48 inserted	37 inserted

12	12	12	12
25	25	25	25
37	37	37	33
48	48	48	37
57	57	57	48
⑨②	92	86	57
86	⑧⑥	92	86
33	33	③③	92
12 inserted	92 inserted	86 inserted	33 inserted

Figure 9-6 Linear insertion sort.

words, the unsorted array "shrinks" from N elements down to none as the sorted one grows from no elements to N, and we can use the same physical space for both arrays, "back to back." This is shown in Figure 9–6.

Figure 9–7 gives a procedure in which the algorithm is in fact a bit simpler than we discussed here. Instead of moving a number of items after the new item's proper place has been found, we start the new item at the bottom of the sorted part of the array, moving it upward by exchanging, until it finds its proper place.

We mentioned that this sort has O(N^2) running time. To see this, consider how many comparisons need to be made to place the K + 1st "arrival." If we assume that all original orderings are equally probable, then on the average K/2 comparisons will be necessary to find the proper place for the K + 1st element. Furthermore, an average of K/2 exchanges will be required to make space.

To sort the whole array, then, involves a number of operations characterized by a series that will sum once again to (N − 1)*N/2, giving us O(N^2).

```
procedure LinearInsertionSort(V: in out vector) is

    NewArrival: KeyType;
    Top:        integer := V'first;
    Bottom:     integer := V'last;
    position:   integer;

begin

    for CurrentBottom in Top+1..Bottom loop

        NewArrival := V(CurrentBottom);

        -- find position for new arrival

        for current in Top..CurrentBottom loop
            position := current;
            exit when NewArrival < V(current);
        end loop;

        -- move others up to make room

        for i in reverse position..CurrentBottom-1 loop
            V(i+1) := V(i);
        end loop;

        -- install new arrival

        V(position) := NewArrival;

    end loop;

end LinearInsertionSort;
```

Figure 9-7   Procedure for linear insertion sort.

9.3.5 Binary Insertion Sort

Linear insertion can be speeded up by noticing that because the first K elements are *already* in order by the time the K+1st arrives, we can find the proper place for the K+1st item by using a *binary* rather than a *linear* search. Since binary search is an O(log(K)) process, the searching part of the algorithm runs much faster.

On the other hand, the moving part of the algorithm is not speeded up at all, since it still takes O(K) time. Since for nontrivial N a squared term will dominate a logarithmic term, the overall algorithm is still O(N^2) even though using binary search will indeed reduce the actual running time somewhat.

9.4   INTERNAL SORTS WITH GROWTH RATE O(N × LOG(N))

Three sort algorithms are introduced here, all with performance O(N × log(N)). These are *Merge Sort*, *Heap Sort*, and *Quick Sort*. You will notice immediately that in each of the three a price is paid for the improved "big O" performance, either in extra space required or in increased complexity of the algorithm, or both.

These sort algorithms show clearly that there are time-space and time-complexity tradeoffs which just cannot be avoided.

9.4.1 Merge Sort

Back in Chapter 2 we gave a sketch of a recursive algorithm to sort a list by merging. In this section we shall develop a non-recursive version of Merge Sort, which sorts an array with performance O(N × log(N)). The price paid for the improved performance is that a second copy of the array is needed.

Consider the general algorithm for merging two *sorted* lists L1 and L2 to create a third list L3 (these are not necessarily linked lists; we are thinking abstractly here). You may recall that the sparse-vector addition algorithm seen in Chapter 4 is a special case of this.

The algorithm proceeds by comparing the key of the first item in L1 with the key of the first item in L2. The item with the smaller key is removed from its list and placed at the end of L3. (If the keys are equal, act as though L1 had the smaller one). At this stage, one of the lists has been shortened by one item.

Now compare the two first items again, removing the one with the smaller key and attaching it to L3. If we continue this process, eventually either L1 or L2 becomes empty. The remaining items in the non-empty list are then just removed and copied to L3. Each list is traversed exactly once, and every item is copied exactly once, so the performance of the merge is directly proportional to the total number of items in the two lists.

Several illustrations of the merge algorithm are given in Figure 9–8. We now need to consider how to use this *merge* to create a *merge sort*.

In any sort, we are given an unsorted array of N items. Let us think of this array as a collection of N *sorted* lists, each with *one* item in it. For simplicity, let's assume that N is an exact power of 2; we'll remove the limitation later.

Now create a "blank" array to use as a result array. Go through the original array, merging each *pair* of items into this result array. So items 1 and 2 are merged into positions 1 and 2 of the result, and so on. When we are all finished, the result array will contain N/2 sorted lists, each with *two* items.

Copy the result array back to the original, then merge, from the original array, each *pair* of length-2 lists into the result. This will give N/4 lists of length 4. Again copy the result array back, and continue merging and copying longer and longer lists, until 2 lists of length N/2 are left in the original array. Merge these into the result array, which is then sorted! This process is illustrated in Figure 9–9.

To see the performance of this algorithm, note that each merge pass does exactly 2N operations—each item is merged once, then copied back once. If N

```
 L1      L2     L3=Merge(L1,L2)

  3       4            3
  5                    4
  9                    9


 L1      L2     L3=Merge(L1,L2)

 13       2            2
          5            5
         10           10
                      13


 L1      L2     L3=Merge(L1,L2)

  2       1            1
  4       3            3
  8       6            4
 10      11            6
 13      15            8
                      10
                      11
                      13
                      15
```

Figure 9-8 Several examples of merging.

Initially List Length=1	After 1st pass List Length=2	After 2nd Pass List Length=4	After 3rd Pass List Length=8	Finally List Length=16
23	14	-1	-1	-9
14	23	0	0	-3
0	-0	14	3	-1
-1	0	23	4	0
3	3	3	7	1
4	4	4	8	2
8	7	7	14	3
7	8	8	23	4
19	12	-3	-9	7
12	19	1	-3	8
1	-3	12	1	10
-3	1	19	2	12
10	-9	-9	10	14
-9	10	2	12	15
2	2	10	15	19
15	15	15	19	23

Figure 9-9   Merge sort (nonrecursive or "bottom-up").

```
-- GO UNTIL ONE SUBARRAY RUNS OUT

while (Left < TopLeft) and (Right < TopRight) loop

    if TempArray(Left) <= TempArray(Right) then
        V(M) := TempArray(Left);
        Left := Left + 1;

    else
        V(M) := TempArray(Right);
        Right := Right + 1;

    end if;
    M := M + 1;

end loop;


-- NOW "COPY TAIL" OF WHICHEVER SUBARRAY REMAINS

while Left < TopLeft loop
    V(M) := TempArray(Left);
    Left := Left + 1;
    M := M + 1;
end loop;

while Right < TopRight loop
    V(M) := TempArray(Right);
    Right := Right + 1;
    M := M + 1;
end loop;
```

Figure 9-10   Fragment implementing a part of merge sort.

is a power of 2, there are log(N) passes, so the growth rate of the whole algorithm is O(N × log(N)). If N is not a power of 2, the number of passes is the
logarithm of the next higher power of 2. You can show this in an exercise.

To turn this algorithm into a procedure, we show first in Figure 9–10 a
fragment which merges two adjacent sections of an array into a result array.
Figure 9–11 shows an entire procedure for Merge Sort.

```
procedure MergeSort(V: in out vector) is

    TempArray        : vector(1..V'length);
    Max              : Integer := V'length;
    CurrentLength    : Integer;  -- LENGTH OF SUBARRAYS
    M                : Integer;  -- POSITION IN RESULT
    Left, TopLeft    : Integer;  -- POSITION AND END OF LEFT
    Right, TopRight  : Integer;  -- POSITION AND END OF RIGHT

begin

    CurrentLength := 1;
    while CurrentLength < Max loop  -- NEW PHASE

        TempArray := V;
        Left := 1;
        M := 1;

        while Left <= Max loop  -- FIND PAIR OF SUBARRAYS
            Right := Left + CurrentLength;

            TopLeft := Right;
            if TopLeft > Max then
                TopLeft := Max + 1;
            end if;

            TopRight := Right + CurrentLength;
            if TopRight > Max then
                TopRight := Max + 1;
            end if;


            -- INSERT FRAGMENT HERE; MERGE SUBARRAYS


            Left := TopRight;  -- NEXT PAIR OF SUBARRAYS
        end loop;

        -- NOW DOUBLE SIZE OF SUBARRAYS
        -- AND GO BACK FOR NEXT PHASE

        CurrentLength := 2 * CurrentLength;
    end loop;

end MergeSort;
```

Figure 9-11   Complete procedure for merge sort.

This algorithm can be speeded up by avoiding the extra copying of the result array back to the original. This is done by alternating the "original" and "result" arrays, using a flag to keep track of which array is which. We leave the development of a program for this as an exercise.

Merge Sort is interesting in its own right as an internal sort, but its greatest utility is as a part of most external sort methods, where the lists to be merged reside on external files instead of on arrays. This will be shown in Chapter 10.

9.4.2 Heap Sort

Heap Sort is an important $N \times \log(N)$ algorithm for internal sorting. It is an unusual method in that no space penalty is exacted for the good performance: indeed, it is an *in situ* sort.

This method uses the concept of a *heap*, which is a rather special binary tree. Recall that an *almost complete binary tree* is one in which all leaves are at the same level, except for some which are one level higher and concentrated at the right side of the tree.

Now let us define a *heap* as an almost complete binary tree in which the key at every node is greater than or equal to the keys of its children. Note that a leaf is a heap by this definition.

One more definition will allow us to proceed: an *almost-heap* is an almost complete binary tree which fails to be a heap only because its *root* key may be smaller than one or both of its children's keys. Figure 9–12 shows some heaps; Figure 9–13 shows some almost-heaps.

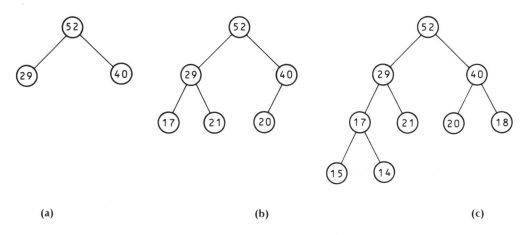

(a)   (b)   (c)

Figure 9-12   Some heaps.

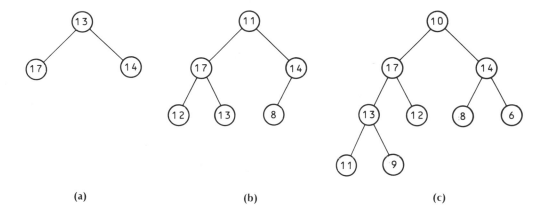

(a)   (b)   (c)

Figure 9-13   Some almost-heaps.

Creating a Heap

Let us show first how to add a new value to an existing heap. Taking the heap from Figure 9–12c as an example, let us add a key 13 to it. Let us temporarily position this new value in the next available leaf in the heap (note that because a heap is an almost complete tree this position is always known). Now, in order to maintain the heap property, the new arrival must be no larger than its parent. If it is, we are finished. Otherwise, we exchange the new arrival with its parent.

This has the effect of moving the new arrival one level up in the heap. Notice that the subtree consisting of the new arrival and its children must still be a heap. But the new arrival may *still* be greater than its new parent. So we just continue the exchange process, moving the new arrival up in the heap until it is no greater than its parent. Convince yourself that we maintain the heap property throughout. Figure 9–14a shows our heap with 13 added. As it happens, 13 is added as a leaf.

Let us now add key 43 to the heap. Notice in Figure 9–14b how the other nodes are displaced in order to preserve the heap property. Similarly, adding 95 to the heap entails putting the 95 at the root, as shown in Figure 9–14c.

Converting an Almost-Heap to a Heap

Let us look at the almost-heap from Figure 9–13c and consider how to convert it into a heap. What we need to do is first exchange the root with the *larger* of its two children—which of course imposes the heap property with respect to the *other* branch. We now have the former root located one level down, and possibly smaller than its children. So we exchange again with the larger child, and

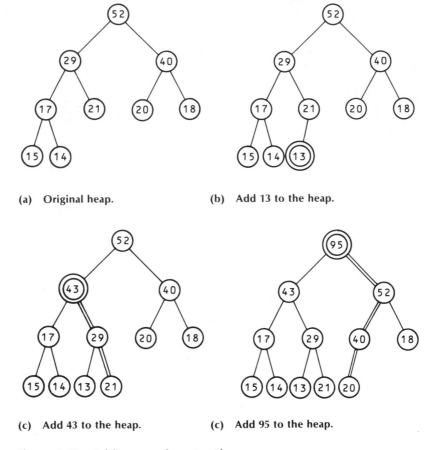

(a) Original heap.   (b) Add 13 to the heap.

(c) Add 43 to the heap.   (c) Add 95 to the heap.

Figure 9-14   Adding new keys to a heap.

continue this process until the former root key finds its proper place (i.e. no smaller than either of its children). Since only the root was out of place to begin with, the process leaves us with a heap. The steps in this process are shown in Figure 9–15.

Sorting a List With a Heap

Let us imagine that we have taken some unsorted list and built a heap one item at a time using the procedure from above. The largest item in the original list is now necessarily at the root of the heap.

Now take this largest key and exchange it with the key in the *rightmost* position of the *lowest level* of the heap. If we then (conceptually) cut this leaf off the tree, what are we left with? If the original heap had N nodes, we are left with an almost-heap of N − 1 nodes (remember, we are ignoring the rightmost lowest leaf).

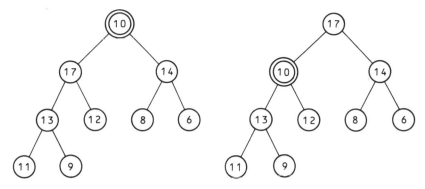

(a) Original almost-heap.

(b) 17 is 10's larger child, so exchange 10,17.

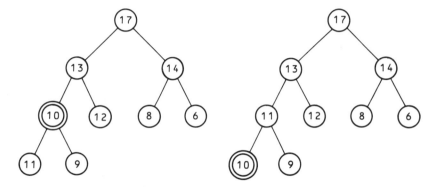

(c) Now 13 is 10's larger child, so exchange 10,13.

(d) Now 11 is 10's larger child, so exchange 10,13; we have a heap!

Figure 9-15   Converting an almost-heap to a heap.

Now we convert the almost-heap to a heap (of N − 1 nodes). It is clear that the second-largest key in the original list is now at the root. Exchange it with the rightmost lowest leaf of the (N − 9-node) heap. Conceptually cut this leaf off, getting an N − 2-node almost-heap. Convert *it* to a heap, then continue the process, until all N keys have been removed from the heap. This process is shown in Figure 9–16. The links to nodes that have been "cut off" are shown as dashed lines.

Looking now at the resulting tree (no longer a heap, of course), we see that if we traverse it *level by level* we visit the keys in ascending order!

The Practicality of Heap Sort

The practicality of Heap Sort as an *in situ* sort can be understood by recalling that an almost complete binary tree can be represented easily in array form.

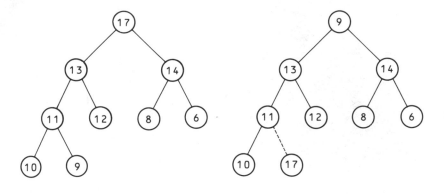

(a)   Original heap.   (b)   Exchange 17,9.

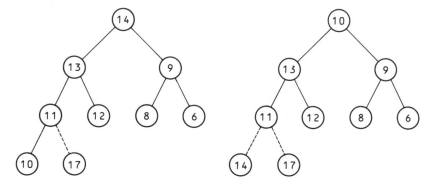

(c)   Convert to heap.   (d)   Exchange 14,10.

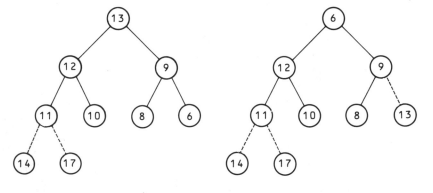

(e)   Convert to heap.   (f)   Exchange 13,6.

Figure 9-16   Sorting with a heap.

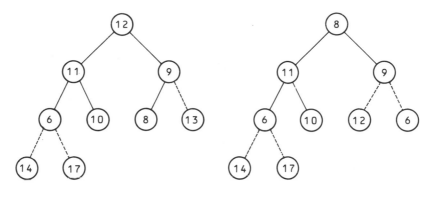

(g)   Convert to heap.   (h)   Exchange 12,8.

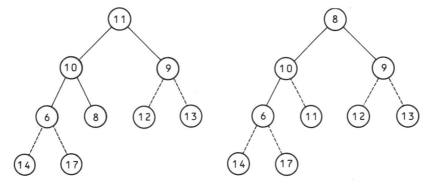

(i)   Convert to heap.   (j)   Exchange 11,8.

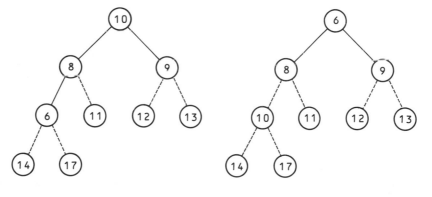

(k)   Convert to heap.   (l)   Exchange 10,6.

Figure 9-16   Sorting with a heap. (*continued*)

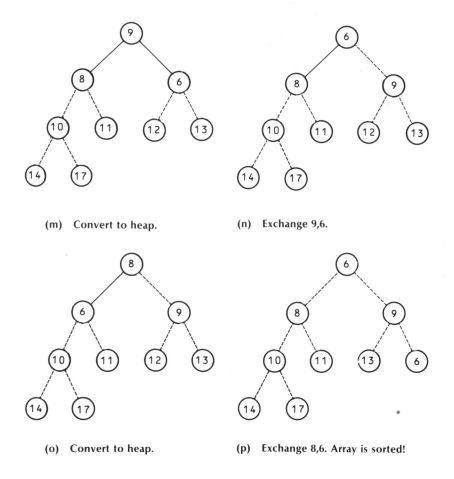

(m)   Convert to heap.   (n)   Exchange 9,6.

(o)   Convert to heap.   (p)   Exchange 8,6. Array is sorted!

Figure 9-16   Sorting with a heap. (*continued*)

Since all levels of the tree are complete except the lowest, we can store such a tree unambiguously, *level by level* in a linear array without using any pointers. In Figure 9–17 we show the heap of Figure 9–12c thus stored. All the "missing" nodes of the tree are concentrated at the right end of the array.

This implementation scheme is useful because the storage mapping function is straightforward and efficient to calculate, and level-by-level traversal of the tree is easy. If we call the array A(1..N) then the i-th node is at A(i). Where are the children of the i-th node? They are at A(2*i) and A(2*i+1) respectively (assuming that they are present at all). Where is the parent of the i-th node? Unless i = 1 (the root node), the parent is at A(i/2) (integer division!).

Furthermore, the i-th level of the tree begins at A(2**(i − 1)), and all items at that level follow immediately. So, looking back at the tree resulting from the

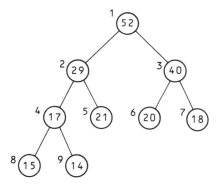

(a)   Heap of Figure 9-12c, with nodes numbered.

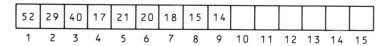

(b)   Array view of the heap.

Figure 9-17   Array and tree views of a heap.

Heap Sort in the previous section, in this implementation that tree would be a sorted array!

We can thus implement Heap Sort for an *arbitrary* unsorted array as follows:

Heap Sort:

1. A(1) is a heap trivially.

2. Make a heap of the entire array by adding the values in A(2) through A(N) in turn. The heap "grows" in the left end of the array; the values yet to be added dwindle in the right end.

3. Remembering that the rightmost lowest key is now at A(N), exchange it with A(1), and convert this almost-heap A(1)..A(N − 1) into a heap.

4. Continue the process in (3) by exchanging A(N − 1) with A(1), converting to a heap, and so on.

The heap is now dwindling in the left end of the array, and the sorted list is growing in the right end!

The various parts of Figure 9–18 show procedures for adding a new value to a heap (Figure 9–18a), converting an almost-heap to a heap (Figure 9–18b), building a heap from an array (Figure 9–18c), sorting a heap (Figure 9–18d),

```
procedure ExtendHeap(V: in out vector) is

--   assumes V(1) .. V(V'last-1) is a heap;
--   extends heap by adding V(V'last) to it.
--   Note that this will appear in a loop with V'last
--   increasing each time through.

   child:  integer := V'last;
   parent: integer := child / 2;

begin

   while (parent > 0)
       and then (V(child) > V(parent)) loop

     Swap(V(child),V(parent));
     child := parent;
     parent := parent / 2;

   end loop;

end ExtendHeap;
```

(a)   Adding a new element to a heap.

Figure 9-18   HeapSort procedures.

and finally a "driver" program called HeapSort which runs the whole process (Figure 9–18e).

What is the performance of Heap Sort? We can estimate it conservatively by noting that since the tree we are using is balanced, its depth is equal to $\log(N) - 1$, where the log is taken to the base 2 and N is the number of nodes rounded up to the next higher power of 2.

Now in the procedure BuildHeap, items are moved upward in the tree by ExtendHeap. Since an item cannot move higher than the root, it cannot move more than $\log(N) - 1$ levels. Since there are—rounded upward—N items, this gives us $O(N \times \log(N))$ performance for BuildHeap. Similarly, in the procedure SortHeap, items are moved downward in the tree by AlmostHeapTo-Heap. No item can move down more than $\log(N)-1$ levels; there are N items, so we have $O(N \times \log(N))$ here as well. Thus the overall performance is $O(N \times \log(N))$.

Suppose the original array is already sorted? Since all the larger items are at the right hand end of the array, they are at the bottom of the tree to be turned into a heap. Thus items will have further to move into their "heap" positions if the array is sorted or nearly so. Heap Sort's worst case performance, then, is for a sorted array. On the other hand, Heap Sort's best case performance is achieved when the original array is sorted *downward*, since in that case it is a heap already!

```
procedure AlmostHeapToHeap(V: in out vector) is

--  assumes V(1) .. V(V'last-1) is an "almost heap",
--  that is, it would be a heap except that V(1) may be
--  smaller than one or both of its children

    L:       integer := V'last;
    parent:  integer := 1;
    child:   natural := 2;
    placed:  boolean := false;

begin

    while (child <= L) and not placed loop

      if child+1 <= L then       -- parent has 2 children

        if    V(parent) >= V(child)
              and V(parent) >= V(child+1) then
          placed := true;

        elsif V(child) > V(child+1) then
          Swap(V(parent),V(child));
          parent := child;    --left child was larger
          child := 2*parent;

        else
          Swap(V(parent),V(child+1));
          parent := child+1; --right child was larger
          child := 2*parent;
        end if;

      else                          --parent has only one child
        if V(parent) >= V(child) then
          Swap(V(parent),V(child));
        end if;

          placed := true;

      end if;

    end loop;

end AlmostHeapToHeap;
```

(b)   **Converting an almost-heap to a heap.**

Figure 9-18   HeapSort procedures (*continued*)

Heap Sort is interesting partly because it can be made to run with a relatively small time per operation: parents and children are calculated by dividing and multiplying by 2, respectively. These operations can be implemented as single-bit shifts in assembly language, or in a high-level language which supports bitwise shifting.

```
procedure BuildHeap(V: in out vector) is

--  given a vector V(1) .. V(V'last), build a heap in place

begin

   for i in 2..V'last loop
      ExtendHeap(V(1..i));
   end loop;

end BuildHeap;
```

(c)   Building a heap in place.

```
procedure SortHeap(V: in out vector) is

--  assuming V(1) .. V(V'last) is a heap, sort it in place.
--  also assume that the heap has at least three elements.

begin

   for i in reverse 3..V'last loop
      Swap(V(1),V(i));
      AlmostHeapToHeap(V(1..i-1));
   end loop;

end SortHeap;
```

(d)   Sorting a heap.

```
procedure HeapSort(V: in out vector) is

      --  insert code for ExtendHeap here

      --  insert code for AlmostHeapToHeap here

      --  insert code for BuildHeap here

      --  insert code for SortHeap here


--  Heapsort driver; just calls BuildHeap and SortHeap.

begin

   BuildHeap(V);
   SortHeap(V);

end HeapSort;
```

(e)   Driver routine.

Figure 9-18   HeapSort procedures (*continued*)

9.4.3 Quicksort

Quicksort is one sorting method that has been shown by much experiment to perform well in the average case: on the average Quicksort requires $O(N \times \log(N))$, even though its worst-case performance is $O(N^2)$.

Quicksort is often called *partition sort*. It is in fact a recursive method, in which the unsorted array is first rearranged so that there is some record, somewhere in the middle of the array, whose key is greater than all keys to its left and less than or equal to all keys to its right.

Once this "middle" record (which is probably *not* really in the middle of the array) is found, the same method can be applied again to sort the section of the array to its left, then to sort the section of array to its right.

This algorithm is thus another example of a "divide and conquer" method, where a structure is divided in two pieces by some criterion, then the two pieces are attacked separately. Each piece is then subdivided, and so on, until the whole structure is processed.

Philosophically this method is in the same category as binary search, and with the binary search tree methods we have seen earlier.

The Quicksort Algorithm

The idea is to take a guess at a "median" or "middle" value, one an element in the array such that half the other elements are less and the other half greater than the median. It would be a true median if exactly half the elements were greater, half less, and we could partition it into equal-size pieces. In general, we won't guess correctly, but whichever value we guess will clearly let us partition the array into two pieces—generally of unequal size—such that one piece has all the smaller elements and the other piece all the larger ones.

How shall we take a guess? Since we're not assuming any prior ordering in the array, any element has as good a chance of being the median as any other. So we might just as well take the first element in the array. In fact, we'll be a little more clever than that; since the first few items in the array could all be the same value, we'll choose the leftmost *distinct* element. The procedure Find-Pivot presented in Figure 9–19 determines the location of the pivot element. (Since our guessed "median" really isn't a median, because in general it doesn't fall in the middle of the array, it's conventional to call it a "pivot" instead.)

Now, having found the location of the pivot, how do we partition? The idea is to start two "cursors" moving: one will move rightward from the left end of the array, the other leftward from the right end. The rightward-moving cursor (which we'll call "up") will keep moving as long as the elements it scans are less than the pivot; the leftward-moving one (which we'll call "down") will keep moving as long as the elements it scans are greater than the pivot.

If the "up" cursor finds a value greater than the pivot and the "down" cursor finds one less than the pivot, those two values are exchanged. Then the cursors are started again from those points.

```
procedure FindPivot(V:      in out vector;
                     pivot: out integer) is

   left:     integer  := V'first;
   right:    integer  := V'last;
   FirstKey: KeyType := V(left);

begin

   pivot:=0;
   for up in left+1 .. right loop

      if    V(up) > FirstKey then
         pivot := up;
         exit;

      elsif V(up) < FirstKey then
         pivot := left;
         exit;

      end if;

   end loop;

end FindPivot;
```

Figure 9-19   Procedure to find pivot point.

Eventually, the two cursors will meet. At the point where they meet, all values to the left are guaranteed to be less than the pivot and all values to the right are guaranteed to be greater than the pivot. We call that meeting point the "partition point," and the procedure Partition in Figure 9–20 computes it.

Now we can write a procedure Quick, which first finds a pivot, then finds the partition point for that pivot. At that stage, the array is partitioned into a section with "smaller" values on the left and a section with "larger" values on the right. But the two sections are not yet sorted. On the other hand, we can sort them by calling Quick recursively, first to sort the left section, then to sort the right section. This recursive procedure appears in Figure 9–21.

All that remains is to write a "driver" called QuickSort, which just calls Quick with the entire initial array as input. The entire procedure is shown in Figure 9–22. In Figure 9–23 you can see the various phases of the process as applied to a ten-element array.

Quicksort performs, for the average case, in $O(N \times log(N))$ time. Interestingly, its worst case, which approaches $O(N^2)$, occurs when the original array is already sorted. In that situation, every attempt to partition the array results in a left subarray of length 1 and all the rest of the items in the right subarray.

```
procedure Partition(V:            in out vector;
                    pivot:        in KeyType;
                    PartitionPoint: out integer) is

  up   : integer := V'first; -- cursors to find
  down : integer := V'last;  --    partition point

begin
  loop

    Swap(V(up),V(down));

    while V(up) < pivot loop
      up := up + 1;
    end loop;

    while pivot <= V(down) loop
      down := down - 1;
    end loop;

    exit when up > down;

  end loop;

  PartitionPoint := up;

end Partition;
```

Figure 9-20   Procedure to partition array.

```
procedure Quick(V: in out vector) is

  PivotPoint:     integer;
  Pivot:          KeyType;
  PartitionPoint: integer;
  left:           integer := V'first;
  right:          integer := V'last;

begin
  FindPivot(V(left..right),PivotPoint);

  if PivotPoint /= 0 then

    Pivot := V(PivotPoint);
    Partition(V(left..right),Pivot,PartitionPoint);

    Quick(V(left..PartitionPoint-1));
    Quick(V(PartitionPoint..right));

  end if;

end Quick;
```

Figure 9-21   The recursive procedure Quick.

```
procedure QuickSort(V: in out vector) is

    -- insert code for FindPivot here

    -- insert code for Partition here

    -- insert code for Quick here


begin  -- body of QuickSort

    Quick(V(V'first..V'last));

end QuickSort;
```

Figure 9-22   QuickSort procedure.

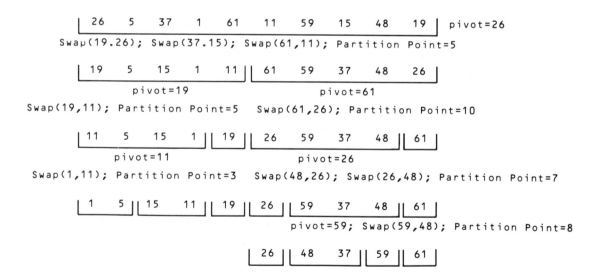

Figure 9-23   QuickSort applied to 10-element array (the reader can complete the algorithm)

9.5   OTHER INTERNAL SORT ALGORITHMS

In this section we introduce three additional sort algorithms whose performance does not fall neatly into either of the preceding categories.

The first algorithm is *Shell Sort*, a generalization of bubble sort, which performs, on the average, in $O(N \times \sqrt{N})$ time. The second is *Quadratic Selection Sort*, an interesting method which trades space for time to give, again, the growth rate of $O(N \times \sqrt{N})$. The third and last internal sort is *Radix Sort*, which is based on the methodology developed for use in punched-card sorting machines, in the days before digital computers. Its performance is $O(N)$, with a high price paid in extra space required and time per operation.

9.5.1   Shell Sort

The Shell sort (named for its inventor, D. Shell), can be viewed as a modification of either the bubble sort or the linear insertion sort. The essential premise of this method is the observation that the bubble sort moves items in an array A to their final position only one "slot" at a time. The Shell sort tries first to put the array in rough order by comparing items that are separated from each other instead of adjacent ones.

This is done by choosing a *distance* and sorting subfiles, each of which is made up of elements separated from each other by that distance. For example, suppose this distance—call it d—is 5 and the total length of the array is 15. We sort the subarray {A(1),A(6),A(11)} (most people use linear insertion to do this). Then the subarray {A(2),A(7),A(12)} is sorted, followed by {A(3),A(8),A(13)}, and so on until {A(5),A(10),A(15)} is done.

Having put all the subarrays in mutual order—which moves small items near the top and large items nearer the bottom in larger steps than in bubble sort—we then reduce the distance. While the optimal selection of distances is still an unsolved problem, some experiments have shown that the best intermingling of subarrays occurs when the distances are all relatively prime. In our example, then, let us choose the next d=3, so the subarrays {A(1),A(4),A(7),A(10),A(13)}, {A(2),A(5),...,A(14)}, and {A(3),A(6),...,A(15)} are sorted.

We continue taking smaller and smaller d's, until we have a phase such that d = 1; this last phase is a final linear insertion on the whole array. Figure 9–24 gives an example of the Shell sort applied to an array; Figure 9–25 shows an Ada procedure for this algorithm.

The performance of Shell Sort is in the neighborhood of $O(N \times \sqrt{N})$; the calculations are beyond the scope of this book.

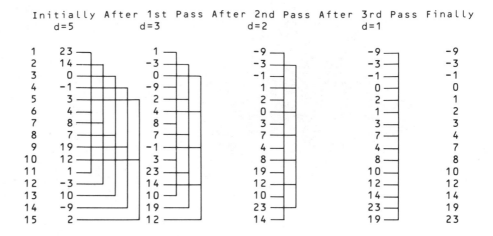

Figure 9-24 Shell sort, applied to a 15-element array.

```
procedure ShellSort(V: in out vector) is

    N:          constant integer:= V'last;
    Distance: integer := N/2;
    j:          integer;

begin

    while Distance > 0 loop

        for i in Distance+1 .. N loop

            j := i - Distance;
            while j > 0 and then V(j) > V(j+Distance) loop
                Swap(V(j),V(j+Distance));
                j := j - Distance;
            end loop;

        end loop;

        Distance := Distance/2;
    end loop;

end ShellSort;
```

Figure 9-25 Procedure for Shell sort.

9.5.2 Quadratic Selection Sort

An interesting sort algorithm trades a penalty in space for a payoff in running time, where the running time is $O(N \times \sqrt{N})$. Let $\sqrt{N}$ be denoted by M. The unsorted array is divided up into segments of M (rounded up to the nearest integer, of course) and copied into a square array M × M. Call this array A′. The algorithm then proceeds as follows:

Quadratic Selection Sort:

1. By comparing and swapping as in the delayed selection sort, get the smallest element in each row of A′ into the first position of that row.
2. Find the smallest element in the first column of A′, and output it to the sorted array.
3. Replace that element in A′ by the smallest element in the row from which it came, and "compress" the row by replacing the element just removed by the current last element in the row.

26 5 37 1 61 11 59 15 48 19 0 -3 7

(a) Original unsorted array.

26	61	48	7
5	11	19	
37	59	0	
1	15	-3	

(c) Row minima located and placed at heads of rows.

7	61	48	26
5	11	19	
0	59	37	
-3	15	1	

(b) Initial square array made from the array above.

7	61	48	26
5	11	19	
0	59	37	
1	15		

Result Array -3

7	61	48	26
5	11	19	
37	59		
1	15		

-3 0

7	61	48	26
5	11	19	
37	59		
1	15		

-3 0 1

(d) A few steps of the algorithm (the reader can complete it).

Figure 9-26 Quadratic selection sort.

4. Continue the process until all rows are empty. The original array is then sorted.

An example of this algorithm in action is shown in Figure 9–26; writing a procedure for it is suggested as an exercise.

What is the running time of quadratic selection? Since when we first create A', each row has at most M elements, and there are M rows, initializing the first column as in step 1 takes at most $M \times M = N$ operations. Step 2 takes $M - 1$ operations; step 3 takes a variable number, but surely no more than $M - 1$. But we carry out steps 2 and 3 once for each item in the original array or N times. So we have the sum of an $O(N)$ term and an $O(N \times M)$ term; for nontrivial N the second term dominates, and thus the overall algorithm is $O(N \times M) = O(N \times \sqrt{N})$.

9.5.3 Radix Sort

This sort is probably best explained in terms of electromechanical punched-card sorting machines. These machines were widely used during the 1930s, 1940s, and 1950s before computers became widespread; their popularity declined through the 1960s and 1970s; they are hardly to be found anymore. The author recalls having to operate such a machine for several consecutive weeks as part of a summer job he held in 1965.

A punched card, as you probably know, has eighty data positions or columns, each with twelve rows. Ten of these rows are numbered 0 through 9. Each position can hold one character of data. If we assume for simplicity that all the data is numeric, then each character is one of the digits 0 through 9, and a digit in a given column is encoded by a single punch in the appropriate row of that column. A numerical value—a sequence of numeric digits—is encoded by a single punch in each of several consecutive columns. Figure 9–27 shows a section of a punched card with a six-digit number punched in it in positions 5 through 10.

The card sorter has thirteen bins or pockets, each capable of holding several hundred cards, and an equally large input hopper. The machine operates on one column at a time. The operator sets an indicator to the desired column, loads the input hopper with a face-up stack of cards, then presses the start button. The machine, with much noise and furious movement of cards, places each card in the bin corresponding to the row in which a punch appears *in the given column*. The thirteenth bin collects those cards with no punch at all. Figure 9–28 shows a diagram of the machine.

How is such a machine used to sort a deck of cards on an entire key? The deck must be run through the card sorter once for each digit of the key! Here is a sketch of an algorithm:

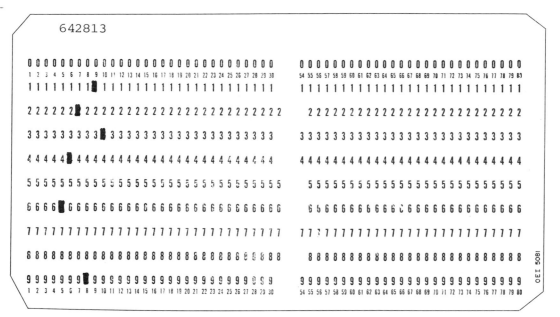

Figure 9-27 A punched card.

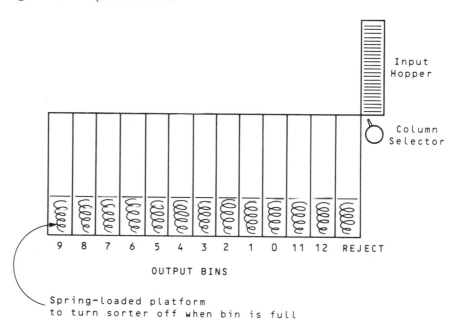

Figure 9-28 Electromechanical punched-card sorter.

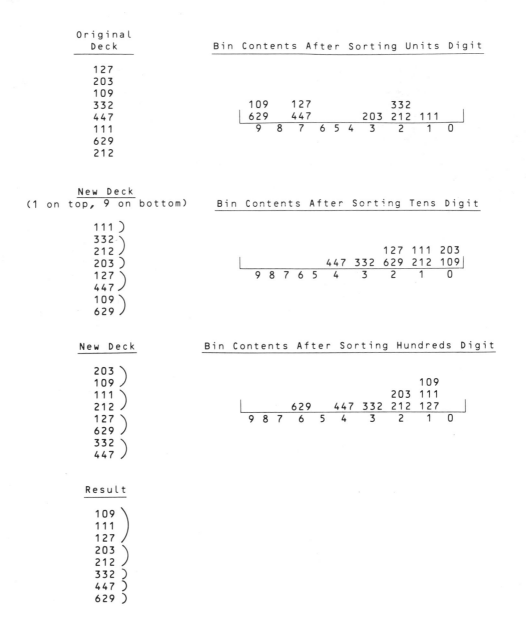

Figure 9-29 Radix sort, as used by a card sorter.

Card Sorter Algorithm:

1. Set column indicator to *rightmost* (low-order) column of key to be sorted.
2. Place deck, face up, in input hopper.
3. Start sorter; wait until input hopper is empty (the machine stops by itself).
4. Move column indicator one column to the left.
5. Remove the decks of cards from each bin, making one deck with the contents of bin 0 on top and the contents of bin 9 on the bottom.
6. If all columns have not yet been processed, move column indicator one position to the left and repeat steps 2 through 5.

In Figure 9–29 we illustrate this sort for an eight-card deck to be sorted on a three-digit key. Be sure you understand why the sort must begin with the rightmost digit and move to the left, and why it won't work the other way around.

This sort algorithm can be adapted to operate on a computer, and works rather well if we realize that the keys are represented as binary sequences (like everything else on most computers!). If the keys are unsigned binary integers, or character strings, we can just treat the keys as bit sequences. We just use two "bins," generally arrays, and sort bit by bit, from the rightmost bit to the leftmost. This sort is called *radix sort* because the number of bins is determined by the radix or base of the digits being sorted.

What is the performance of this algorithm? The number of passes is determined, clearly, by the number of bits in the key. For a fixed-size key, the number of passes is fixed. Each pass examines each record exactly once, so the total number of operations is a constant (the number of passes) times the number of records (N); in other words this sort has growth rate O(N). It is not very widely used because of the extra space required for the bins and because the usually large number of passes means that the O(N) growth rate may well be dominated by the very large constant of proportionality.

9.6 SUMMARY

In this chapter you have seen a number of sorting methods, along with performance-estimation discussions. You should be equipped to make a sensible choice of a method for whatever sorting problem faces you.

Clearly, if you only need to sort a small list, the best method is the one that's easiest for you to write, since in that case your time is more expensive than the computer's. On the other hand, if you have a large list to sort, particularly as part of an application that will be run frequently, it pays to think the problem through and choose wisely, because the computer time used in the sort will no longer be negligible.

Bear in mind that all of the methods in this chapter are designed to support *internal* sorts. The next chapter takes up another important sorting problem, namely, sorting lists too large to fit in main memory all at once. Methods for solving this problem are called *external* sorts, involving auxiliary space on disk or tape.

9.7   EXERCISES

1. Refer to the bubble sort procedure presented in Section 9.3.3. Define "trip length" as the number of *upward* moves an element in the array must make on its way to its final position. Show that the number of passes required by the bubble-sort algorithm depends upon the maximum of all the trip lengths in the array.

2. In the bubble sort algorithm of Section 9.3.3, we begin at the top of the array and move elements downward. Write a procedure for a bubble sort in which we start at the *bottom* of the array and move elements *upward*.

3. In the modified bubble sort often called "shaker sort", we run successive passes *alternately* in the upward and downward directions. Write a procedure for this sort. Why does this method sometimes offer improved performance?

4. Calculate the number of passes in the merge sort when the number of elements in the array is not an exact power of 2.

5. Write a modified merge sort procedure in which it is not necessary to re-copy the array after each pass. Hint: do this by "switching" alternately the input and output arrays.

6. Write a procedure implementing the quadratic selection sort of Section 9.5.2.

7. Write a procedure implementing a decimal radix sort, assuming that the keys are all the same length and are represented as strings of digits.

8. Write a procedure implementing binary radix sort, as suggested in Section 9.5.3. Note that since only two bins are required, only one additional array is needed because the array can be filled from both ends, all "0" elements inserted from the top of the array, all "1" elements from the bottom.

Chapter 10

SORTING EXTERNAL FILES

10.1 GOAL STATEMENT

We have studied a number of sorting algorithms, all of which assume that the file to be sorted is sufficiently small to fit in the computer's main memory. Given the actual size of many real-world files, and the size of main memory on most actual machines, it is clear that not all files can fit in main memory. Let us thus direct our attention to sorting large files stored on external devices.

External sorting algorithms are based on the *merging* process, introduced as the Merge Sort algorithm in the previous chapter. The underlying principle of these algorithms is to break the file up into unsorted subfiles, sort the subfiles, then merge the sorted subfiles into larger and larger sorted subfiles until the entire file is sorted. That is why these algorithms are often called Sort/Merge algorithms.

Sort/Merge algorithms generally begin with a *distribution* phase, which creates a number of sorted subfiles on external devices; this is followed by a series of merge phases, to produce one sorted file at the end.

This chapter is somewhat less formal than the others. We have chosen to omit programs for most of the algorithms, because the idea of the chapter is just to give a quick overview of external sorting issues.

10.2   THE TWO-WAY MERGE

The merge process for sequential files stored externally is so fundamental to the whole class of Sort/Merge algorithms that it makes sense to study it first. The external merge is very similar to the internal merge as applied to items in an array or linked list.

We start with two previously-sorted sequential files F1 and F2, and merge them to produce a new sorted file F3. Assuming the two input files to be sorted in ascending order on key k, then, informally, we begin by reading one record from each file and writing the one with the smaller k to the output file. If that record came from F1, we read a new record from F1; if it came from F2, we read a new record from F2. Then we just continue the process.

Eventually, F1 or F2 becomes empty first. At this point, we copy the remaining records from the *other* file onto F3. This is known as "copying the tail." When we are finished, F3 will be a single sorted file.

Calling this process TwoWayMerge, we show an Ada procedure in Figure 10–1.

10.3   THE K-WAY MERGE

A merge does not have to be limited to two files. If we have K sorted files, these can be merged simultaneously to produce a K+1-st sorted file. Informally, we start the process by reading a record from each of the K files, writing to the output file F(K + 1) whichever record has the smallest key, then reading a new record from whichever file the output record came from. When one of the K input files runs out of records, we continue the process with the remaining K − 1 files until only one file is left with records on it, then we copy its tail.

A diagram of this process is shown in Figure 10–2; we leave writing the program as an exercise.

Since in this merge process only very limited main memory is required (just the space for one record per file, plus program space), the number of files we can merge is limited only by the number of sequential external files available to us.

10.4   SIMPLE MERGE SORTING

The preceding section assumed that we had K sorted files available. We can turn the K-Way Merge process into a Sort by determining how to produce the K sorted files required. In the ensuing discussion, we will use the term "tapes" to designate external devices. It is clear that these need not literally be magnetic

```
procedure TwoWayMerge(F1, F2: File_Type; F3: out File_Type) is

    R1, R2: RecordType;

    -- ASSUME FILE MANAGEMENT (OPEN, CLOSE) DONE BY CALLER

begin
    get(F1, R1);   -- ASSUME F1 AND F2 EACH HAVE AT LEAST ONE RECORD
    get(F2, R2);

    loop

        if KeyPart(R1) < KeyPart(R2) then
            put(F3, R1);    -- WRITE OUT THE SMALLER
            if End_of_File(F1) then
                put(F3,R2); -- WRITE OUT THE OTHER RECORD
                exit;
            else
                get(F1, R1);
            end if;

        else
            put(F3, R2);    -- WRITE OUT THE SMALLER
            if End_of_File(F2) then
                put(F3,R1); -- WRITE OUT THE OTHER RECORD
                exit;
            else
                get(F2, R2);
            end if;
        end if;

    end loop;


    while not End_of_File(F1) loop
        get(F1, R1);
        put(F3, R1);
    end loop;

    while not End_of_File(F2) loop
        get(F2, R2);
        put(F3, R2);
    end loop;

end TwoWayMerge;
```

Figure 10-1   A procedure for TwoWayMerge.

tape units, since often disk files are used instead. But the classical tape sort is our paradigm here.

Suppose first that we are in the happy situation where, given an N − record unsorted file, we have enough tapes $K + 1$ and main store (measured in records) R such that $R = N/K$. The problem then becomes a simple one: use K tapes; read R records at a time from the $K + 1$st tape, sort them by

F1:

F2:

F3:

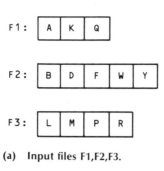

(a)   Input files F1,F2,F3.

F4:

(b)   Output file F4, after merging.

Figure 10-2   A three-way merge.

an appropriate *internal* sort(perhaps Heap Sort or Quicksort), then write this sorted file onto its own output tape; merge these K sorted files onto the K + 1st tape.

Unfortunately this situation does not occur very often; typically we are limited both in the amount of main store and the number of tapes or other devices we have. A solution, then, is as follows:

K-Way Distribution:

1. Determine R, the number of records which we can reasonably sort internally.

2. Determine K, the total number of tapes we can use; let K be an even number.

3. Sort R records at a time internally, writing the results in turn onto each of K/2 tapes, with file markers at their ends.

4. Continue the process in (3), writing additional files onto the K/2 tapes.

We now have the situation depicted in Figure 10–3, where each of K/2 tapes has, say, M sorted subfiles on it (some of the tapes will probably have only M − 1 files, since we will run out of input records before we've put the M-th file on all K/2 tapes). We have concluded a process known as *distribution*: we have *distributed* the sorted subfiles onto tapes which can be merged repeatedly until a single sorted file is achieved.

Once the distribution is accomplished, we merge from the K/2 tapes onto the other K/2 tapes, in what is called a *phase* of the Sort/Merge algorithm.

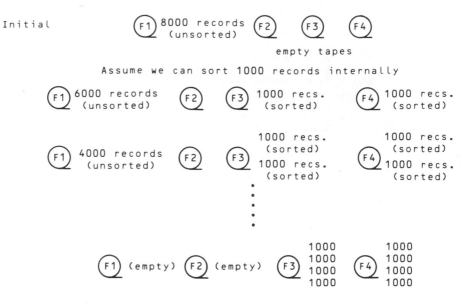

Figure 10-3   Distribution by internal sorting, k=4.

K-Way Sort/Merge, one phase:

1. Rewind all the tapes.
2. Do a K/2-way merge using the first file from each tape, writing the output onto one of the K/2 empty tapes.
3. Repeat the process in (2) for each of the rest of the K/2 empty tapes.
4. Repeat (1) through (3), merging in rotation onto the K/2 files until the original K/2 files are empty.

We have now created files of R*(K/2) records on K/2 of the tapes. This process of "bouncing" between groups of K/2 tapes is continued through additional phases, until finally there is at most one file on each of K/2 tapes; these can be merged in one final pass onto the output tape. This is illustrated in Figure 10–4.

10.5   THE "NATURAL" DISTRIBUTION

Suppose we are severely limited in the main store we can use? Then we cannot easily use the internal-sort method of distribution. Another method of distributing sorted subfiles onto tapes is to take advantage of the fact that most files arrive for sorting with their records in random order, which, oddly enough,

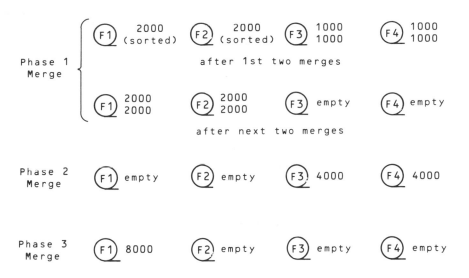

Figure 10-4   Merge process, starting with the distribution from Figure 10-3.

means that there is already a certain amount of order in them. Using now the term *run* to denote a series of records which already happen to be in the correct order, we can see that *any* file consists of a sequence of runs (in the worst case, the file is in *reverse* order, where no run is longer than one record). Figure 10–5 shows a file divided into the "runs" which naturally occur in it.

We distribute our file onto K/2 tapes by simply reading a record at a time, comparing each key against the previous one to see if order is maintained, i.e. if the new record is part of the current run. If we are sorting low-to-high, then, the new record will fail to be part of the current run if its key is less than the previous key. We continue writing records onto a tape as long as they are part of a run. A record which is not part of the current run obviously begins a new run, in which case we switch to a new output tape.

We now continue distributing runs onto tapes in rotation, just as we distributed sorted subfiles in the previous example. When all runs are exhausted, we are ready to merge as described in the previous section. This distribution is shown in Figure 10–6, for the file given in Figure 10–5.

The advantage of the "natural" distribution is that time and space are saved since we don't have to sort internally; the chief disadvantage is that runs are of unequal length and we cannot predict how many of them there will be. There may, then, be many more merge phases required since runs may be very short—in the worst case, only one record long!

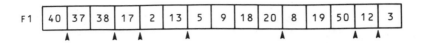

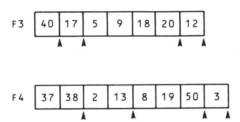

Figure 10-5   An unsorted file (note the runs, marked by ˆ).

Figure 10-6   Distribution of the runs from Figure 10-5 onto two tapes. (note the runs, marked by ˆ).

10.6   POLYPHASE SORTING

In the preceding examples we have merged by using K/2 tapes for input and K/2 tapes for output in each of the merge phases. Another approach is to notice that it is not really necessary to empty all K/2 tapes before beginning a new phase: we can in fact use K-1 tapes for input and *one* for output, then start a new phase whenever *any* tape is empty! When a tape becomes empty, we just make *it* the output, and the remaining K-1 tapes (which still have runs on them) as input. This is known as *polyphase merging*. A polyphase merge using three tapes for input and one for output is shown in Figure 10–7, using the same example file.

10.7   FIBONACCI DISTRIBUTION FOR POLYPHASE MERGING

The polyphase distribution of the previous section assigned runs to the K-1 tapes in strict rotation, resulting in an (approximately) equal number of runs on each tape. It turns out that polyphase merging can be improved by a more optimal distribution of runs. This can be seen by working backwards from the ideal situation where the last phase consists of merging *one* run from each of K − 1 tapes onto the K-th, leaving K-1 empty tapes and one sorted one. How could we have arrived at that situation?

F1 empty

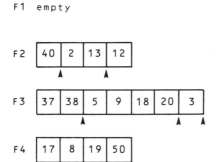

(a) Initial distribution of file from Figure 10-5.

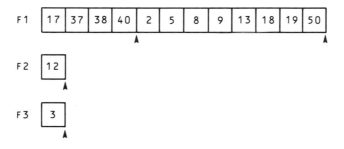

F4 empty

(b) First merge phase.

F2 empty

F3 empty

(c) Second merge phase.

Figure 10-7 Polyphase merge.

F1   empty

F2 | 2 | 3 | 5 | 8 | 9 | 12 | 13 | 17 | 18 | 19 | 37 | 38 | 40 | 50 |

F3   empty

F4   empty

(d)   Third merge phase.

Figure 10-7   Polyphase merge (*continued*)

Let us look at the example where $K = 6$. Numbering the configurations such that the *last* one is denoted Last, then configuration Last-1 is the one with one run on each of K-1 tapes. What should configuration Last-2 be? It should be one with two runs on each of K-2 tapes, one tape with one run, and one with none. How about configuration Last-3? We should have three tapes with four runs, one with three, one with two, and one with none. Several more configurations are given in Figure 10–8.

The reader may have suspected by now that there might be a systematic way to determine how a file with a given number of initial runs might be distributed to reach this ideal situation. Indeed, if we rewrite the configurations just to show the five tapes used for input and arrange the rows in descending numbers of runs, we can see that certain relationships exist among these num-

| | | | TAPE | FILE | | | |
PHASE	F1	F2	F3	F4	F5	F6	TOTAL NO. OF RUNS
Last-5	16	15	14	12	8	0	65
Last-4	8	7	6	4	0	8	33
Last-3	4	3	2	0	4	4	17
Last-2	2	1	0	2	2	2	9
Last-1	1	0	1	1	1	1	5
Last	0	1	0	0	0	0	1

Figure 10-8   Ideal last six phases of six-tape polyphase merge sort.

0	1	0	0	0	0	1
1	1	1	1	1	1	5
2	2	2	2	2	1	9
3	4	4	4	3	2	17
4	8	8	7	6	4	33
5	16	15	14	12	8	65
6	31	30	28	24	16	129
7	61	59	55	47	31	253

Figure 10-9 "Perfect" distribution of runs onto five tapes for polyphase merge sort.

bers. The rearranged table is shown in Figure 10–9; the relationships are given in Figure 10–10. They are closely related to the *Fibonacci sequences*.

The numbers of runs for "perfect" distribution can be gotten from tables and built into a program. The distribution goes as follows:

Fibonacci Distribution:

1. Given K-1 tapes, start with the second line of the table, trying to match the distribution if possible (one run per tape).
2. Repeat the next steps as long as records remain on the input tape.
3. Increment the line of the table needing to be matched.
4. Try to match the distribution required by this line.

Eventually the input file will run out of runs. Since files do not ordinarily have *exactly* the right number of runs to match a line of the table, we shall be part way through matching a line when the input runs out. In this case, to get the merge process going, we imagine that the remaining runs to match the table

$$A_5^{L+1} = A_1^L$$
$$A_4^{L+1} = A_1^L + A_1^{L-1}$$
$$A_3^{L+1} = A_1^L + A_1^{L-1} + A_1^{L-2}$$
$$A_2^{L+1} = A_1^L + A_1^{L-1} + A_1^{L-2} + A_1^{L-3}$$
$$A_2^{L+1} = A_1^L + A_1^{L-1} + A_1^{L-2} + A_1^{L-3} + A_1^{L-4}$$

substituting f_L for A_1 gives

$$f_{L+1} = f_L + f_{L-1} + f_{L-2} + f_{L-3} + f_{L-4} \text{ for } L \geq 4$$

$$f_4 = 1$$

$$f_L = 0 \text{ for } L < 4$$

These are the Fibonacci numbers of order 4.

Figure 10-10 Relationships between entries in Figure 10-9.

line have in fact been placed on the tapes; they are just empty runs. This gives us a fictitious "perfect" distribution; we merge the empty or "dummy" runs with the real ones until we reach the next lower line of the table, then continue from there.

10.8   SUMMARY

This chapter has presented some typical methods for sorting external files. As in so many other areas of computing, we have been able only to scratch the surface of this important application area; entire books can easily be devoted to the subject.

Indeed, on most large-mainframe systems, sort/merge subprograms are supplied as part of the standard libraries, and these have—it may be assumed—been thoroughly optimized to the underlying hardware and peripheral configuration.

On the other hand, *someone* has to write these standard procedures, and you may turn out to be that someone at some point in your career. Besides, understanding the underlying algorithms of sort/merge programs will enable you better to assess the performance of the one available on your system, and to "tune" it if necessary.

10.9   EXERCISES

1. Estimate the performance of the various merge-sort algorithms discussed in the chapter.

2. Write a program to carry out the simple merge sort discussed in section 10.4. If your computer does not allow (convenient) use of tapes, use disk files to simulate them.

3. Implement a polyphase sort as discussed in section 10.6. Use the "natural" distribution. Use disk files to simulate the tapes, if necessary.

4. Implement polyphase sort using the Fibonacci distribution, as presented in section 10.7.

BIBLIOGRAPHY

This bibliography is far from exhaustive and of course reflects the subjective judgments of its author. It is divided into three sections: other textbooks on data structures, books on the Ada language *per se,* and other relevant references. The Ada list is annotated, because the listed books are very recent and quite varied in their approach to the language. The additional references are mainly a selection of papers with important original results, and recent surveys with extensive bibliographies of their own.

Books on Data Structures

Aho, A.H., J.E. Hopcroft, and **J.D. Ullman.** *Data Structures and Algorithms.* Reading, Mass.: Addison-Wesley, 1983.

Baron, R.J., and **L.G. Shapiro.** *Data Structures and their Implementation.* Boston: PWS Publishers, 1980.

Beidler, J. *An Introduction to Data Structures.* Boston: Allyn and Bacon, 1982.

Berztiss, A.T. *Data Structures: Theory and Practice.* 2d. ed. New York: Academic Press, 1975.

Coleman, D. *A Structured Programming Approach to Data.* New York: Springer Verlag, 1979.

Deo, N. *Graph Theory with Applications to Engineering and Computer Science.* Englewood Cliffs, N.J.: Prentice-Hall, 1975.

Elson, M. *Data Structures.* Chicago: Science Research Associates, 1975.

Harary, F. *Graph Theory.* Reading, Mass.: Addison-Wesley, 1969.

Horowitz, E., and **S. Sahni.** *Fundamentals of Data Structures.* Rockville, Md.: Computer Science Press, 1977.

Horowitz, E., and **S. Sahni.** *Fundamentals of Data Structures in Pascal.* Rockville, Md.: Computer Science Press, 1984.

Knuth, D.E. *Fundamental Algorithms,* 2d. ed. Reading, Mass.: Addison-Wesley, 1973.

Knuth, D.E. *Sorting and Searching.* Reading, Mass.: Addison-Wesley, 1973.

Lewis, T.G., and **M.Z. Smith.** *Applying Structures.* Boston: Houghton Mifflin, 1976.

Reingold, E.M., and **W.J. Hansen.** *Data Structures.* Boston: Little, Brown, 1983.

Tenenbaum, A.M., and M.J. Augenstein. *Data Structures and PL/1 Programming*. Englewood Cliffs, N.J.: Prentice-Hall, 1979.

Tenenbaum, A.M., and M.J. Augenstein. *Data Structures Using Pascal*. Englewood Cliffs, N.J.: Prentice-Hall, 1981.

Tremblay, J.P., and P.G. Sorenson. *An Introduction to Data Structures with Applications*. 2d. ed. New York: McGraw-Hill, 1984.

Wirth, N. *Algorithms+Data Structures=Programs*. Englewood Cliffs, N.J.: Prentice-Hall, 1976.

Books on the Ada Programming Language

American National Standards Institute. *Ada Programming Language*. ANSI/MIL-STD-1815A, Washington, D.C.: Government Printing Office, 1983.
This is the official language standard for Ada—the "Bible."

Barnes, J.G.P. *Programming in Ada*, 2d. ed. Reading, Mass.: Addison-Wesley, 1984.
Introduces Ada in small steps to reasonably experienced programmers.

Booch, G. *Software Engineering with Ada*. Menlo Park, Cal.: Benjamin/Cummings, 1983.
Introduces a useful and interesting diagram notation for designing packages.

Buhr, R.J.A. *System Design with Ada*. Englewood Cliffs, N.J.: Prentice-Hall, 1984.
Focuses on system design *using* Ada; not to be used to *learn* Ada.

Cherry, G.W. *Parallel Programming in ANSI Standard Ada*. Reston, Va.: Reston Publishing Co., 1984.
Focuses mainly on tasking and parallel programming in Ada.

Gehani, N. *Ada: An Advanced Introduction*. Englewood Cliffs, N.J.: Prentice-Hall, 1983.
This is a really good *second* book on Ada. Takes a very sophisticated, comparative approach.

Gehani, N. *Ada: Concurrent Programming*. Englewood Cliffs, N.J.: Prentice-Hall, 1984.
This is a comprehensive and well-thought-out analysis of concurrent programming in general and Ada tasking in particular. Not a text on Ada.

Habermann, A.N., and D.E. Perry. *Ada for Experienced Programmers*. Reading, Mass.: Addison-Wesley, 1983.
This book is strongest in its side-by-side Ada and Pascal solutions.

Hibbard, P., et al. *Studies in Ada Style*. 2d. ed. New York: Springer Verlag, 1984.
A series of very interesting case studies for nontrivial Ada applications. Not a text.

Nissen, J., and P. Wallis, eds. *Portability and Style in Ada*. Cambridge: Cambridge University Press, 1984.
A compendium of really good recommendations for good, portable Ada programming style. Not a text.

Olsen, E.W., and S.B. Whitehill. *Ada for Programmers*. Reston, Va.: Reston Publishing Co., 1983.
A good first text.

Price, D. *Introduction to Ada*. Englewood Cliffs, N.J.: Prentice-Hall, 1984.
A good first text.

Shumate, K. *Understanding Ada*. New York: Harper & Row, 1984.
A good first text.

Wiener, R., and R. Sincovec. *Programming in Ada*. New York: John Wiley, 1983.
Focuses a lot on language syntax; doesn't discuss packages much.

Wiener, R., and **R. Sincovec.** *Software Engineering with Modula-2 and Ada.* New York: John Wiley, 1984.
Good, side-by-side discussion of package design in Ada and module design in Modula-2. Not an Ada text.

Other References

Adelson-Velskii, G.M., and **E.M. Landis.** "An Algorithm for the Organization of Information." *Dokl. Akad. Nauk SSSR, Mathemat.* (1962): 146:2, pp 263–266. (Balanced binary search trees).

Bauer, F.L., and **K. Samelson.** "Sequential Formula Translation." *Comm. ACM* (1960): 2:2, pp. 76–83. (Translating with a stack).

Comer, D. "The Ubiquitous B-Tree." *Comp. Surveys* (1979): 11:2, pp. 121–137.

Eppinger, J.L. "An Empirical Study of Insertion and Deletion in Binary Search Trees." *Comm. ACM.* (1973): 26:9, pp. 663–669.

Feldman, M.B. "Information Hiding in Pascal: Packages and Pointers." *Byte.* (1981): 6:11, pp. 493–498.

Feldman, M.B. "Abstract Types, Ada Packages, and the Teaching of Data Structures." *Proc. Fifteenth SIGCSE Technical Symposium on Computer Science Education.* (1984): pp. 183–189.

Guttag, J.V., E. Horowitz, and **D.R. Musser.** "Abstract Data Types and Software Validation." *Comm. ACM.* (1978): 21:12, pp. 1048–1064.

Hoare, C.A.R. [1962]: "Quicksort," *Comp. Journal,* 5:1, pp. 10–15.

Liskov, B.H., and **S.N. Zilles.** "Specification Techniques for Data Abstractions." *IEEE Trans. on Software Engrng.,* (1975): SE-1:1, pp. 7–18.

Liskov, B.H., and **S.N. Zilles.** "Abstraction Mechanisms in CLU," *Comm. ACM.* (1977): 20:8, pp. 564–576. (Specification vs. implementation).

Lukasiewicz, J. *Aristotle's Syllogistic from the Standpoint of Modern Formal Logic.* Clarendon Press, England: 1951.

Martin, W. "Sorting." *Comp. Surveys,* (1971): 3 (4): 147.

Maurer, W.D. "An Improved Hash Code for Scatter Storage." *Comm. ACM.* (1968): 11:1. (Quadratic hashing).

Maurer, W.D., and **T. Lewis.** "Hash Table Methods." *Comp. Surveys.* (1975): 7:1, pp. 5 19.

Nievergelt, J. "Binary Search Trees and File Organization." *Comp. Surveys.* (1974): 6:3, pp. 195–207.

Perlis, A., and **C. Thornton.** "Symbol Manipulation by Threaded Lists." *Comm. ACM.* (1960): 3:4, pp. 195–204. (Threading binary trees).

Shaw, M. "The Impact of Abstraction Concerns on Modern Programming Languages." *Proc. IEEE.* (1980): 68:9, pp. 1119–1130.

Shell, D.L. "A High Speed Sorting Procedure." *Comm. ACM,* 2:7. (1959): pp. 30–32. (Shell sort).

Shell, D.L. "Optimizing the Polyphase Sort." *Comm. ACM.* (1971): 14:11, pp. 713–719.

Singleton, R.C. "Algorithm 347: an Algorithm for Sorting with Minimal Storage." *Comm. ACM.* (1969): 12:3, pp. 185–187 (Quicksort).

Stroustrup, B. "Classes: an Abstract Data Type Facility for the C Language." *SIGPLAN Notices.* (1982): 17:1, pp. 354–356.

Williams, J.W.J. "Algorithm 232 (Heapsort)." *Comm. ACM.* (1964): 7:6, pp. 347–348.

Index

Abstract data type (ADT)
    complex number. *See* Complex number ADT
    defined, 4–5
    discussed, 5–7
    fraction. *See* Fraction ADT
    matrix. *See* Matrix ADT
    one-way linked list. *See* One-way linked list
        ADT
    queue. *See* Queue ADT
    rational number. *See* Fraction ADT
    set. *See* Set ADT
    stack. *See* Stack ADT
    table handler. *See* Table handler ADT
    text string. *See* Text string ADT
    two-way linked list, 116, 117
    vector. *See* Vector ADT
Abstraction vs. implementation, 1–4
ACBT. *See* Almost complete binary tree
Access types, 100
Access variables, 100
Acyclic directed graph, 169
Ada
    access types, 100
    access variables, 100
    array attributes, 41
    array implementation, 63
    array slice, 41
    array type, unconstrained, 85–86
    attribute inquiries, 86, 87, 91
    attributes, 20

    control structures, 46–53
    dispose operation, simulated, 128, 133–135
    dynamic memory management, 99–101, 102
    exceptions, 87, 88, 89, 90
    garbage collection, 101
    input/output instantiation, 86, 87
    keywords, 8, 15–16
    named type equivalence, 85
    new operation, 100–101, 102
    new operation, simulated, 128, 132–135
    null value, 100
    packages, 9–16
    parameters, 15–16
    pointers, 99–101, 102
    raise statement, 89
    record types, 93–95
    recursive data structures, 98
    variable types, 6
Ada-related programming support environment
    (APSE), 15
Adel'son-Vel'skii and Landis (AVL) tree, 207, 215
Adjacency list, for directed graph, 172
Adjacency matrix, for directed graph, 171, 173
Adjacency set, of graph node, 165
ADT. *See* Abstract data type
Algol, array implementation, 63
Algorithms
    binary search, 39
    binary search tree, 205
    breadth-first search, 178

Algorithms (*continued*)
  card sorter, 287
  defined, 33
  depth-first search, 175
  discussed, 33–34
  expression evaluation, 152
  factorial, 34
  Fibonacci distribution, 299
  growth rates. *See* Big O performance
  heap sort, 273
  infix to expression tree, 217
  infix to RPN, 156
  inserting linear list, 112
  K-way distribution, 293
  permutations, 37
  quadratic selection sort, 283
  recursive. *See* Recursive algorithms
  recursive merge sort, 42
  retrieval, sparse vector element, 77
  simple scanner, 181
  sorting, defined, 254
  sparse vector addition, 120
  storage, sparse vector element, 78
  string reversal, 36
  See also External sorts; Internal sorts
Almost complete binary tree (ACBT), 190–191
  as almost-heap, 266–267
Almost-heap
  conversion to heap, 267–268, 269, 275
  defined, 266–267
Antisymmetry
  of directed graph, 166, 168
  of tree, 188
APSE. *See* Ada-related programming support environment
Arcs, of graph, 165
Array attributes, 41
Array slice, 41
Array type, unconstrained, 85–86
Arrays
  ABCTs implemented as, 190, 192
  densely-packed, 71–75
  downward sorted, 254
  one-dimensional. *See* Vectors
  queues implemented as, 140–143, 144, 145
  of records, declaration of, 93–95
  rectangular, 66–69
  sparse. *See* Sparse matrices; Sparse vectors
  stacks implemented as, 147–148, 149
  two-dimensional and higher-dimensional. *See* Matrices
  upward sorted, 254
Ascending sort, 254
Associativity, of operators, 153–156
Attribute inquiries, 86, 87, 91
Attributes, of Ada, 20
AVL. *See* Adel'son-Vel'skii and Landis

B-trees, 211, 215–217
Backus, John, 63
Balanced binary tree, 191, 192–193
Band matrices, 73, 75
  bandwidth of, 73
Basic
  array implementation, 63
  cursor-oriented linked allocation, 99
  record types, implementation of, 93–95
  recursion not allowed, 35
  variable types, 6
Benchmarks, 43
Big O performance
  adjacency list, for directed graph, 172
  adjacency matrix, for directed graph, 171
  algorithm growth rates, 44–45
  balanced BST, 215
  binary insertion sort, 254, 262
  binary search, 54
  bubble sort, 254, 257–259
  bucket hashing, 248–249
  counting loop, 47–49, 50
  create operation, 55, 59
  decision, 46–47
  delayed selection sort, 254, 256–257
  delete operation, 58–59, 239, 241
  digital search trees, 212, 214
  factorials, 53
  hash tables, 239, 241
  heap sort, 262, 274
  linear insertion sort, 254, 259–261
  linked list implementation, 148
  merge sort, 54, 262, 263, 265
  multiplicatively-controlled loop, 49–52
  pop operation, 147, 148
  push operation, 147, 148

quadratic selection sort, 281, 283, 284
queues, 143, 145
quicksort, 262, 277, 278
radix sort, 281, 287
report operation, 58–59, 221, 239, 241
search operation, 56, 58–59, 208, 239, 241
searches, hybrid, 250
set permutations, 54
shell sort, 281
simple selection sort, 254, 255–256
sparse matrix operations, 121
sparse vector operations, 119–121
stacks, 147, 148
statement, simple, 45
statements, sequence of, 46
string reversal, 53–54
subprogram call, 53
table operations, 55, 56, 58–59, 206–207, 208, 221, 239, 241
update operation, 56, 58, 59, 206–207, 221, 239, 241
Binary insertion sort, 262
Binary search, 39–42, 54
Binary search trees (BSTs)
    defined, 201, 202–203
    delete operation, 208–211
    report operation, 203–204
    search operation, 207–208
    threading, 228–235
    traversals, 203–204
    update operation, 205–207
    see also Binary trees; Cross-reference generator; Expression trees; Lexical scanner
Binary trees
    defined, 189, 190
    implementation, 193, 194
    properties, 189–193
    traversals, 193, 195, 196, 197
    see also Binary search trees; Expression trees
Bit map, of a set, 19
Blocking factor, for records, 3–4
Body, of Ada package, 10–15
Boolean type, 6
Breadth-first search, for directed graph, 176, 177, 178
BSTs. See Binary search trees
Bubble sort, 257–259
Bucket hashing, 248–249

C language
    dynamic memory management, 99–101, 102
    lack of garbage collection, 132
    limitations on functions and procedures, 24–25
    overloading not allowed, 23–24
    pointers, 26, 99–101, 102
    record types, 93–95
    recursion allowed, 35
Calculator, hand-held, 149–150
Card sorting machines, 281, 284–287
Cardinality, of set, 20
Cell. See Node
Chained hashing, 248–249
CHARACTER type, 6
Characteristic function, of set, 19
Children, of node, 188
Circular array implementation of queue, 143, 144, 145
Closed hashing, 245–248
Clustering, in hash table, 247, 248
Cobol
    recursion not allowed, 35
    variable types, 6
Collisions in hash tables, resolving, 244–249
Column-major implementation of matrices, 67–70
Columns, of matrices, 66
Compilation
    of Ada packages, 15
    using expression trees, 195–201
Complement, of a set, 18
Complete binary tree, 189–190, 191
Complex number ADT
    complex sum, 25–26
    creation and decomposition, 27–28
    extensions using **new** and **dispose,** 132–135
    specification as block comment, 29, 30
    type definition and variable declaration, 25–27
COMPLEX type, 6
Concatenation, of text objects, 21, 124, 127
Concordance, 218
Conformability
    of matrices, 91
    of vectors, 87, 89
Connectivity, of directed graph, 169, 170
Constant growth rate, 44–45. See also Big O performance
Control structures, 46–53
Create operation, 55, 56, 59

Creation, process of, 2–3
Cross lists, 122
Cross-reference generator
    main program, 218, 220, 222
    scanner, 224, 226–228, 229, 230
    table handler, 220–224, 225
    see also Lexical scanner
Cursor, 129
Cursor-oriented implementation, 131
Cycle, of directed graph, 169

Data structure, 6
    in package specification, 10–11
Data type, 5–6
    in package, 9–10
Delayed selection sort, 256–257
Delete operation, 55
    for array, 57, 58–59
    for BST, 208–211
    for hash table, 239, 241, 250
    and sparse vectors, 77–78
Densely-packed structures, 71–75
Depth
    of recursion, 53
    of tree, 188, 189, 190
Depth-first search, for directed graph, 175–176,
    177
Dereferencing operation, 27
Descendants, of node, 188
Descending sort, 254
Diagonal-major structure, of band matrices, 73
Dictionary, using digital search tree, 212–215
Difference, between sets, 18
Digital search trees, 211–215
Directed graphs (Digraphs)
    defined, 165
    implementations, 170–174
    lexical scanner example, 179–182
    properties, 166–170
    traversals, 175–178
    see also Trees
dispose operation, simulated, 128, 133–135
Distribution phase, of sort merge algorithm, 290,
    293
Division hash function, 243
Downward sorted array, 254
Dummy node, 113–115

Dyadic function, 8
Dynamic memory management, 99–101, 102. *See
    also* heap
Dynamic memory space. *See* Heap
Dynamic storage pool. *See* Heap

Edges, of graph, 165
Empty set, 17
Encapsulation, 6
English text scanner. *See* Cross-reference genera-
    tor
Enumeration types, 179, 226–228
Equality, of sets, 17
Exceptions, in Ada, 87, 88, 89, 90
Expression trees
    infix-to-tree translator program, 217–218, 219,
        220, 221
    manual construction, 195, 196, 197, 198–199,
        200
    traversals, 199, 200–201
    see also Binary trees; Binary search trees
Expression-to-tree translator program, 217–218,
    219, 220, 221
External sorts
    defined, 254
    Fibonacci distribution, for polyphase merging,
        296–300
    K-way merge, 291, 293
    natural distribution, 294, 295–296
    perfect distribution, 298–300
    polyphase merge sort, 296–300
    simple merge sort, 291, 292, 293–294, 295
    two-way merge, 291, 293

Factorials, 34–35, 53
Fibonacci distribution, for polyphase merging,
    296–300
FIFO. *See* First-In, First-out
Finite-state machine, 181–182, 226–228
First-In, First-Out (FIFO) structure, 139
Folding hash function, 243, 244
Fortran
    array implementation, 63
    cursor-oriented linked allocation, 99
    pointers not supported, 126
    record types, implementation of, 93–95
    recursion not allowed, 35

storage allocation, 63–66
variable types, 6
Forward Polish notation, 150
Fraction ADT
    body, 11, 13
    example program, 17
    functions, 7–9
    I/O, 15–16
    specification, 11, 12, 13–14
    type definition, 11
Full binary tree, 190

Garbage collection
    in Ada, 101
    in other languages, 131–135
General trees
    B-trees, 211, 215–217
    digital search, 211–215
Graphs
    defined, 165
    state, 226–227
    transition, 226–227
    see also Directed graphs
Growth rates. See Big O performance

Hand-held calculator, 149–150
Hash functions
    division, 243
    folding, 243, 244
    mid-square, 243
    partitioning, 243, 244
    truncation, 242
    see also Hash tables
Hash tables, 240–241
    collisions in, resolving, 244–249
    see also Hash functions
Head, of queue, 139–146
Head pointer, 109–111
Heap, 27, 29, 99–101, 102
    manager, 100
    simulation, 127–131, 132
    see also Heap sort
Heap sort
    bit shifts in, 275
    conversion of almost-heap to heap, 267–268,
        269, 275

definitions, 266–267
heap creation, 267, 268
list sorting, 268, 269, 270–272
practicality of, 269, 272–275
use of ABCT, 190, 192, 266–267
Height-balanced binary tree, 191, 192
High-level language (HLL), 2
HP-3000 storage allocation, 66
Hybrid search strategies, 250

IBM, 63
IBM System/370 storage allocation, 64, 65, 67
Implementation, vs. abstraction, 1–4
in parameter, 15–16
in situ sort, 254. See also Heap sort
In-degree
    of directed graph, 170
    of tree node, 186
Infix notation
    example, 150
    infix-to-RPN translator program, 156–161
    infix-to-tree translator program, 217–218, 219,
        220, 221
    manual conversion to RPN, 153–156
    see also Expression trees
Inner product, of vectors, 84
Inorder traversal, of binary tree, 195, 196, 197
Instantiation, input/output, 86, 87
INTEGER type, 6
Interior node, of tree, 187
Internal sorts
    binary insertion, 262
    bubble, 257–259
    defined, 254
    delayed selection, 256–257
    heap sort. See Heap sort
    linear insertion, 259–261
    merge sort, 262–266
    quadratic selection, 283–284
    quicksort, 277–280
    radix, 284–287
    shell, 281–282
    simple selection, 255–256
Interpreters, use of expression trees, 195–201
Intersection, of sets, 18
Irreflexivity
    of directed graph, 166, 167
    of tree, 187

Key-to-address transformation. *See* Hash functions
Keywords, 8, 15–16
K-way merge, 291, 293

Landis, 207
Language scanner. *See* Cross-reference generator
Last-In, First-Out (LIFO) structure, 139
Leaf, of tree, 187, 190, 191
Left child, of node, 189
Level, of node, 188
Lexical scanner, 179–182. *See also* Cross-reference generator
LIFO. *See* Last-In, First-Out
Linear growth rate, 44–45. *See also* Big O performance
Linear insertion sort, 259–261
Linear probing, of hash table, 245, 247
Linked lists
    node, defined, 101, 102
    one-way, ADT. *See* One-way linked list ADT
    one-way, creating, 103–104
    ordered, 112–115
    queues as, 143–144, 145–146
    sparse matrices as, 121–123
    sparse vectors as, 117–121
    stacks as, 148
Linked structures, 99–103. *See also* Linked lists
Lists
    cross, 122
    orthogonal, 122
    see also Linked lists
Logarithmic growth rate, 44–45. *See also* Big O performance
Logical records, 3–4, 5
LOGICAL type, 6
Lower triangular matrices, 71–73
Lukasiewicz, Jan, 150

Magnetic tape, 3–4
Magnetic tape sorts. *See* External sorts
Matrices
    band, 73, 75
    defined, 66
    densely-packed, 71–75
    implementation of, 66–70

lower triangular, 71–73
    planes, 69–70
    rectangular, 66–69
    sparse. *See* Sparse matrices
    symmetric, 73, 74
    upper triangular, 73
    see also Matrix ADT
Matrix ADT
    exception handling, 90, 92
    functions, 91–93
    sparse matrix operations, 121–123
    specification, 89–91
Merge sort, 42–43, 54, 262–266. *See also* External sorts
Mid-square hash function, 243
Modula-2
    dynamic memory management, 99–101, 102
    lack of garbage collection, 132
    limitations on functions and procedures, 24–25
    overloading not allowed, 23–24
    pointers, 26, 99–101, 102
    record types, 93–95
    recursion allowed, 35
Monadic function, 8
Multi-list structure, 122–123

N log N growth rate, 44–45. *See also* Big O performance
Named type equivalence, 85
Natural distribution, for merge sort, 294, 295–296
new operation, 100–101, 102
    simulated, 128, 132–135
Nodes
    children of, 188
    descendants of, 188
    dummy, 113–115
    of graph, 165
    in one-way linked lists, 105–111
    in two-way linked lists, 116, 117
    left child of, 189
    level of, 188
    of linked lists, 101, 102
    parents of, 188
    right child of, 189
    as siblings, 188
    of sparse matrices, 121
    of trees, 185–189

Non-linear probing, of hash table, 247–248
Nonterminal node, of tree, 187
Null, 115
Null value, 100

O ( ) performance. *See* Big O Performance
One-way linked list ADT
    declarations, 105–106
    dummy node implementation, 112–115
    operations, 106–107, 108, 109–111
    specification, 107, 109, 110
Open hashing, 248–249
Operator overloading. *See* Overloading
Order of magnitude. *See* Big O performance
Ordered children, of tree, 189
Ordered hashing, 249
Ordered list, 112–115
Orthogonal lists, 122
out parameter, 15–16
Out-degree
    of directed graph, 170
    of tree node, 187
Overloading, 11, 16, 21, 23–24, 87

Packages
    compiling, 15
    general structure, 9–10
    private type, 12–14
    specification and body, 10–12, 15
Packages, program text for
    Complex, 30, 133
    CircularQueues, 145
    FractionI.O., 16
    Fractions, 12
    LinkedQueues, 146
    Matrices, 90
    NaturalSets, 18
    OneWayLists, 110
    Queues, 140, 142
    ShortTextHandler, 125
    Stacks, 147, 149
    TableHandler, 55, 204, 246
    TextHandler, 22
    Vectors, 88
Packaging, 6–7
Palindrome, 35–37

Parent, of node, 188
Parenthesis-free notation. *See* Reverse Polish notation
Parenthesized notation. *See* Infix notation
Parser. *See* Expression trees; Cross-reference generator; Lexical scanner
Partition sort. *See* Quicksort
Partitioning hash function, 243, 244
Pascal
    ADT definition, 6
    array implementation, 63
    complex number ADT, 25–29
    dispose operation, simulated, 128, 133–135
    dynamic memory management, 99–101, 102
    lack of garbage collection, 132
    limitations on functions and procedures, 24–25
    new operation, simulated, 128, 132–135
    overloading not allowed, 23–24
    pointers, 26–28, 99–101, 102
    record types, 93–95
    recursion allowed, 35
    specification as block comment, 29, 30
    text strings, 20
    variable types, 6
Pass, on array, 255
Path, of directed graph, 168
PDP-11 storage allocation, 64
Perfect distribution, for polyphase merge sort, 298–300
Performance prediction. *See* Big O performance
Permutations, of a set, 37–39, 40, 54
Phase, of sort merge algorithm, 293–294
Physical records, 3–4, 5
PL/1
    array implementation, 63
    dynamic memory management, 99–101, 102
    lack of garbage collection, 132
    limitations on functions and procedures, 24–25
    overloading not allowed, 23–24
    pointers, 26, 99–101, 102
    record types, 93–95
    recursion allowed, 35
    text strings, 20
    variable types, 6
Planes, in matrices, 69–70
Pointers, 26–28, 99–101, 102, 106
    head, 109–111
    tail, 109, 111

Points, of graph, 165
Polynomial growth rate, 49. *See also* Big O performance
Polyphase merge sort, 296–300
Pop operation, on stack, 147–149, 217–218, 220, 221
Postfix notation. *See* Reverse Polish notation
Postorder traversal, of binary tree, 195, 196, 197
Precedence, of operators, 153–156
Preorder traversal, of binary tree, 195, 196, 197
Primitive types, for variables, 6
Priority, of operators, 153–156
Private type, in Ada package, 12–14
Probing, of hash tables, 244–248
Product, of vector with scalar, 84
Punched-card sorting machines, 281, 284–287
Push operation, on stack, 147–149, 217–218, 220, 221

Quadratic growth rate, 44–45. *See also* Big O performance
Quadratic hashing, 248
Quadratic selection sort, 283–284
Queue ADT
    array implementation, 140–143, 144, 145
    Big O performance, 143, 145
    linked list implementation, 143–144, 145–146
    package sketch, 139–140
Queues
    breadth-first search, for directed graph, 176, 177, 178
    as FIFO structures, 139
    operations on, 139–140, 141
    parts of, 139
    see also Queue ADT; stacks
Quicksort, 277–280

Radix sort, 284–287
raise statement, 89
Rational number ADT. *See* Fraction ADT
REAL type, 6
Record types, 93–95
Records, logical vs. physical, 3–4, 5
Rectangular matrix, 66–69
Recursive algorithms
    binary search, 39–42, 54

    defined, 34
    delete, for BST, 208–211
    depth of recursion, 53
    factorials, 34–35, 53
    merge sort, 42–43, 54
    report, for BST, 203–204
    search, for BST, 207–208
    set permutations, 37–39, 40, 54
    string reversal, 35–37, 53–54
    traversals, of binary tree, 193, 195, 196, 197
    update, for BST, 205–207
Reflexivity, of directed graph, 166, 167
Report operation, 55
    for array, 58, 59
    for BST, 203–204
    for hash table, 241
Reserved words, 8
Reverse Polish notation (RPN)
    example, 150
    expression evaluation, 151–153
    infix-to-RPN translator program, 156–161
    manual conversion from infix, 153–156
    see also Expression trees
Right child, of node, 189
Root, of tree, 185, 186, 187, 191
Row-major implementation of matrices, 67–70
Rows, of matrices, 66
RPN. *See* Reverse Polish notation

Scanner. *See* Expression trees; Cross-reference generator; Lexical scanner
Scatter storage technique. *See* Hash tables
Search operation, 55
    for array, 56, 58–59
    for BST, 207–208
    for hash table, 239, 241, 246, 249, 250
    and sparse vectors, 77–78
Searches
    binary, 39–42, 54
    BST. *See* Binary search trees
    hash table. *See* Hash functions; Hash tables
    hybrid strategies, 250
    sequential. *See* Table handler ADT
Set ADT
    body, 19–20
    specification, 18, 19

Sets
    defined, 16
    operations and representations, 17–20
    permutations of, 37–39, 40, 54
    see also Set ADT
Shell sort, 281–282
Siblings, nodes as, 188
Simple merge sort, 291, 292, 293–294, 295
Simple selection sort, 255–256
Sorts
    external. See External sorts
    internal. See Internal sorts
    stable, 206
    terminology, 254
Sparse matrices
    adjacency list, for directed graph, 172
    as cross lists, 122
    defined, 74
    as linked lists, 121–123
    as multi-list structures, 122–123
    see also Linked lists
Sparse vectors
    declarations for, 75–77, 79
    defined, 74
    in heap simulation, 128, 130–131
    as linked lists, 83, 117–121
    table operations, 77–83
    see also Digital search trees; Linked lists
Specification, for Ada package, 10–15
Spelling checker, using digital search tree,
        212–215
Stack ADT
    array implementation, 147–148, 149
    package sketch, 147
Stacks
    as LIFO structures, 139
    operations on, 147–149, 217–218, 220, 221
    parts of, 147
    see also Expression-to-tree translator program;
        Queues; Reverse Polish notation; Stack
        ADT
State graph, 174, 226–227. See also Lexical scan-
        ner
State table, for directed graph, 174
Storage allocation, for vectors, 63–66
Storage mapping function, 65
Strictly binary tree, 189
String ADT. See Text string ADT

String reversal, 35–37, 53–54
STRING type, 6
Strings. See Text strings
Strong connectivity, of directed graph, 170
Structure, of Ada package, 9–10
Structures
    densely-packed, 71–75
    FIFO, 139
    graphs, directed. See Directed graphs
    LIFO, 139
    linear, 98
    linked, 99–103
    multi-list, 122–123
    one-dimensional. See Vectors
    queues. See Queues
    rectangular, 66–69
    sparse. See Sparse matrices; Sparse vectors
    stacks. See Stacks
    trees. See Trees
    two-dimensional and higher-dimensional. See
        Matrices; Sparse matrices
    see also Linked lists
Subscript, 63
    range of, 65
Subtree, 187, 188, 193
Sum, of vectors, 84
Symmetric matrices, 73, 74
Symmetry, of directed graph, 166, 168
Synonyms, of keys, 241
System/370 storage allocation, 64, 65, 67

Table handler ADT
    Big O performance, 56, 58–59
    operations, defined, 55
    ordered array implementation, 58–59
    specification, 55, 56
    unordered array implementation, 56–58, 59
Table operations. See Create operation; Delete
        operation; Report operation; Search op-
        eration; Update operation
Tail, of queue, 139–146
Tail pointer, 109–111
Tape, magnetic, 3–4
Tensors, 63
Terminal node, of tree, 187
Text scanner. See Cross-reference generator

Text string ADT
    body, 21, 23
    one-way linked list extensions, 123–126, 127
    specification, 20–21, 22
    type definition, 20–21
Text string reversal. *See* String reversal
Text strings
    operations on, 20–21
    see also Text string ADT
Threading, tree, 228–235
Transition graph, 226–227
Transivity, of directed graph, 167, 169
Transpose, of a matrix, 91
Traversals
    of binary search tree, 203–204
    of binary tree, 193, 195, 196, 197
    of directed graph, 175–176, 177, 178
    of expression tree, 199, 200, 201
Trees
    B-trees, 211, 215–217
    binary. *See* Binary trees
    binary search. *See* Binary search trees
    defined, 185–187
    digital search, 211–215
    expression. *See* Expression trees
    properties of, 187–189
    threading, 228–235
    see also Directed graphs
Truncation hash function, 242
2-3 trees, 216, 217
Two-way linked list ADT, 116, 117
Two-way merge, 291, 292
Type. *See* Abstract data type; Array type; Data
        type; Record types; Variable type
Type equivalence, 85

UCSD Pascal. *See* Pascal
Unconstrained array type, 85–86
Union, of sets, 18
Universe, 16–17
Update operation, 55
    for array, 56, 58, 59
    for BST, 205–207
    for hash table, 239, 241, 246, 249, 250
    and sparse vectors, 77–78
Upward sorted array, 254
use keyword, 15–16

Variable type, 5–6
Vector ADT
    exception handling, 87, 88, 89, 90
    functions, 86–89
    sparse vector operations, 117–121
    specification, 87, 88
Vectors
    defined, 63
    implementation of, 63–66
    operations on, 84–89
    sparse. *See* Sparse vectors
    storage allocation, 63–66
    see also Vector ADT
Vertices, of graph, 165

Wasted node, 113–115
Weighted adjacency matrix, for directed graph,
        173
Weights, for directed graph, 173, 179
with keyword, 15–16